THE MONTANIST ORACLES
AND TESTIMONIA

The
Montanist Oracles
and Testimonia

Ronald E. Heine

North American Patristic Society
Patristic Monograph Series
14

BT
1435
.M66
1989

ISBN 0-86554-333-X

The paper used in this publication meets
the minimum requirements of American National Standard
for Information Sciences—Permanence of Paper
for Printed Library Materials, ANSI Z39.48-1984.

Library of Congress Cataloging-in-Publication Data

The Montanist oracles and testimonia / [edited by] Ronald E. Heine.
  xiv + 190 pp. 6 × 9″ (15 × 23cm.)
(Patristic monograph series ; 14)
  English, Greek, and Latin.
  Bibliography : p. xiii
  Includes indexes.
  ISBN 0-86554-333-X (Mercer University Press : alk. paper)
  1. Montanism—History—Sources. I. Heine, Ronald E.
II. Series: Patristic monograph series ; no. 14.
BT1435.M66   1989
270.1—dc20
                              89-32706
                                 CIP

C O N T E N T S

Part III
Testimonia
from the Fourth Century and Later

Indexes 181

Acknowledgments

I wish to take this opportunity to express my appreciation to William R. Schoedel who first suggested this work to me, and to Robert L. Wilken who read the work and offered helpful suggestions concerning some of the translations. I must, however, bear full responsibility for any errors the work may contain. My indebtedness to the textual scholars from whose editions these excerpts have been drawn is recorded with each entry. I also express a special word of appreciation to Dean Huffman who provided me with the computer hardware for work on these texts and also provided assistance in some of the more technical aspects of working with computers.

—*Ronald E. Heine*

To
William R. Schoedel

Introduction

Sometime in the second half of the second century Montanus, a newly baptized Christian in Phyrgia, began to prophesy.[1] He was quickly joined in this by two women, Priscilla and Maximilla. These three formed the leadership of a group of followers who rapidly became a disturbing presence in the Church and, eventually in some areas, an independent sect.

The followers of Montanus and his two prophetesses were characterized by their belief that the prophetic trio had received revelations while in a state of ecstasy, and by their practice of a more rigorous life-style than was demanded in the Church. In later literature the Montanists are sometimes charged with holding heretical doctrines regarding Christ or the Trinity, but there is no evidence such charges were leveled at them in the earliest period nor that there was any basis for such charges in the early period. Tertullian insisted that they held the same doctrines concerning the rule of faith as the Catholics, and that it was only in the area of discipline that they deviated from the Church by their stricter style of life (*Virg. Vel.* 1; cf. Epiphanius, *Pan.* 48.1.4; Cyprian, *Ep.* 75.19).

The followers of Montanus were most frequently referred to as Cataphrygians by their opponents, the title indicating the Phrygian provenance of the heresy. The designation "the new prophecy" may have been a title the Montanists used of themselves. Tertullian, at least, seems to use it in this way. They were also later called Montanists after the name of their leader.

There is evidence in early Christian literature that the Montanists produced numerous treatises. All have perished, however, except those treatises written by Tertullian after his adoption of Montanism. Our knowledge of the Montanists,

---

[1]The exact date is uncertain because Eusebius and Epiphanius disagree. Eusebius places the beginning of Montanus's prophecy around A.D. 171 and Epiphanius places it about twenty years earlier. See T. D. Barnes, "The Chronology of Montanism," JTS n.s. (1970): 403-408.

therefore, is dependent on a few oracles attributed to Montanus and the prophetesses which have been preserved in early Christian literature, on the descriptions of Montanist beliefs and practices given by their critics, and on the treatises of Tertullian from his Montanist period. These sources range in time of composition from a few years after the death of the prophetess Maximilla to the Middle Ages.

Eusebius and Epiphanius are the most important writers for our knowledge of the rise of Montanism in Phrygia and the beliefs and practices of the earliest Phrygian Montanists because of the sources they preserve in their writings. Eusebius quotes from two early sources concerning the Montanists in Phrygia. The first and most extensive is from an unnamed author, subsequently dubbed "the Anonymous" by modern scholars, who claimed to have taken part in oral controversy with the Montanists in Galatia, and to have written his account of them thirteen years after Maximilla's death. Eusebius's second source, from Apollonius, was composed forty years after Montanus began prophesying.

Epiphanius indicates that he used both oral and written sources in his section on the Montanists (*Pan.* 48.15). He does not, however, indicate when or whom he is quoting. R. A. Lipsius and H. G. Voigt have argued convincingly that Epiphanius drew on a source from the late second or early third century for his description of Montanism.[2] I have set forth arguments elsewhere suggesting that the provenance of this source was Phrygia.[3]

The writings of Tertullian which come from his Montanist period are also of special importance. They should not be used, however, to reconstruct Phrygian Montanism. Tertullian's views sometimes disagree with what we know of Montanism elsewhere, and appear to be modifications he himself has introduced. There is also evidence to suggest that Montanism reached Tertullian via Rome where other innovations had already been introduced.[4]

There are numerous other writers who refer to the Montanists. Sometimes they introduce new information from reliable sources, but often the descriptions of the Montanists in the later writers are either somewhat garbled rehashings of the accounts in the three writers we have mentioned, or are based on the kind of gossipy

---

[2]R. A. Lipsius, *Zur Quellenkritik des Epiphanios* (Wien, 1865); H. G. Voigt, *Eine verschollene Urkunde des antimontanistischen Kampfes. Die Berichte des Epiphanius über die Kataphryger und Quintillianer* (Leipzig, 1891). Lipsius considered the source to run from *Pan.* 48.2 to 48.13. Voigt moved the beginning of the source back to the middle of 48.1, while continuing to mark its ending at 13 as Lipsius. I follow the boundaries of the source as marked off by Voigt.

[3]In an article entitled "The Role of the Gospel of John in the Montanist Controversy" to appear in *The Second Century*.

[4]See the previously mentioned article for my arguments in this regard.

hearsay that accumulates around controversies, and especially around religious controversies.

The sources descriptive of Montanism were collected, edited, and translated into French by Pierre de Labriolle.[5] This collection has subsequently been the primary sourcebook for the study of Montanism,[6] and has served as the basis for my own work presented here. This edition differs from Labriolle's in the following ways.

First, for the sake of space, I have omitted ninety-six texts which Labriolle includes.[7] These, with one exception,[8] all come from the fourth century or later. A large number of the texts omitted tell us nothing about Montanism, but simply mention it in a list of heresies. Second, where possible I have used more recent critical editions of the sources than were available to Labriolle. The most obvious difference between my edition and that of Labriolle, however, is in the order in which the texts are presented. Labriolle structured his book according to the chronology of the writings in which the material appeared. I have introduced several divisions within the materials based on the conclusions that various modern scholars have reached, and on conclusions that I have reached after working closely with these texts for an extended period of time.

First, there are three major divisions of the materials. Part 1 contains the oracles. If these are authentic, they must come first. I have distinguished within part 1 between those oracles which most scholars today would agree to be authentic, and those which are questionable and probably inauthentic and, therefore, not to be taken into account in an attempt to understand the earliest leaders of Montanism. I include number 11 among the authentic as a possible oracle of Quintilla, but not of Priscilla. Epiphanius does not know which prophetess may

---

[5]*Les sources de l'histoire du Montanisme* (Paris, 1913).

[6]S. Gero, "Montanus and Montanism according to a Medieval Syriac Source," JTS n.s. (1977): 520-24, has discovered and published a description of Montanism found in the chronicle of Michael the Syrian composed in the late twelfth century which was overlooked by Labriolle.

[7]The following is the list of testimonia included by Labriolle that I have omitted. The numbers refer to Labriolle's section numbers. 1, 65, 74, 77[2], 80, 81, 82, 85, 87, 93, 94, 95, 96, 97, 98, 99, 101, 104, 110, 111, 112, 128, 129, 130, 131, 133, 137, 141, 142, 143, 146, 147, 148, 150, 151, 154, 155, 156, 157, 158, 159, 160, 161, 162, 163, 164, 166, 168, 170, 171, 173, 176, 177, 180, 181, 182, 183, 184, 185, 187, 188, 189, 190, 191, 192, 193, 194, 195, 196, 197, 198, 200, 201, 203, 205, 206, 207, 209, 210, 211, 212, 214, 216, 217, 218, 219, 220, 221, 222, 223, 225, 226, 227, 228, 229.

[8]That is, Labriolle's first source, from the *Ascension of Isaiah,* which, it seems to me, has a very tenuous relationship to Montanism if any at all.

have uttered it. The oracle does not come from his second or third century source, but from his account of the Quintillians which is confused in various ways.

Part 2 contains testimonia dating from the second and third centuries, and part 3 has the testimonia from the fourth century and later. The division falls naturally here because it is in the fourth century that the Trinitarian and Christological controversies color the perception of what Montanus and his followers had believed. In part 3 the texts are quoted according to the chronology of the writers.

Part 2 contains the most significant deviations from Labriolle's text. In this section I have used two criteria in grouping the materials. The first is the locale where the sources were written or to which they were written. There were three major geographical centers of Montanism in the second and third centuries. Phyrgia, where it arose and was, perhaps, strongest; Rome, where it seems to have gone quite early and stirred up significant debates; and North Africa where it made its most famous convert in Tertullian. The other criterion used for the ordering of the materials in part 2 has been the chronology of the sources quoted in the writings, as opposed to the chronology of the writings themselves. This appears primarily in the section concerning Montanism in Phrygia, where Eusebius and Epiphanius have preserved significant early sources. I have pulled these sources out of Eusebius and Epiphanius, both fourth century authors, and quoted them in the order in which they appeared in the second and third centuries. This way of structuring the material will, it seems to me, help bring precision and clarity to our picture of the beliefs and practices of the earliest Montanists.

I have included selection 20 from the *Martyrdom of Polycarp* because it is debated whether it has reference to a Montanist martyr. If it does, it is the earliest reference to Montanism we possess. I think it does not.[9]

There are also several inscriptions which may be related to Montanism which have been omitted from this collection of texts. These have not been included for the following reasons. First, the connection with Montanism is very tenuous for many of these inscriptions. This is especially true of the so-called "Christians for/to Christians" inscriptions from Phrygia, which are readily accessible in the study of E. Gibson. Second, all the epigraphical evidence related to Montanism is to be included in a forthcoming study by W. Tabbernee.

---

[9]See the arguments presented by W. Tabbernee, "Early Montanism and Voluntary Martyrdom," *Colloquium* (1985): 40-41.

Select Bibliography

Aland, Kurt. "Bemerkungen zum Montanismus und zur frühchristlichen Eschatologie." *Kirchengeschichtliche Entwürfe*. Gütersloh, 1960.

Ash, James L. "The Decline of Ecstatic Prophecy in the Early Church." *Theological Studies* 37 (1976): 227-52.

Barnes, Timothy D. "The Chronology of Montanism." *The Journal of Theological Studies* n.s. 21 (1970): 403-408.

Ford, J. Massyngberde. "St. Paul, The Philogamist (I Cor. VII in Early Patristic Exegesis)." *New Testament Studies* 11 (1964): 326-48.

_____. "Was Montanism a Jewish-Christian Heresy?" *Journal of Ecclesiastical History* 17 (1966): 145-58.

Gibson, Elsa. *The "Christians for Christians" Inscriptions of Phrygia*. Harvard Theological Studies 32. Missoula MT: Scholars Press, 1978.

Groh, Dennis E. "Utterance and Exegesis: Biblical Interpretation in the Montanist Crisis." *The Living Text*. Edited by Dennis E. Groh and Robert Jewett. New York: University Press of America, 1985.

Heine, Ronald E. "The Role of the Gospel of John in the Montanist Controversy." *The Second Century*. Forthcoming.

Johnson, Gary J. "Roman Bithynia and Christianity to the Mid-Fourth Century." Ph.D. dissertation, The University of Michigan, 1984.

Klawiter, Frederick C. "The New Prophecy in Early Christianity: The Origin, Nature, and Development of Montanism, A.D. 165-220." Ph.D. dissertation, The University of Chicago, 1975.

_____. "The Role of Martyrdom and Persecution in Developing the Priestly Authority of Women in Early Christianity: A Case Study of Montanism." *Church History* 49 (1980): 251-61.

Labriolle, Pierre de. *La crise montaniste*. Paris: Ernest Leroux, 1913.

_____. *Les sources de l'histoire du Montanisme*. Collectanea Friburgensia, no. 24. Paris: Ernest Leroux, 1913.

Powel, Douglas. "Tertullianists and Cataphrygians." *Vigiliae Christianae* 29 (1975): 33-54.

Schepelern, Wilhelm. *Der Montanismus und die Phrygischen Kulte.* Tübingen: J. C. B. Mohr, 1929.

Tabbernee, William. "Early Montanism and Voluntary Martyrdom." *Colloquium: The Australian and New Zealand Theological Review* 17 (1985): 33-43.

Abbreviations

CC	*Corpus Christianorum*
CSEL	*Corpus Scriptorum Ecclesiasticorum Latinorum*
GCS	*Die griechischen christlichen Schriftsteller*
OECT	*Oxford Early Christian Texts*
PG	Migne, *Patrologiae Graecae*
PL	Migne, *Patrologiae Latinae*
SC	*Sources chrétiennes*

Part I

The Montanist Oracles

Authentic Oracles

Oracles Attributed to Montanus

1. Epiphanius, *Panarion* 48.11 (GCS 31, ed. Holl 233.18-19).

Ἔτι δὲ προστίθησιν ὁ αὐτὸς Μοντανὸς οὕτως λέγων "ἐγὼ κύριος ὁ θεὸς ὁ παντοκράτωρ καταγινόμενος ἐν ἀνθρώπῳ."

2. Ibid. (Holl 235.1-2).

Εἶτα πάλιν φησὶ τὸ ἐλεεινὸν ἀνθρωπάριον Μοντανὸς ὅτι "οὔτε ἄγγελος οὔτε πρέσβυς, ἀλλ' ἐγὼ κύριος ὁ θεὸς πατὴρ ἦλθον."

3. Ibid. 48.4 (Holl, 224.22-225.2).

Εὐθὺς γὰρ ὁ Μοντανός φησιν "ἰδού, ὁ ἄνθρωπος ὡσεὶ λύρα κἀγὼ ἐφίπταμαι ὡσεὶ πλῆκτρον· ὁ ἄνθρωπος κοιμᾶται κἀγὼ γρηγορῶ· ἰδού, κύριός ἐστιν ὁ ἐξιστάνων καρδίας ἀνθρώπων καὶ διδοὺς καρδίαν ἀνθρώποις."

4. Ibid. 48.10 (Holl 232.19-233.1).

Λέγει γὰρ [Μοντανὸς] ἐν τῇ ἑαυτοῦ λεγομένῃ προφητείᾳ "τί λέγεις τὸν ὑπὲρ ἄνθρωπον σῳζόμενον; λάμψει γὰρ (φησίν) ὁ δίκαιος ὑπὲρ τὸν ἥλιον ἑκατονταπλασίονα, οἱ δὲ μικροὶ ἐν ὑμῖν σῳζόμενοι λάμψουσιν ἑκατονταπλασίονα ὑπὲρ τὴν σελήνην."

Oracles Attributed to Maximilla

5. Eusebius, H.E. 5.16.17 (GCS 9.1, ed. E. Schwartz 466.18-20).

Καὶ μὴ λεγέτω ἐν τῷ αὐτῷ λόγῳ τῷ κατὰ 'Αστέριον 'Ορβανὸν τὸ διὰ Μαξιμίλλης πνεῦμα "διώκομαι ὡς λύκος ἐκ προβάτων· οὐκ εἰμὶ λύκος, ῥῆμά εἰμι καὶ πνεῦμα καὶ δύναμις."

6. Epiphanius, *Panarion* 48.2.4 (Holl 221.25-222.2).

Φάσκει γὰρ ἡ λεγομένη παρ' αὐτοῖς Μαξίμιλλα ἡ προφῆτις ὅτι, φησί "μετ' ἐμὲ προφήτης οὐκέτι ἔσται, ἀλλὰ συντέλεια."

Authentic Oracles

Oracles Attributed to Montanus

1. Epiphanius, *Panarion* 48.11.

But in addition, this same Montanus adds the following words: "I am the Lord God, the Almighty dwelling in man."

2. Ibid.

Then again this miserable little man Montanus says: "Neither angel nor envoy, but I the Lord God the Father have come" (cf. Isa 63:9).

3. Ibid. 48.4.

For Montanus says, for instance: "Behold, man is like a lyre, and I flit about like a plectron; man sleeps, and I awaken him;[1] behold, it is the Lord who changes the hearts of men and gives men a heart."

4. Ibid. 48.10.

For [Montanus] says in his so-called prophecy: "Why do you call the more excellent man saved? For the just, he says, will shine a hundred times brighter than the sun, and the little ones among you who are saved will shine a hundred times brighter than the moon."

Oracles Attributed to Maximilla

5. Eusebius, *Ecclesiastical History* 5.16.17.

And let not the spirit which speaks through Maximilla say, in the same book according to Asterius Orbanus: "I am pursued like a wolf from the sheep. I am not a wolf (cf. Matt 7:15). I am word, and spirit, and power" (cf. 1 Cor 2:4).

6. Epiphanius, *Panarion* 48.2.4.

For the one they call Maximilla, the prophetess, declares: "After me there will no longer be a prophet,[2] but the end."

---

[1] Cf. Ps. Justin, *Cohortatio ad Graecos* 8; Athenagoras, *Legatio* 9; Hippolytus, *De antichristo* 2; Tertullian, *Adversus Marcionem* 4.22.

[2] The MSS. are divided between "prophet" and "prophetess." Labriolle chose "prophetess."

7. Ibid. 48.12.4 (Holl 235.19-21).

Εὐθὺς γὰρ αὕτη ἡ Μαξίμιλλα ἡ παρὰ τοῖς τοιούτοις κατὰ Φρύγας οὕτω καλουμένοις—ἀκούσατε, ὦ παῖδες Χριστοῦ, τί λέγει· "ἐμοῦ μὴ ἀκούσητε, ἀλλὰ Χριστοῦ ἀκούσατε."

8. Ibid. 48.13.1 (Holl 237.9-13).

Φάσκει δὲ πάλιν ἡ αὐτὴ Μαξίμιλλα, ἡ τῆς παρακολουθίας γνῶσις καὶ διδασκαλία, ἵνα καὶ χλευαστικῶς εἴπω, ὅτι "ἀπέστειλέ με κύριος τούτου τοῦ πόνου καὶ τῆς συνθήκης καὶ τῆς ἐπαγγελίας αἱρεστιστὴν μηνυτὴν ἑρμηνεύτην, ἠναγκασμένον, θέλοντα καὶ μὴ θέλοντα, γνωθεῖν γνῶσιν θεοῦ."

Cf. ibid. 48.13.7 (Holl 238.13-14).

Καὶ γὰρ καὶ Μαξίμιλλα τοὺς θέλοντας καὶ μὴ θέλοντας ἔλεγεν ἀναγκάζειν, κτλ.

Oracles Attributed to Priscilla/Prisca

9. Tertullian, de resurrectio carnis 11.2 (CSEL 47, ed. Kroymann, p. 39).

De quibus luculente et paracletus per prophetidem Priscam: "Carnes sunt, et carnem oderunt."

10. Idem, de exhortatione castitatis 10.5 (CSEL 70, ed. Kroymann, pp. 145-46).

Item per sanctam prophetidem Priscam ita evangelizatur, quod sanctus minister sanctimoniam noverit ministrare. "Purificantia enim concordat, ait, et visiones vident, et ponentes faciem deorsum etiam voces audiunt salutares, tam manifestas quam et occultas."

An Oracle Attributed to Quintilla (or Priscilla)

11. Epiphanius, Panarion 49.1 (Holl 241,23-242.8).

Φασὶ γὰρ οὗτοι οἱ Κυϊντιλλιανοὶ εἴτ' οὖν Πρισκιλλιανοὶ ἐν τῇ Πεπούζῃ ἢ Κυϊντίλλαν ἢ Πρίσκιλλαν (οὐκ ἔχω [γὰρ] ἀκριβῶς λέγειν), μίαν δὲ ἐξ αὐτῶν ὡς προεῖπον ἐν τῇ Πεπούζῃ κεκαθευδηκέναι καὶ τὸν Χριστὸν πρὸς αὐτὴν ἐληλυθέναι συνυπνωκέναι τε αὐτῇ τούτῳ τῷ τρόπῳ, ὡς ἐκείνη ἀπατωμένη ἔλεγεν· "ἐν ἰδέᾳ, φησί, γυναικός, ἐσχηματισμένος ἐν στολῇ λαμπρᾷ ἦλθε πρός με Χριστὸς καὶ ἐνέβαλεν ἐν ἐμοὶ τὴν σοφίαν καὶ ἀπεκάλυψέ μοι τουτονὶ τὸν τόπον εἶναι ἅγιον καὶ ὧδε τὴν Ἱερουσαλὴμ ἐκ τοῦ οὐρανοῦ κατιέναι."

7. Ibid. 48.12.4.

For hear, O children of Christ, what this Maximilla who belongs to such as are thus called Cataphrygians says in a straightforward manner: "Hear not me, but hear Christ."

8. Ibid. 48.13.1.

And again the same Maximilla, who claims to be the gnosis of persuasion and doctrine, to speak derisively, declares: "The Lord has sent me as partisan, revealer, and interpreter of this suffering, covenant, and promise. I am compelled to come to understand the knowledge of God whether I want to or not."

Cf. ibid. 48.13.7.

For indeed even Maximilla said she compelled those who were willing and those who were not. . . .

Oracles Attributed to Priscilla/Prisca

9. Tertullian, *On the Resurrection of the Flesh* 11.2.

The Paraclete has also said well of them through the prophetess Prisca: "They are flesh, and they hate the flesh."

10. Tertullian, *Exhortation to Chastity* 10.5.

Likewise the holy prophetess Prisca preaches that the holy minister should know how to administer purity of life. "For purification produces harmony," she says, "and they see visions, and when they turn their faces downward they also hear salutary voices, as clear as they are secret."

An Oracle Attributed to Quintilla (or Priscilla)

11. Epiphanius, *Panarion* 49.1.

For these Quintillians, or Priscillians, say that in Pepuza either Quintilla or Priscilla, I cannot say precisely, but one of them, as I said before, had been asleep in Pepuza and the Christ came to her and slept with her in the following manner, as that deluded woman described it. "Having assumed the form of a woman," she says, "Christ came to me in a bright robe and put wisdom in me, and revealed to me that this place is holy, and that it is here that Jerusalem will descend from heaven."[3]

---

[3]The authenticity of this oracle has been questioned by recent scholars. See D. E. Groh, "Utterance and Exegesis: Biblical Interpretation in the Montanist Crisis," in *The Living Text,* ed. D. E. Groh and R. Jewett (New York: University Press of America, 1985) 80-81. Tertullian surely did not know this oracle, for although he was a chiliast, he never spoke of the events of the end involving Pepuza, but only Jerusalem.

Oracles of Unidentified Prophets or Prophetesses

12. Tertullian, *de pudicitia* 21.7 (CSEL 20, ed. Reifferscheid and Wissowa, p. 269).

Hoc ego magis et agnosco et dispono, qui ipsum paracletum in prophetis novis habeo dicentem: "Potest ecclesia donare delictum, sed non faciam, ne et alia delinquant."

13. Tertullian, *de fuga* 9.4 (CSEL 76, ed. Bulhart, p. 32).

Spiritum vero si consulas quid magis sermone illo Spiritus probat? Namque omnes paene ad martyrium exhorta[n]tur, non ad fugam, ut et illius commemoremur: "Publicaris," inquit, "bonum tibi est; qui enim non publicatur in hominibus, publicatur in Domino. Ne confundaris, iustitia te producit in medium. Quid confunderis laudem ferens? Potestas fit, cum conspiceris ab hominibus."

14. Ibid.

Sic et alibi: "Nolite in lectulis nec in aborsibus et febribus mollibus optare exire, sed in martyriis, uti glorificetur qui est passus pro vobis."

Cf. Tertullian, *de anima* 55.5 (ed. Waszink [Amsterdam, 1947] p. 74).

Si pro deo occumbas, ut paracletus monet, non in mollibus febribus et in lectulis, sed in martyriis, si crucem tuam tollas et sequaris dominum, ut ipse praecepit. Tota paradisi clavis tuus sanguis est.

Questionable Oracles

15. Μοντανιστοῦ καὶ Ὀρθοδόξου διαλέξις (Labriolle, *Les sources*, p. 97).

Λέγει [Μοντανός]· "Ἐγώ εἰμι ὁ πατὴρ καὶ ἐγώ εἰμι ὁ υἱὸς καὶ ἐγὼ ὁ παράκλητος."

Cf. ibid. (Labriolle, *Les sources*, p. 101).

"Ἐγώ εἰμι καὶ ὁ πατὴρ καὶ ὁ υἱὸς καὶ τὸ πνεῦμα."

Oracles of Unidentified Prophets or Prophetesses

12. Tertullian, *On Modesty* 21.7.

This I recognize and will more than you, for I have the Paraclete himself who says in the new prophets: "The Church can pardon sin, but I will not do it, lest they also commit other offences."

13. Tertullian, *Concerning Flight* 9.4.

But if you consult the Spirit, what does he approve more than that word of the Spirit? For nearly all his words exhort to martyrdom, not to flight, as we are also reminded by his saying: "It is good for you to be publicly exposed. For he who is not exposed among men is exposed in the Lord. Do not be disturbed; righteousness brings you before the public. Why are you disturbed when you are receiving praise? There is opportunity when you are observed by men."

14. Ibid.

So he also says elsewhere: "Wish not to choose to die in your beds, nor in miscarriages and mild fevers, but in martyrdoms, that he who has suffered for you may be glorified."

Cf. Tertullian, *On the Soul* 55.5.

If you should die for God, as the Paraclete instructs, not in mild fevers and on your beds, but in martyrdoms; if you take up your cross and follow the Lord as he himself commands, your blood is the complete key of Paradise.

Questionable Oracles

15. *Dialogue of a Montanist and an Orthodox Christian.*

[Montanus] says: "I am the Father, and I am the Son, and I am the Paraclete."

Cf. ibid.

"I am the Father, and the Son, and the Spirit."[4]

---

[4]The context of this statement shows that these were not taken to be claims Montanus made about himself, but Christological assertions similar to those of the Sabellians. The statement in full is: "Show me where it is written in the Gospels: 'I am the Father, and the Son, and the Spirit.' "

Cf. ibid (Labriolle, *Les Sources,* p. 103).

Μοντανὸς δὲ λέγει· "Ἐγώ εἰμι ὁ πατὴρ καὶ ὁ υἱὸς καὶ τὸ ἅγιον πνεῦμα."

16. Didymus, *de trinitatis* 3.41.1 (PG 39.984).

Μοντανὸς γάρ, φησίν, εἶπεν· "Ἐγώ εἰμι ὁ πατὴρ καὶ ὁ υἱὸς καὶ ὁ παράκλητος."

17. Fragment of the *Odes of Montanus* (Labriolle, *Les sources,* p. 3).

Μοντανοῦ ἐκ τῶν ᾠδῶν.

Μίαν ὁ Χριστὸς ἔχει τὴν φύσιν καὶ τὴν ἐνέργειαν καὶ πρὸ τῆς σαρκὸς καὶ μετὰ τῆς σαρκός, ἵνα μὴ διάφορος γένηται, ἀνόμοια καὶ διάφορα πράττων.

18. Origen, *Contra Celsum* 7.9 (GCS 2, ed. Koetschau, 160.30-161.19).

Ἐπεὶ δὲ καὶ τὸν τρόπον τῶν ἐν Φοινίκῃ καὶ Παλαιστίνῃ μαντείων ἐπαγγέλλεται φράσειν ὁ Κέλσος ὡς ἀκούσας καὶ πάνυ καταμαθὼν, φέρε καὶ ταῦτα κατανοήσωμεν. πρῶτον δὴ λέγει πλείονα εἶναι εἴδη προφητειῶν, μὴ ἐκτιθέμενος αὐτά· οὐδὲ γὰρ εἶχεν, ἀλλὰ ψευδῶς ἐπανετείνετο. ὃ δέ φησιν εἶναι τελεώτατον παρὰ τοῖς τῇδε ἀνδράσιν ἴδωμεν. πολλοὶ, φησὶ, καὶ ἀνώνυμοι ῥᾷστα ἐκ τῆς προστυχούσης αἰτίας καὶ ἐν ἱεροῖς καὶ ἔξω ἱερῶν, οἱ δὲ καὶ ἀγείραντες καὶ ἐπιφοιτῶντες πόλεσιν ἢ στρατοπέδοις, κινοῦνται δῆθεν ὡς θεσπίζοντες. πρόχειρον δ' ἑκάστῳ καὶ σύνηθες εἰπεῖν· ἐγὼ ὁ θεός εἰμι ἢ θεοῦ παῖς ἢ πνεῦμα θεῖον. ἥκω δέ· ἤδη γὰρ ὁ κόσμος ἀπόλλυται, καὶ ὑμεῖς, ὦ ἄνθρωποι, διὰ τὰς ἀδικίας οἴχεσθε. ἐγὼ δὲ σῶσαι θέλω· καὶ ὄψεσθέ με αὖθις μετ' οὐρανίου δυνάμεως ἐπανιόντα. μακάριος ὁ νῦν με θρησκεύσας, τοῖς δ' ἄλλοις ἅπασι πῦρ αἰώνιον ἐπιβαλῶ καὶ πόλεσι καὶ χώραις. καὶ ἀνθρώποις οἳ μὴ τὰς ἑαυτῶν ποινὰς ἴσασι, μεταγνώσονται μάτην καὶ στενάξουσι· τοὺς δέ μοι πεισθέντας αἰωνίους φυλάξω. εἶτα τούτοις ἑξῆς φησι· ταυτ' ἐπανατεινάμενοι προστιθέασιν ἐφεξῆς ἄγνωστα καὶ πάροιστρα καὶ πάντη ἄδηλα, ὧν τὸ μὲν γνῶμα οὐδεὶς ἂν ἔχων νοῦν εὑρεῖν δύναιτο· ἀσαφῆ γὰρ καὶ τὸ μηδὲν, ἀνοήτῳ δὲ ἢ γόητι παντὶ περὶ παντὸς ἀφορμὴν ἐνδίδωσιν, ὅπῃ βούλεται, τὸ λεχθὲν σφετερίζεσθαι.

19. Origen, *in epistolam ad Titum* PG 14.1306).

Requisierunt sane quidem, utrum haeresim an schisma oporteat vocari eos qui Cataphryges nominantur, obsecrantes falsos prophetas et dicentes: "Ne accedas ad me quoniam mundus sum: non enim accepi uxorem, nec est sepulchrum patens guttur meum, sed sum Nazareus Dei, non bibens vinum, sicut illi."

Cf. ibid.

Montanus says: "I am the Father, and the Son, and the Holy Spirit."

16. Didymus, *On the Trinity* 3.41.1.

For Montanus said: "I am the Father, and the Son, and the Paraclete."

17. Fragment of the *Odes of Montanus*.

From the Odes of Montanus.

The Christ has one nature and energy both before and after the flesh, that he not be different when he does dissimilar and different things.

18. Origen, *Against Celsus* 7.9.

Now since Celsus also professes to make known the manner of the prophecies in Phoenicia and Palestine since he has heard them and has examined them very carefully, come let us also consider these matters. First, he says there are several kinds of prophecies, although he does not quote examples, for he did not have any, for he brandished them falsely. But let us see what he says is the most perfect kind among the men here. Many, he says, who are nameless, prophesy readily for any reason whatever, both in temples and outside them; some beg and go about to cities and military camps, and pretend to be moved as if delivering an oracle. And each one commonly and customarily says: "I am God," or "a son of God," or "a divine spirit, and I have come. For the world is already perishing, and you, gentlemen, are ruined because of your offences. But I want to save you; and you will see me coming again with heavenly power. Blessed is he who has worshipped me now, but I will cast eternal fire on all the others both in the cities and in the countrysides. And men who have not become acquainted with their own recompenses will repent in vain and groan; but I will protect forever those who have obeyed me." Then Celsus says: "After they have brandished these words, they subsequently add words that are unintelligible, and frenzied, and totally obscure, whose meaning no intelligent person could discover, for they are obscure and void of meaning, but they afford opportunity to every fool or sorcerer to appropriate what was said concerning anything in whatever way he wishes."

19. Origen, *On the epistle to Titus*.

Indeed some have properly raised the question whether those who have the name Cataphrygians ought to be called a heresy or a schism. They invoke false prophets and say: "Do not approach me, for I am pure; for I have not taken a wife, nor is my throat an open sepulchre, but I am a Nazirite of God; like them, I do not drink wine."

Part II

Testimonia from the Second and Third Centuries

Testimonia Concerning Montanism in Phrygia

The Martyrdom of Polycarp

20. *Martyrium Polycarpi* 4 (OECT, ed. Musurillo, 4).

Εἷς δὲ ὀνόματι Κόϊντος, Φρύξ, προσφάτως ἐληλυθὼς ἀπὸ τῆς Φρυγίας, ἰδὼν τὰ θηρία ἐδειλίασεν. οὗτος δὲ ἦν ὁ παραβιασάμενος ἑαυτόν τε καί τινας προσελθεῖν ἑκόντας. τοῦτον ὁ ἀνθύπατος πολλὰ ἐκλιπαρήσας ἔπεισεν ὀμόσαι καὶ ἐπιθῦσαι. διὰ τοῦτο οὖν, ἀδελφοί, οὐκ ἐπαινοῦμεν τοὺς προσιόντας ἑαυτοῖς, ἐπειδὴ οὐχ οὕτως διδάσκει τὸ εὐαγγέλιον.

The Letter of the Churches of Vienne and Lyon

21. Eusebius, H.E. 5.3.4 (GCS, ed. Schwartz, p. 432).

Τῶν δ' ἀμφὶ τὸν Μοντανὸν καὶ Ἀλκιβιάδην καὶ Θεόδοτον περὶ τὴν Φρυγίαν ἄρτι τότε πρῶτον τὴν περὶ τοῦ προφητεύειν ὑπόληψιν παρὰ πολλοῖς ἐκφερομένων (πλεῖσται γὰρ οὖν καὶ ἄλλαι παραδοξοποιίαι τοῦ θείου χαρίσματος εἰς ἔτι τότε· κατὰ διαφόρους ἐκκλησίας ἐκτελούμεναι πίστιν παρὰ πολλοῖς τοῦ κἀκείνους προφητεύειν παρεῖχον) καὶ δὴ διαφωνίας ὑπαρχούσης περὶ τῶν δεδηλωμένων, αὖθις οἱ κατὰ τὴν Γαλλίαν ἀδελφοὶ τὴν ἰδίαν κρίσιν καὶ περὶ τούτων εὐλαβῆ καὶ ὀρθοδοξοτάτην ὑποτάττουσιν, ἐκθέμενοι καὶ τῶν παρ' αὐτοῖς τελειωθέντων μαρτύρων διαφόρους ἐπιστολάς, ἃς ἐν δεσμοῖς ἔτι ὑπάρχοντες τοῖς ἐπ' Ἀσίας καὶ Φρυγίας ἀδελφοῖς διεχάραξαν, οὐ μὴν ἀλλὰ καὶ Ἐλευθέρῳ τῷ τότε Ῥωμαίων ἐπισκόπῳ, τῆς τῶν ἐκκλησιῶν εἰρήνης ἕνεκα πρεσβεύοντες.

Apolinarius

22. Ibid. 4.27 (Schwartz, p. 388).

Τοῦ δ' Ἀπολιναρίου πολλῶν παρὰ πολλοῖς σῳζομένων τὰ εἰς ἡμᾶς ἐλθόντα ἐστὶν τάδε· λόγος ὁ πρὸς τὸν προειρημένον βασιλέα καὶ Πρὸς Ἕλληνας συγγράμματα πέντε καὶ Περὶ ἀληθείας ά β´ καὶ Πρὸς Ἰουδαίους ά β´ καὶ ἃ μετὰ ταῦτα συνέγραψε κατὰ τῆς τῶν Φρυγῶν αἱρέσεως, μετ' οὐ πολὺν καινοτομηθείσης χρόνον, τότε γε μὴν ὥσπερ ἐκφύειν ἀρχομένης,

Testimonia Concerning Montanism in Phrygia

The Martyrdom of Polycarp

20. *The Martyrdom of Polycarp* 4.

But one, named Quintus, a Phrygian recently come from Phrygia, was afraid when he saw the beasts. Now he was the one who had compelled himself and some others to appear before the tribunal voluntarily. When the proconsul had earnestly entreated him many times, he persuaded him to swear and offer sacrifice. For this reason, then, brothers, we do not praise those who come forward of themselves, since the gospel does not so teach.

The Letter of the Churches of Vienne and Lyon

21. Eusebius, *Ecclesiastical History* 5.3.4.

Just then the disciples of Montanus and Alcibiades and Theodotus in Phrygia first published among many their opinion about prophecy (for the many other wonders of the divine charisma still being accomplished up to that time in various Churches caused many to believe that those men too prophesied). And when there was discord concerning the men mentioned, the brothers in Gaul again submitted their own judgment also on these matters, which was pious and very orthodox, exhibiting also various letters of the martyrs who had been perfected among them, which they had written to the brothers in Asia and Phrygia while they were still in prison, but also to Eleutherus who was bishop of the Romans at that time, being ambassadors for the sake of the peace of the Churches.

Apolinarius

22. Ibid. 4.27.

Of the numerous writings of Apolinarius which many have preserved, those which have reached us are the following. A treatise to the above mentioned king, and five books *To the Greeks*, two *Concerning the Truth*, two *To the Jews*, and after these those which he composed against the heresy of the Phrygians which had made its innovations a little earlier. It was

ἔτι τοῦ Μοντανοῦ ἅμα ταῖς αὐτοῦ ψευδοπροφήτισιν ἀρχὰς τῆς παρεκτροπῆς ποιουμένου.

The Anonymous

23. Ibid. 5.16-17 (Schwartz, pp. 458-72).

16. (1) Πρὸς μὲν οὖν τὴν λεγομένην κατὰ Φρύγας αἵρεσιν ὅπλον ἰσχυρὸν καὶ ἀκαταγώνιστον ἐπὶ τῆς Ἱεραπόλεως τὸν Ἀπολινάριον, οὗ καὶ πρόσθεν μνήμην ὁ λόγος πεποίητο, ἄλλους τε σὺν αὐτῷ πλείους τῶν τηνικάδε λογίων ἀνδρῶν ἡ τῆς ἀληθείας ὑπέρμαχος ἀνίστη δύναμις, ἐξ ὧν καὶ ἡμῖν ἱστορίας πλείστη τις ὑπόθεσις καταλέλειπται. (2) ἀρχόμενος γοῦν τῆς κατ' αὐτῶν γραφῆς, τῶν εἰρημένων δή τις πρῶτον ἐπισημαίνεται ὡς καὶ ἀγράφοις τοῖς κατ' αὐτῶν ἐπεξέλθοι ἐλέγχοις· προοιμιάζεται γοῦν τοῦτον τὸν τρόπον· (3) "ἐκ πλείστου ὅσου καὶ ἱκανωτάτου χρόνου, ἀγαπητὲ Ἀυίρκιε Μάρκελλε, ἐπιταχθεὶς ὑπὸ σοῦ συγγράψαι τινὰ λόγον εἰς τὴν τῶν κατὰ Μιλτιάδην λεγομένων αἵρεσιν, ἐφεκτικώτερόν πως μέχρι νῦν διεκείμην, οὐκ ἀπορίᾳ τοῦ δύνασθαι ἐλέγχειν μὲν τὸ ψεῦδος, μαρτυρεῖν δὲ τῇ ἀληθείᾳ, δεδιὼς δὲ καὶ ἐξευλαβούμενος μή πῃ δόξω τισὶν ἐπισυγγράφειν ἢ ἐπιδιατάσσεσθαι τῷ τῆς τοῦ εὐαγγελίου καινῆς διαθήκης λόγῳ, ᾧ μήτε προσθεῖναι μήτε ἀφελεῖν δυνατὸν τῷ κατὰ τὸ εὐαγγέλιον αὐτὸ πολιτεύεσθαι προῃρημένῳ. (4) προσφάτως δὲ γενόμενος ἐν Ἀγκύρᾳ τῆς Γαλατίας καὶ καταλαβὼν τὴν κατὰ τόπον ἐκκλησίαν ὑπὸ τῆς νέας ταύτης, οὐχ, ὡς αὐτοί φασιν, προφητείας, πολὺ δὲ μᾶλλον, ὡς δειχθήσεται, ψευδοπροφητείας διατεθρυλημένην, καθ' ὅσον δυνατόν, τοῦ κυρίου παρασχόντος, περὶ αὐτῶν τε τούτων καὶ τῶν προτεινομένων ὑπ' αὐτῶν ἕκαστά τε διελέχθημεν ἡμέραις πλείοσιν ἐν τῇ ἐκκλησίᾳ, ὡς τὴν μὲν ἐκκλησίαν ἀγαλλιαθῆναι καὶ πρὸς τὴν ἀλήθειαν ἐπιρρωσθῆναι, τοὺς δ' ἐξ ἐναντίας πρὸς τὸ παρὸν ἀποκρουσθῆναι καὶ τοὺς ἀντιθέτους λυπηθῆναι. (5) ἀξιούντων οὖν τῶν κατὰ τόπον πρεσβυτέρων ὅπως τῶν λεχθέντων κατὰ τῶν ἀντιδιατιθεμένων τῷ τῆς ἀληθείας λόγῳ ὑπόμνημά τι καταλείπωμεν, παρόντος καὶ τοῦ συμπρεσβυτέρου ἡμῶν Ζωτικοῦ τοῦ Ὀτρηνοῦ, τοῦτο μὲν οὐκ ἐπράξαμεν, ἐπηγγειλάμεθα δέ, ἐνθάδε γράψαντες, τοῦ κυρίου διδόντος, διὰ σπουδῆς πέμψειν αὐτοῖς."

(6) ταῦτα καὶ ἑξῆς τούτοις ἕτερα κατ' ἀρχὰς εἰπὼν τοῦ λόγου, τὸν αἴτιον τῆς δηλουμένης αἱρέσεως προϊὼν τοῦτον ἀνιστορεῖ τὸν τρόπον· "ἡ τοίνυν ἔνστασις αὐτῶν καὶ πρόσφατος τοῦ ἀποσχίσματος αἵρεσις πρὸς τὴν ἐκκλησίαν τὴν αἰτίαν ἔσχε τοιαύτην. (7) κώμη τις εἶναι λέγεται ἐν τῇ κατὰ τὴν Φρυγίαν Μυσίᾳ, καλουμένη Ἀρδαβαῦ τοὔνομα· ἔνθα φασί τινα τῶν νεοπίστων πρώτως, Μοντανὸν τοὔνομα, κατὰ Γρᾶτον Ἀσίας ἀνθύπατον, ἐν ἐπιθυμίᾳ ψυχῆς ἀμέτρῳ φιλοπρωτείας δόντα πάροδον εἰς ἑαυτὸν τῷ ἀντικειμένῳ πνευματοφορηθῆναί τε καὶ αἰφνιδίως

beginning to spring up as it were, at that time, when Montanus, together with his false prophetesses, was making the beginnings of his deviations.

The Anonymous

23. Ibid. 5.16-17.

16. (1) Against the so-called Cataphyrgian heresy, the power which defends the truth raised up a mighty and unconquerable warrior at Hierapolis in Apolinarius, who has been mentioned previously, and with him many other learned men at that time. These men have also left us an abundance of raw material for history. (2) One of these men, in beginning his treatise against them, first indicates that he had also attacked them with oral refutations. He speaks in this manner in his preface: (3) "For a very long and considerable time, dear Avircius Marcellus, you have enjoined me to compose a treatise against the heresy of those who follow Miltiades. I was rather hesitant until now, not because I lacked the ability to refute the lie and bear testimony to the truth, but from fear and concern lest in any way I appear to some to add a new writing or add to the word of the new covenant of the gospel to which one who has chosen to live according to the gospel itself can neither add nor substract (cf. Rev 22:18-19). (4) But when I had just arrived in Ancyra of Galatia and perceived that the Church there had been deafened not by this new prophecy, as they call it, but much rather, as will be demonstrated, by false prophecy, to the best of our ability, with the Lord's help, we lectured for many days in the Church both concerning these very people and also on the particulars of the things put forward by them. As a result, the Church rejoiced and was encouraged in the truth, but our opponents were repelled for the present, and our antagonists grieved. (5) Although the presbyters of the place thought it worthwhile that we leave behind some written reminder of what was said against the opponents of the word of truth, Zoticus of Otrous, our fellow presbyter also being present, we did not do this, but we promised that after we had written it here, as the Lord should grant, we would send it to them with haste."

(6) After he had made these and other remarks after them at the beginning of his treatise, he proceeds and records the cause of the heresy under discussion in this way. "Their opposition and recent heresy of schism in relation to the Church had the following cause. (7) There is said to be a village called Ardabav in Phrygian Mysia. There, they say, first, when Gratus was proconsul of Asia, a recent convert to the faith named Montanus, in his soul's immense ambitious desire, gave the adversary access to himself and was carried away as by the Spirit, and suddenly experiencing some kind of possession and spurious ecstasy, he was inspired and be-

ἐν κατοχῇ τινι καὶ παρεκστάσει γενόμενον ἐνθουσιᾶν ἄρξασθαί τε λαλεῖν καὶ ξενοφωνεῖν, παρὰ τὸ κατὰ παράδοσιν καὶ κατὰ διαδοχὴν ἄνωθεν
τῆς ἐκκλησίας ἔθος δῆθεν προφητεύοντα. (8) τῶν δὲ κατ᾽ ἐκεῖνο καιροῦ ἐν
τῇ τῶν νόθων ἐκφωνημάτων ἀκροάσει γενομένων οἱ μὲν ὡς ἐπὶ ἐνεργουμένῳ
καὶ δαιμονῶντι καὶ ἐν πλάνης πνεύματι ὑπάρχοντι καὶ τοὺς ὄχλους
ταράττοντι ἀχθόμενοι, ἐπετίμων καὶ λαλεῖν ἐκώλυον, μεμνημένοι τῆς
τοῦ κυρίου διαστολῆς τε καὶ ἀπειλῆς πρὸς τὸ φυλάττεσθαι τὴν τῶν ψευδοπροφητῶν ἐγρηγορότως παρουσίαν· οἱ δὲ ὡς ἁγίῳ πνεύματι καὶ προφητικῷ
χαρίσματι ἐπαιρόμενοι καὶ οὐχ ἥκιστα χαυνούμενοι καὶ τῆς διαστολῆς
τοῦ κυρίου ἐπιλανθανόμενοι, τὸ βλαψίφρον καὶ ὑποκοριστικὸν καὶ λαοπλάνον πνεῦμα προυκαλοῦντο, θελγόμενοι καὶ πλανώμενοι ὑπ᾽ αὐτοῦ, εἰς
τὸ μηκέτι κωλύεσθαι σιωπᾶν. (9) τέχνῃ δέ τινι, μᾶλλον δὲ τοιαύτῃ μεθόδῳ
κακοτεχνίας ὁ διάβολος τὴν κατὰ τῶν παρηκόων ἀπώλειαν μηχανησάμενος
καὶ παρ᾽ ἀξίαν ὑπ᾽ αὐτῶν τιμώμενος ὑπεξήγειρέν τε καὶ προσεξέκαυσεν
αὐτῶν τὴν ἀποκεκοιμημένην ἀπὸ τῆς κατ᾽ ἀλήθειαν πίστεως διάνοιαν, ὡς
καὶ ἑτέρας τινὰς δύο γυναῖκας ἐπεγεῖραι καὶ τοῦ νόθου πνεύματος
πληρῶσαι, ὡς καὶ λαλεῖν ἐκφρόνως καὶ ἀκαίρως καὶ ἀλλοτριοτρόπως, ὁμοίως
τῷ προειρημένῳ. καὶ τοὺς μὲν χαίροντας καὶ χαυνουμένους ἐπ᾽ αὐτῷ
μακαρίζοντος τοῦ πνεύματος καὶ διὰ τοῦ μεγέθους τῶν ἐπαγγελμάτων
ἐκφυσιοῦντος, ἔσθ᾽ ὅπῃ δὲ καὶ κατακρίνοντος στοχαστικῶς καὶ ἀξιο-
πίστως αὐτοὺς ἄντικρυς, ἵνα καὶ ἐλεγκτικὸν εἶναι δοκῇ (ὀλίγοι δ᾽ ἦσαν
οὗτοι τῶν Φρυγῶν ἐξηπατημένοι), τὴν δὲ καθόλου καὶ πᾶσιν τὴν ὑπὸ τὸν
οὐρανὸν ἐκκλησίαν βλασφημεῖν διδάσκοντος τοῦ ἀπηυθαδισμένου πνεύματος, ὅτι μήτε τιμὴν μήτε πάροδον εἰς αὐτὴν τὸ ψευδοπροφητικὸν ἐλάμ-
βανε πνεῦμα, (10) τῶν γὰρ κατὰ τὴν Ἀσίαν πιστῶν πολλάκις καὶ πολλαχῇ
τῆς Ἀσίας εἰς τοῦτο συνελθόντων καὶ τοὺς προσφάτους λόγους ἐξετα-
σάντων καὶ βεβήλους ἀποφηνάντων καὶ ἀποδοκιμασάντων τὴν αἵρεσιν, οὕτω
δὴ τῆς τε ἐκκλησίας ἐξεώσθησαν καὶ τῆς κοινωνίας εἴρχθησαν."
(11) ταῦτα ἐν πρώτοις ἱστορήσας καὶ δι᾽ ὅλου τοῦ συγγράμματος τὸν
ἔλεγχον τῆς κατ᾽ αὐτοὺς πλάνης ἐπαγαγών ἐν τῷ δευτέρῳ περὶ τῆς
τελευτῆς τῶν προδεδηλωμένων ταῦτά φησιν· (12) "ἐπειδὴ τοίνυν καὶ
προφητοφόντας ἡμᾶς ἀπεκάλουν, ὅτι μὴ τοὺς ἀμετροφώνους αὐτῶν προφήτας
ἐδεξάμεθα (τούτους γὰρ εἶναί φασιν οὕσπερ ἐπηγγείλατο τῷ λαῷ πέμψειν ὁ κύριος), ἀποκρινάσθωσαν ἡμῖν πρὸς θεοῦ· ἔστιν τις, ὦ βέλτιστοι,
τούτων τῶν ἀπὸ Μοντανοῦ καὶ τῶν γυναικῶν λαλεῖν ἀρξαμένων ὅστις ὑπὸ
Ἰουδαίων ἐδιώχθη ἢ ὑπὸ παρανόμων ἀπεκτάνθη; οὐδείς. οὐδέ γέ τις αὐτῶν
κρατηθεὶς ὑπὲρ τοῦ ὀνόματος ἀνεσταυρώθη; οὐ γὰρ οὖν. οὐδὲ μὴν οὐδὲ
ἐν συναγωγαῖς Ἰουδαίων τῶν γυναικῶν τις ἐμαστιγώθη ποτὲ ἢ ἐλιθοβο-
λήθη; οὐδαμόσε οὐδαμῶς. (13) ἄλλῳ δὲ θανάτῳ τελευτῆσαι λέγονται
Μοντανός τε καὶ Μαξίμιλλα. τούτους γὰρ ὑπὸ πνεύματος βλαψίφρονος
ἑκατέρους ὑποκινήσαντος λόγος ἀναρτῆσαι ἑαυτοὺς οὐχ ὁμοῦ, κατὰ δὲ

gan to speak and say strange things, prophesying, as he pretended, contrary to the custom related to the tradition and succession of the Church from the beginning. (8) Of those who heard those spurious utterances at that moment, some, being irritated as at one who is inspired and possessed by a devil and a spirit of error and is troubling the multitudes, rebuked him and forbid him to speak, remembering the command of the Lord and his warning to maintain an alert guard against the coming of false prophets (cf. Matt 7:15). Others, however, as if exalted by a holy spirit and a prophetic gift, and, above all, conceited and unmindful of the Lord's command, provoked the maddening, cajoling spirit which deceived the people, being beguiled and mislead by it so that silence could no longer be imposed. (9) But by some art, or rather by such a ruse of false artifice, the devil, after he had devised the destruction of the disobedient and was honored unworthily by them, secretly excited and inflamed their understanding which had departed from the true faith. Consequently he also raised up two other women and filled them with the spurious spirit, so that, like the man mentioned earlier, they spoke in a frenzied manner, unsuitably, and abnormally. And the spirit blessed those who rejoiced and were conceited in him, and puffed them up on the basis of the greatness of his promises. And, in a way, he also openly condemned them in a pointed and plausible manner, so that he might also appear to be critical (but few were those of the Phrygians who were deceived). And the boldly speaking spirit taught the whole Church in general everywhere to blaspheme, because the spirit of false prophecy received neither honor from it nor access to it. (10) For the faithful in Asia met for this purpose many times and in many places in Asia. They examined the recent sayings carefully, declared them to be profane, and rejected the heresy. So at length they were thrust out of the Church and excluded from the fellowship.''

(11) After he has narrated these things in the first pages and has advanced the refutation of their error through the whole work, he speaks as follows about the end of the aforesaid persons in the second book. (12) ''Since then they also call us prophet-slayers because we did not receive their prophets who spoke immoderately (for they say these were those whom the Lord promised to send to the people [cf. Matt 23:34]), let them answer us before God. Who, noble sirs, of these who began to speak from Montanus and the women, is there who has been persecuted by the Jews or slain by the lawless? Not one. Or has anyone of them been arrested and crucified for the name? Certainly not. Or was anyone of the women ever beaten or stoned in the synagogues of the Jews (cf. Matt 23:34)? In no way anywhere. (13) But both Montanus and Maximilla are said to have died by another death. For the story is that each of these, deranged by a maddening

τὸν τῆς ἑκάστου τελευτῆς καιρὸν φήμη πολλὴ καὶ οὕτω δὲ τελευτῆσαι
καὶ τὸν βίον καταστρέψαι Ἰούδα προδότου δίκην, (14) καθάπερ καὶ τὸν
θαυμαστὸν ἐκεῖνον τὸν πρῶτον τῆς κατ᾿ αὐτοὺς λεγομένης προφητείας
οἷον ἐπίτροπόν τινα Θεόδοτον πολὺς αἱρεῖ λόγος ὡς αἱρόμενόν ποτε καὶ
ἀναλαμβανόμενον εἰς οὐρανοὺς παρεκστῆναί τε καὶ καταπιστεῦσαι ἑαυτὸν τῷ τῆς ἀπάτης πνεύματι καὶ δισκευθέντα κακῶς τελευτῆσαι· φασὶ
γοῦν τοῦτο οὕτως γεγονέναι. (15) ἀλλὰ μὴ ἄνευ τοῦ ἰδεῖν ἡμᾶς ἐπί-
στασθαί τι τῶν τοιούτων νομίζωμεν, ὦ μακάριε· ἴσως μὲν γὰρ οὕτως, ἴσως
δὲ οὐχ οὕτως τετελευτήκασιν Μοντανός τε καὶ Θεόδοτος καὶ ἡ προ-
ειρημένη γυνή.

(16) αὖθις δ᾿ ἐν τῷ αὐτῷ φησιν λόγῳ τοὺς τότε ἱεροὺς ἐπισκόπους
πεπειρᾶσθαι μὲν τὸ ἐν τῇ Μαξιμίλλῃ πνεῦμα διελέγξαι, κεκωλύσθαι δὲ
πρὸς ἑτέρων, συνεργούντων δηλαδὴ τῷ πνεύματι· (17) γράφει δὲ οὕτως·
"καὶ μὴ λεγέτω ἐν τῷ αὐτῷ λόγῳ τῷ κατὰ Ἀστέριον Ὀρβανὸν τὸ διὰ
Μαξιμίλλης πνεῦμα 'διώκομαι ὡς λύκος ἐκ προβάτων· οὐκ εἰμὶ λύκος· ῥῆμά
εἰμι καὶ πνεῦμα καὶ δύναμις,' ἀλλὰ τὴν ἐν τῷ πνεύματι δύναμιν ἐναργῶς
δειξάτω καὶ ἐλεγξάτω καὶ ἐξομολογεῖσθαι διὰ τοῦ πνεύματος καταναγ-
κασάτω τοὺς τότε παρόντας εἰς τὸ δοκιμάσαι καὶ διαλεχθῆναι τῷ πνεύματι λαλοῦντι, ἄνδρας δοκίμους καὶ ἐπισκόπους, Ζωτικὸν ἀπὸ Κουμάνης
κώμης καὶ Ἰουλιανὸν ἀπὸ Ἀπαμείας, ὧν οἱ περὶ Θεμίσωνα τὰ στόματα
φιμώσαντες οὐκ εἴασαν τὸ ψευδὲς καὶ λαοπλάνον πνεῦμα ὑπ᾿ αὐτῶν
ἐλεγχθῆναι." (18) ἐν ταὐτῷ δὲ πάλιν ἕτερα μεταξὺ πρὸς ἔλεγχον τῶν
τῆς Μαξιμίλλης ψευδοπροφητειῶν εἰπών, ὁμοῦ τόν τε χρόνον καθ᾿ ὃν ταῦτ᾿
ἔγραφεν, σημαίνει καὶ τῶν προρρήσεων αὐτῆς μέμνηται δι᾿ ὧν πολέμους
ἔσεσθαι καὶ ἀκαταστασίας προεμαντεύσατο, ὧν καὶ τὴν ψευδολογίαν
εὐθύνει, ὧδε λέγων·

(19) "καὶ πῶς οὐ καταφανὲς ἤδη γέγονεν καὶ τοῦτο τὸ ψεῦδος; πλείω
γὰρ ἢ τρισκαίδεκα ἔτη εἰς ταύτην τὴν ἡμέραν ἐξ οὗ τετελεύτηκεν ἡ
γυνή, καὶ οὔτε μερικὸς οὔτε καθολικὸς κόσμῳ γέγονεν πόλεμος, ἀλλὰ καὶ
Χριστιανοῖς μᾶλλον εἰρήνη διάμονος ἐξ ἐλέου θεοῦ."

(20) καὶ ταῦτα δ᾿ ἐκ τοῦ δευτέρου συγγράμματος. καὶ ἀπὸ τοῦ τρίτου
δὲ σμικρὰς παραθήσομαι λέξεις, δι᾿ ὧν πρὸς τοὺς αὐχοῦντας ὡς ἄρα
πλείους καὶ αὐτῶν μεμαρτυρηκότες εἶεν, ταῦτα φησιν· "ὅταν τοίνυν ἐν
πᾶσι τοῖς εἰρημένοις ἐλεγχθέντες ἀπορήσωσιν, ἐπὶ τοὺς μάρτυρας κατα-
φεύγειν πειρῶνται, λέγοντες πολλοὺς ἔχειν μάρτυρας καὶ τοῦτ᾿ εἶναι
τεκμήριον πιστὸν τῆς δυνάμεως τοῦ παρ᾿ αὐτοῖς λεγομένου προφητικοῦ
πνεύματος. τὸ δ᾿ ἐστὶν ἄρα, ὡς ἔοικεν, παντὸς μᾶλλον οὐκ ἀληθές. (21)
καὶ γὰρ τῶν ἄλλων αἱρέσεών τινες πλείστους ὅσους ἔχουσι μάρτυρας,

spirit, hung themselves, but not together. There was, however, much gossip at the time of each one's death, and they were said to have died thus and to have ended their life like the traitor Judas. (14) In the same way also a widespread report suggests that that marvelous man, the first trustee as it were of their so-called prophecy, a certain Theodotus, when he was once lifted up and taken up into heaven, went into spurious ecstasy and entrusted himself to the spirit of deceit, and having been thrown down, died miserably. They say, at least, that it happened in this way. (15) But since we did not see them, we do not consider ourselves to have any knowledge of such things. For perhaps Montanus and Theodotus and the woman mentioned earlier died like this, but perhaps they did not.''

(16) And again, in the same book he says that the holy bishops at that time attempted to refute the spirit in Maximilla, but were hindered by others who were clearly working with the spirit. (17) He writes as follows. ''And let not the spirit which speaks through Maximilla say, in the same book according to Asterius Orbanus: 'I am pursued like a wolf from the sheep. I am not a wolf (cf. Matt 7:15). I am word, and spirit, and power' (cf. 1 Cor 2:4). But let him demonstrate clearly and prove the power in the spirit, and let him constrain through the spirit those men to acknowledge him, who were present then to examine and converse with the spirit when it spoke. They were esteemed men and bishops, Zoticus from the village of Cumane, and Julian from Apamea. The party of Themiso muzzled their mouths and did not permit the false and people-deceiving spirit to be refuted by them.'' (18) And again, after he has said other things in the same book to refute the false prophesies of Maximilla, in the same place he indicates the time he wrote these things and recalls her predictions through which she foretold that there would be wars and anarchy, the falsehood of which he also censures, speaking as follows.

(19) ''And how has it not already become manifest that this too is false? For there have been more than thirteen years to this day since the woman died, and there has been neither a local nor a general war in the world, but by the mercy of God there is rather an enduring peace even for Christians.''

(20) These words come from the second book. But I will also quote a few words from the third book, where he addresses in the following way those who boast that perhaps they also have more martyrs. ''Whenever they are at a loss because they have been refuted in all the things said, they attempt to take refuge in the martyrs by saying that they have many martyrs, and that this is a trustworthy proof of the power of the so-called prophetic spirit among them. But this is perhaps, as it appears, further from being true than anything. (21) For indeed some of the other heresies have the

καὶ οὐ παρὰ τοῦτο δήπου συγκαταθησόμεθα, οὐδὲ ἀλήθειαν ἔχειν αὐτοὺς ὁμολογήσομεν. καὶ πρῶτοί γε οἱ ἀπὸ τῆς Μαρκίωνος αἱρέσεως Μαρκιανισταὶ καλούμενοι πλείστους ὅσους ἔχειν Χριστοῦ μάρτυρας λέγουσιν, ἀλλὰ τόν γε Χριστὸν αὐτὸν κατ' ἀλήθειαν οὐχ ὁμολογοῦσιν." καὶ μετὰ βραχέα τούτοις ἐπιφέρει λέγων· (22) "ὅθεν τοι καὶ ἐπειδὰν οἱ ἐπὶ τὸ τῆς κατ' ἀλήθειαν πίστεως μαρτύριον κληθέντες ἀπὸ τῆς ἐκκλησίας τύχωσι μετά τινων τῶν ἀπὸ τῆς τῶν Φρυγῶν αἱρέσεως λεγομένων μαρτύρων, διαφέρονταί τε πρὸς αὐτοὺς καὶ μὴ κοινωνήσαντες αὐτοῖς τελειοῦνται διὰ τὸ μὴ βούλεσθαι συγκαταθέσθαι τῷ διὰ Μοντανοῦ καὶ τῶν γυναικῶν πνεύματι. καὶ ὅτι τοῦτ' ἀληθές, καὶ ἐπὶ τῶν ἡμετέρων χρόνων ἐν Ἀπαμείᾳ τῇ πρὸς Μαιάνδρῳ τυγχάνει γεγενημένον ἐν τοῖς περὶ Γάϊον καὶ Ἀλέξανδρον ἀπὸ Εὐμενείας μαρτυρήσασι πρόδηλον."

17. (1) Ἐν τούτῳ δὲ τῷ συγγράμματι καὶ Μιλτιάδου συγγραφέως μέμνηται, ὡς λόγον τινὰ καὶ αὐτοῦ κατὰ τῆς προειρημένης αἱρέσεως γεγραφότος· παραθέμενος γοῦν αὐτῶν λέξεις τινάς, ἐπιφέρει λέγων· "ταῦτα εὑρὼν ἔν τινι συγγράμματι αὐτῶν ἐνισταμένων τῷ Μιλτιάδου τοῦ ἀδελφοῦ συγγράμματι, ἐν ᾧ ἀποδείκνυσιν περὶ τοῦ μὴ δεῖν προφήτην ἐν ἐκστάσει λαλεῖν, ἐπετεμόμην."

(2) ὑποκαταβὰς δ' ἐν ταὐτῷ τοὺς κατὰ τὴν καινὴν διαθήκην προπεφητευκότας καταλέγει, ἐν οἷς καταριθμεῖ Ἀμμίαν, τινὰ καὶ Κυδραῖον, λέγων οὕτως· "ἀλλ' ὅ γε ψευδοπροφήτης ἐν παρεκστάσει, ᾧ ἕπεται ἄδεια καὶ ἀφοβία, ἀρχομένου μὲν ἐξ ἑκουσίου ἀμαθίας, καταστρέφοντος δὲ εἰς ἀκούσιον μανίαν ψυχῆς, ὡς προείρηται. (3) τοῦτον δὲ τὸν τρόπον οὔτε τινὰ τῶν κατὰ τὴν παλαιὰν οὔτε τῶν κατὰ τὴν καινὴν πνευματοφορηθέντα προφήτην δεῖξαι δυνήσονται, οὔτε Ἄγαβον οὔτε Ἰούδαν οὔτε Σίλαν οὔτε τὰς Φιλίππου θυγατέρας, οὔτε τὴν ἐν Φιλαδελφίᾳ Ἀμμίαν οὔτε Κοδρᾶτον, οὔτε εἰ δή τινας ἄλλους μηδὲν αὐτοῖς προσήκοντας καυχήσονται."

(4) καὶ αὖθις δὲ μετὰ βραχέα ταῦτά φησιν· "εἰ γὰρ μετὰ Κοδρᾶτον καὶ τὴν ἐν Φιλαδελφίᾳ Ἀμμίαν, ὥς φασιν, αἱ περὶ Μοντανὸν διεδέξαντο γυναῖκες τὸ προφητικὸν χάρισμα, τοὺς ἀπὸ Μοντανοῦ καὶ τῶν γυναικῶν τίνες παρ' αὐτοῖς διεδέξαντο, δειξάτωσαν· δεῖν γὰρ εἶναι τὸ προφητικὸν χάρισμα ἐν πάσῃ τῇ ἐκκλησίᾳ μέχρι τῆς τελείας παρουσίας ὁ ἀπόστολος ἀξιοῖ. ἀλλ' οὐκ ἂν ἔχοιεν δεῖξαι τεσσαρεσκαιδέκατον ἤδη που τοῦτο ἔτος ἀπὸ τῆς Μαξιμίλλης τελευτῆς."

(5) οὗτος μὲν δὴ τοσαῦτα· ὅ γέ τοι πρὸς αὐτοῦ δεδηλωμένος Μιλτιάδης καὶ ἄλλας ἡμῖν τῆς ἰδίας περὶ τὰ θεῖα λόγια σπουδῆς μνήμας καταλέ-

greatest possible number of martyrs, and I presume we shall not agree with them for this reason, nor acknowledge that they possess the truth. And first of all those of the heresy of Marcion, called Marcionites, claim to have the greatest possible number of martyrs of Christ, but they do not confess the Christ himself according to the truth.'' And after some brief remarks, he adds to these words, saying: (22) ''For this reason also, whenever those from the Church who have been called to martyrdom for the true faith happen to be with any of the so-called martyrs from the heresy of the Phrygians, they separate to themselves and die not in fellowship with them because they are not willing to agree with the spirit which speaks through Montanus and the woman. And that this is true is obvious in what has happened even in our times in Apamea on the Menander in those who were martyred with Gaius and Alexander from Eumeneia.''

17. (1) He also mentioned the writer Miltiades[1] in this work, since he too had written a certain treatise against the heresy under discussion. After he has quoted some of their statements, he adds, saying: ''I have abridged these words, having found them in a writing of theirs when they attacked the writing of our brother Miltiades, in which he proves that a prophet does not have to speak ecstatically.''

(2) And further down in the same work he lists those who have prophesied according to the New Testament, among whom he reckons a certain Ammia and Quadratus, speaking as follows: ''But the false prophet speaks in spurious ecstasy, which licentiousness and impiety accompany. He begins with voluntary ignorance, but ends up in involuntary madness of soul. (3) But they will not be able to prove that any prophet either of those in the Old Testament or the New was inspired in this way; they shall boast neither of Agabus, nor Judas (cf. Acts 11:28; 21:10; 15:32; 21:9), nor Silas, nor the daughters of Philip, nor of Ammia in Philadelphia, nor Quadratus, nor if indeed there are any others who have no relation to them at all.''

(4) And again, a little later he speaks as follows: ''For if, as they say, the women who were disciples of Montanus received the prophetic gift as successors of Quadratus and Ammia in Philadelphia, let them point out who among them succeeded the followers of Montanus and the women, for the apostle is of the opinion that the prophetic gift must be in the whole Church until the final coming (cf. Eph 4:11; 1 Cor 1:7; 13:8-12). But they would not be able to point to anyone, although this is now the fourteenth year, I suppose, since the death of Maximilla.''

(5) These are the things he relates, The Miltiades he has referred to has also left us other records of his zeal concerning the divine oracles both in

---

[1]The MSS, have Alcibiades. Most editors emend the text to read Miltiades.

λοιπεν ἔν τε οἷς πρὸς Ἕλληνας συνέταξε λόγοις καὶ τοῖς πρὸς Ἰουδαίους, ἑκατέρᾳ ἰδίως ὑποθέσει ἐν δυσὶν ὑπαντήσας συγγράμμασιν, ἔτι
δὲ καὶ πρὸς κοσμικοὺς ἄρχοντας ὑπὲρ ἧς μετήει φιλοσοφίας πεποίηται
ἀπολογίαν.

Apollonius

24. Ibid. 5.18 (Schwartz, pp. 472-78).

18. (1) Τῆς δὲ κατὰ Φρύγας καλουμένης αἱρέσεως καὶ Ἀπολλώνιος,
ἐκκλησιαστικὸς συγγραφεύς, ἀκμαζούσης εἰς ἔτι τότε κατὰ τὴν Φρυγίαν
ἔλεγχον ἐνστησάμενος, ἴδιον κατ' αὐτῶν πεποίηται σύγγραμμα, τὰς μὲν
φερομένας αὐτῶν προφητείας ψευδεῖς οὔσας κατὰ λέξιν εὐθύνων, τὸν δὲ
βίον τῶν τῆς αἱρέσεως ἀρχηγῶν ὁποῖός τις γέγονεν, διελέγχων· αὐτοῖς
δὲ ῥήμασιν περὶ τοῦ Μοντανοῦ ταῦτα λέγοντος ἄκουε.
(2) "ἀλλὰ τίς ἐστιν οὗτος ὁ πρόσφατος διδάσκαλος, τὰ ἔργα αὐτοῦ
καὶ ἡ διδασκαλία δείκνυσιν. Οὗτός ἐστιν ὁ διδάξας λύσεις γάμων, ὁ
νηστείας νομοθετήσας, ὁ Πέπουζαν καὶ Τύμιον Ἱερουσαλὴμ ὀνομάσας
(πόλεις δ' εἰσὶν αὗται μικραὶ τῆς Φρυγίας), τοὺς πανταχόθεν ἐκεῖ
συναγαγεῖν ἐθέλων, ὁ πρακτῆρας χρημάτων καταστήσας, ὁ ἐπ' ὀνόματι
προσφορῶν τὴν δωροληψίαν ἐπιτεχνώμενος, ὁ σαλάρια χορηγῶν τοῖς
κηρύσσουσιν αὐτοῦ τὸν λόγον, ἵνα διὰ τῆς γαστριμαργίας ἡ διδασκαλία
τοῦ λόγου κρατύνηται."
(3) καὶ ταῦτα μὲν περὶ τοῦ Μοντανοῦ· καὶ περὶ τῶν προφητίδων δὲ
αὐτοῦ ὑποκαταβὰς οὕτω γράφει· "Δείκνυμεν οὖν αὐτὰς πρώτας τὰς
προφήτιδας ταύτας, ἀφ' οὗ τοῦ πνεύματος ἐπληρώθησαν, τοὺς ἄνδρας
καταλιπούσας. πῶς οὖν ἐψεύδοντο Πρίσκιλλαν παρθένον ἀποκαλοῦντες;
(4) εἶτ' ἐπιφέρει λέγων· "δοκεῖ σοι πᾶσα γραφὴ κωλύειν προφήτην λαμβάνειν δῶρα καὶ χρήματα; ὅταν οὖν ἴδω τὴν προφῆτιν εἰληφυῖαν καὶ
χρυσὸν καὶ ἄργυρον καὶ πολυτελεῖς ἐσθῆτας, πῶς αὐτὴν μὴ παραι-
τήσωμαι;
(5) αὖθις δ' ὑποκαταβὰς περί τινος τῶν κατ' αὐτοὺς ὁμολογητῶν ταῦτά
φησιν· "ἔτι δὲ καὶ Θεμίσων, ὁ τὴν ἀξιόπιστον πλεονεξίαν ἠμφιεσμένος,
ὁ μὴ βαστάσας τῆς ὁμολογίας τὸ σημεῖον, ἀλλὰ πλήθει χρημάτων ἀποθέ-
μενος τὰ δεσμά, δέον ἐπὶ τούτῳ ταπεινοφρονεῖν, ὡς μάρτυς καυχώμενος,
ἐτόλμησεν, μιμούμενος τὸν ἀπόστολον, καθολικήν τινα συνταξάμενος
ἐπιστολήν, κατηχεῖν μὲν τοὺς ἄμεινον αὐτοῦ πεπιστευκότας, συναγωνί-
ζεσθαι δὲ τοῖς τῆς κενοφωνίας λόγοις, βλασφημῆσαι δὲ εἰς τὸν κύριον
καὶ τοὺς ἀποστόλους καὶ τὴν ἁγίαν ἐκκλησίαν."
(6) καὶ περὶ ἑτέρου δὲ αὖθις τῶν κατ' αὐτοὺς τετιμημένων ὡς δὴ μαρτύρων οὕτω γράφει· "ἵνα δὲ μὴ περὶ πλειόνων λέγωμεν, ἡ προφῆτις ἡμῖν
εἰπάτω τὰ κατὰ Ἀλέξανδρον, τὸν λέγοντα ἑαυτὸν μάρτυρα, ᾧ συνε-
στιᾶται, ᾧ προσκυνοῦσιν καὶ αὐτῷ πολλοί· οὗ τὰς λῃστείας καὶ τὰ ἄλλα

treatises which he composed to the Greeks and to the Jews, having engaged each subject separately in two books. In addition he also composed an apology to the world leaders on behalf of the philosophy which he followed.

Apollonius

24. Ibid. 5.18.

18. (1) Apollonius, a writer of the Church, also entered upon a refutation of the heresy which is called Cataphrygian at the time when it was still flourishing in Phrygia. He composed his own work against them, refuting word for word as false their prophecies which were being circulated, and he exposed what kind of life the leaders of the heresy lived. Listen to him as he makes the following assertions about Montanus in his own words.

(2) "But the works and teachings of this recent teacher show what he is. He is the one who taught the dissolution of marriages, who legislated fasts, who named Pepuza and Tymion Jerusalem (now these are small towns of Phrygia), who wanted people to gather there from everywhere, who appointed revenue collectors, who contrived the acceptance of bribes in the name of offerings, who provided salaries for those who preached his doctrine that the teaching of his doctrine might prevail through gluttony."

(3) These are his words about Montanus. Further on he also writes as follows about his prophetesses: "We show, therefore, that these first prophetesses themselves left their husbands the moment they were filled with the spirit. Did they not lie, then, when they called Priscilla a virgin?"

(4) Then he adds, saying: "Does it not seem to you that all Scripture forbids a prophet to receive gifts and money (Cf. *Did.* 11.12)? When, then, I see that the prophetess has received gold and silver and expensive clothes, how shall I not reject her?"

(5) And again, further on he speaks as follows concerning one of their confessors: "And in addition also Themiso, who clothed himself with an arrogance worthy of respect, who did not endure the sign of the confession, but by means of a large sum of money avoided bonds, when he ought to have been abased by this, boasted as a martyr and, having composed a general epistle in imitation of the apostle, dared to instruct those whose faith was better than his own, and to contend with vain words, and to blaspheme against the Lord, the apostles, and the holy Church."

(6) And again he writes in this manner also of another of those honored among them as martyrs: "But that we may not speak too long, let the prophetess tell us the things about Alexander, who calls himself a martyr, with whom she lives, whom many also worship. It is not necessary that we

τολμήματα ἐφ᾽ οἷς κεκόλασται, οὐχ ἡμᾶς δεῖ λέγειν, ἀλλὰ ὁ ὀπισθόδομος ἔχει. (7) τίς οὖν τίνι χαρίζεται τὰ ἁμαρτήματα; πότερον ὁ προφήτης τὰς ληστείας τῷ μάρτυρι ἢ ὁ μάρτυς τῷ προφήτῃ τὰς πλεονεξίας; εἰρηκότος γὰρ τοῦ κυρίου μὴ κτήσησθε χρυσὸν μήτε ἄργυρον μηδὲ δύο χιτῶνας, οὗτοι πᾶν τοὐναντίον πεπλημμελήκασιν περὶ τὰς τούτων τῶν ἀπηγορευμένων κτήσεις. δείξομεν γὰρ τοὺς λεγομένους παρ᾽ αὐτοῖς προφήτας καὶ μάρτυρας μὴ μόνον παρὰ πλουσίων, ἀλλὰ καὶ παρὰ πτωχῶν καὶ ὀρφανῶν καὶ χηρῶν κερματιζομένους. (8) καὶ εἰ πεποίθησιν ἔχουσιν, στήτωσαν ἐν τούτῳ καὶ διορισάσθωσαν ἐπὶ τούτοις, ἵνα ἐὰν ἐλεγχθῶσιν, κἂν τοῦ λοιποῦ παύσωνται πλημμελοῦντες. δεῖ γὰρ τοὺς καρποὺς δοκιμάζεσθαι τοῦ προφήτου· ἀπὸ γὰρ τοῦ καρποῦ τὸ ξύλον γινώσκεται. (9) ἵνα δὲ τοῖς βουλομένοις τὰ κατὰ Ἀλέξανδρον ἦ γνώριμα, κέκριται ὑπὸ Αἰμιλίου Φροντίνου ἀνθυπάτου ἐν Ἐφέσῳ, οὐ διὰ τὸ ὄνομα, ἀλλὰ δι᾽ ἃς ἐτόλμησεν ληστείας, ὢν ἤδη παραβάτης· εἶτ᾽ ἐπιψευσάμενος τῷ ὀνόματι τοῦ κυρίου, ἀπολέλυται, πλανήσας τοὺς ἐκεῖ πιστούς. καὶ ἡ ἰδία παροικία αὐτόν, ὅθεν ἦν, οὐκ ἐδέξατο διὰ τὸ εἶναι αὐτὸν ληστήν, καὶ οἱ θέλοντες μαθεῖν τὰ κατ᾽ αὐτὸν ἔχουσιν τὸ τῆς Ἀσίας δημόσιον ἀρχεῖον· (10) ὃν ὁ προφήτης συνόντα πολλοῖς ἔτεσιν ἀγνοεῖ. τοῦτον ἐλέγχοντες ἡμεῖς δι᾽ αὐτοῦ καὶ τὴν ὑπόστασιν ἐξελέγχομεν τοῦ προφήτου. τὸ ὅμοιον ἐπὶ πολλῶν δυνάμεθα ἀποδεῖξαι, καὶ εἰ θαρροῦσιν, ὑπομεινάτωσαν τὸν ἔλεγχον."

(11) πάλιν τε αὖ ἐν ἑτέρῳ τόπῳ τοῦ συγγράμματος περὶ ὧν αὐχοῦσι προφητῶν ἐπιλέγει ταῦτα· "ἐὰν ἀρνῶνται δῶρα τοὺς προφήτας αὐτῶν εἰληφέναι, τοῦθ᾽ ὁμολογησάτωσαν ὅτι ἐὰν ἐλεγχθῶσιν εἰληφότες, οὐκ εἰσὶ προφῆται, καὶ μυρίας ἀποδείξεις τούτων παραστήσομεν. ἀναγκαῖον δέ ἐστιν πάντας καρποὺς δοκιμάζεσθαι προφήτου. προφήτης, εἰπέ μοι, βάπτεται; προφήτης στιβίζεται; προφήτης φιλοκοσμεῖ; προφήτης τάβλαις καὶ κύβοις παίζει; προφήτης δανείζει; ταῦτα ὁμολογησάτωσαν πότερον ἔξεστιν ἢ μή, ἐγὼ δ᾽ ὅτι γέγονεν παρ᾽ αὐτοῖς, δείξω."

(12) ὁ δ᾽ αὐτὸς οὗτος Ἀπολλώνιος κατὰ τὸ αὐτὸ σύγγραμμα ἱστορεῖ ὡς ἄρα τεσσαρακοστὸν ἐτύγχανεν ἔτος ἐπὶ τὴν τοῦ συγγράμματος αὐτοῦ γραφὴν ἐξ οὗ τῇ προσποιήτῳ αὐτοῦ προφητείᾳ ὁ Μοντανὸς ἐπικεχείρηκεν, (13) καὶ πάλιν φησὶν ὡς ἄρα Ζωτικός, οὗ καὶ ὁ πρότερος συγγραφεὺς ἐμνημόνευσεν, ἐν Πεπούζοις προφητεύειν δὴ προσποιουμένης τῆς Μαξιμίλλης ἐπιστὰς διελέγξαι τὸ ἐνεργοῦν ἐν αὐτῇ πνεῦμα πεπείραται, ἐκωλύθη γε μὴν πρὸς τῶν τὰ ἐκείνης φρονούντων. (14) καὶ Θρασέα δέ τινος τῶν τότε μαρτύρων μνημονεύει. ἔτι δὲ ὡς ἐκ παραδόσεως τὸν σωτῆρά φησιν

mention his robberies and other shameless acts for which he has been punished; they are a matter of public record. (7) Who forgives the sins for whom? Does the prophetess forgive the martyr of robbery, or does the martyr forgive the prophetess for greed? For although the Lord has said, 'Possess not gold nor silver nor two coats' (cf. Matt 10:9-10), these, completely to the contrary, have transgressed concerning the possession of these forbidden things. For we will show that the so-called prophets and martyrs among them collect money not only from the rich, but also from the poor, the orphans, and the widows. (8) And if they are confident, let them stop at this and offer an explanation for these things, so that if they are convicted, they may at any rate cease sinning for the future. For the fruits of the prophet must be tested, for the tree is known by its fruit (cf. Matt 12:33; 7:15-20). (9) But that the matters related to Alexander might be well known to those who wish, he was condemned by Aemilius Pompinus, proconsul in Ephesus, not for the name, but for the robberies he had dared, already being a transgressor. Then, after he had falsely called himself by the name of the Lord and deceived the faithful there, he was released. And his own diocese whence he had come would not receive him because he was a robber. Those who wish to learn about the matters related to him have the public archive of Asia. (10) The prophet is ignorant of the man with whom he lived for many years. By exposing this man, through him we also expose the real nature of the prophet. We can demonstrate the same thing in the case of many, and if they have the courage, let them submit to the scrutiny.

(11) And again in another passage of the work he writes these things in addition about the prophets of which they boast: "If they deny that their prophets have taken gifts, let them agree that if they be convicted of having taken them, they are not prophets, and we will present countless proofs of these things. And all the fruits of a prophet must be tested. Tell me, does a prophet dye his hair? Does a prophet paint his eyelids? Does a prophet love ornaments? Does a prophet play at dice-boards and with dice? Does a prophet lend money at usury? Let them admit whether these things are right or not, and I will show that they have been done among them."

(12) And this same Apollonius relates in the same work that at the moment he wrote his work it was the fortieth year from the time Montanus had set to work at his pretended prophecy. (13) And again he says that Zoticus, whom the former writer also mentioned, having appeared when Maximilla was pretending to prophesy in Pepuza, had attempted to refute the spirit which was at work in her; he was prevented, however, by those who agreed with her.

(14) And he also mentions a certain Thraseas among the martyrs at that time. And he says further, as though from tradition, that the Savior had

προστεταχέναι τοῖς αὐτοῦ ἀποστόλοις ἐπὶ δώδεκα ἔτεσιν μὴ χωρισθῆναι τῆς Ἱερουσαλήμ, κέχρηται δὲ καὶ μαρτυρίαις ἀπὸ τῆς Ἰωάννου Ἀποκαλύψεως, καὶ νεκρὸν δὲ δυνάμει θείᾳ πρὸς αὐτοῦ Ἰωάννου ἐν τῇ Ἐφέσῳ ἐγηγέρθαι ἱστορεῖ, καὶ ἄλλα τινά φησιν, δι' ὧν ἱκανῶς τῆς προειρημένης αἱρέσεως πληρέστατα διηύθυνεν τὴν πλάνην. ταῦτα καὶ ὁ Ἀπολλώνιος.

Serapion

25. Ibid. 5.19 (Schwartz, pp. 478-80).

19. (1) Τῶν δὲ Ἀπολιναρίου κατὰ τῆς δηλωθείσης αἱρέσεως μνήμην πεποίηται Σεραπίων, ὃν ἐπὶ τῶν δηλουμένων χρόνων μετὰ Μαξιμῖνον ἐπίσκοπον τῆς Ἀντιοχέων ἐκκλησίας γενέσθαι κατέχει λόγος· μέμνηται δ' αὐτοῦ ἐν ἰδίᾳ ἐπιστολῇ τῇ πρὸς Καρικὸν καὶ Πόντιον, ἐν ᾗ διευθύνων καὶ αὐτὸς τὴν αὐτὴν αἵρεσιν, ἐπιλέγει ταῦτα·
(2) "ὅπως δὲ καὶ τοῦτο εἰδῆτε ὅτι τῆς ψευδοῦς ταύτης τάξεως τῆς ἐπικαλουμένης νέας προφητείας ἐβδέλυκται ἡ ἐνέργεια παρὰ πάσῃ τῇ ἐν κόσμῳ ἀδελφότητι, πέπομφα ὑμῖν καὶ Κλαυδίου Ἀπολιναρίου, τοῦ μακαριωτάτου γενομένου ἐν Ἱεραπόλει τῆς Ἀσίας ἐπισκόπου, γράμματα."
(3) ἐν ταύτῃ δὲ τῇ τοῦ Σεραπίωνος ἐπιστολῇ καὶ ὑποσημειώσεις φέρονται διαφόρων ἐπισκόπων, ὧν ὁ μέν τις ὧδέ πως ὑποσεσημείωσται·
"Αὐρήλιος Κυρίνιος μάρτυς ἐρρῶσθαι ὑμᾶς εὔχομαι,"
ὁ δέ τις τοῦτον τὸν τρόπον· "Αἴλιος Πούπλιος Ἰούλιος ἀπὸ Δεβελτοῦ κολωνίας τῆς Θρᾴκης ἐπίσκοπος· ζῇ ὁ θεὸς ὁ ἐν τοῖς οὐρανοῖς, ὅτι Σωτᾶς ὁ μακάριος ὁ ἐν Ἀγχιάλῳ ἠθέλησε τὸν δαίμονα τὸν Πρισκίλλης ἐκβαλεῖν, καὶ οἱ ὑποκριταὶ οὐκ ἀφῆκαν."
(4) καὶ ἄλλων δὲ πλειόνων τὸν ἀριθμὸν ἐπισκόπων συμψήφων τούτοις ἐν τοῖς δηλωθεῖσιν γράμμασιν αὐτόγραφοι φέρονται σημειώσεις. καὶ τὰ μὲν κατὰ τούτους ἦν τοιαῦτα.

The Unidentified Source of Epiphanius

26. Epiphanius, *Panarion* 48.1-13 (GCS, ed. Holl, pp. 219-38).
[1. (1) Ἀπὸ τούτων ἑτέρα πάλιν αἵρεσις ἀνακύπτει τῶν Φρυγῶν καλουμένη, σύγχρονος γενομένη τούτοις καὶ αὐτοὺς διαδεχομένη. (2) οὗτοι γὰρ γεγόνασι περὶ τὸ ἐννεακαιδέκατον ἔτος Ἀντωνίνου τοῦ εὐσεβοῦς τοῦ μετὰ Ἀδριανόν, καὶ ὁ Μαρκίων δὲ καὶ οἱ περὶ Τατιανὸν καὶ οἱ ἀπ' αὐτοῦ διαδεξάμενοι Ἐγκρατῖται ἐν χρόνοις Ἀδριανοῦ καὶ μετὰ Ἀδριανόν.
(3) οὗτοι γὰρ οἱ κατὰ Φρύγας καλούμενοι δέχονται καὶ αὐτοὶ πᾶσαν γραφὴν παλαιᾶς καὶ νέας διαθήκης καὶ νεκρῶν ἀνάστασιν ὁμοίως λέγουσι,

commanded his apostles not to be removed from Jerusalem for twelve years. And he also has used testimonies from the Apocalypse of John, and he relates that a dead man had been raised by divine power by John himself in Ephesus. He also says certain other things through which he sufficiently and very fully set right the error of the previously mentioned heresy. These have been Apollonius' remarks.

Serapion

25. Ibid. 5.19.

19. (1) Serapion, whom tradition asserts to have been bishop of the Church of Antioch after Maximinus in the times being discussed, has mentioned the works of Apolinarius against the heresy under discussion. He mentions him in his own epistle to Caricus and Pontius, in which he adds the following statements in the course of correcting the same heresy. (2) "But that you might know that the activity of this false order of the so-called new prophecy has been abhorred by the whole brotherhood throughout the world, I have sent you also the writings of the most blessed Claudius Apolinarius, who was bishop in Hierapolis of Asia."

(3) The signatures of various bishops are also produced in this epistle of Serapion. One of them has signed somewhat as follows: "I Aurelius Cyrenaeus, a martyr, pray that you are in good health." Another writes in this manner: "I Aelius Publius Julius, bishop of Debeltum, a colony of Thrace. As God in the heavens lives, the blessed Sotas in Anchialus wanted to cast out the demon of Priscilla, and the hypocrites did not permit it."

(4) The autograph signatures of a large number of other bishops who agree with these are produced in the letter under discussion.

And such were the remarks so far as these men were concerned.

The Unidentified Source of Epiphanius

26. Epiphanius, *Panarion* 48.1-13.

[1. (1) Again another heresy emerged from these. It is called that of the Phrygians, being contemporaneous with the former heretics, and succeeding them. (2) For these came into existence about the nineteenth year of Antoninus the Pious who was after Hadrian. Now both Marcion and the Encratites, disciples and successors of Tatian, arose in the time of Hadrian and after Hadrian.

(3) For those called Cataphrygians themselves also accept all the Scripture of the Old and the New Testament, and likewise say that there is a resurrection of the dead. But they boast that they have a prophet named

Μοντανὸν δέ τινα προφήτην αὐχοῦσιν ἔχειν καὶ Πρίσκιλλαν καὶ Μαξίμιλλαν προφήτιδας· οἷς προσέχοντες τὸν νοῦν ἐξετράπησαν.]
(4) περὶ δὲ πατρὸς καὶ υἱοῦ καὶ ἁγίου πνεύματος ὁμοίως φρονοῦσι τῇ ἁγίᾳ καθολικῇ ἐκκλησίᾳ, ἀπέσχισαν δὲ ἑαυτούς, "προσέχοντες πνεύμασι πλάνης καὶ διδασκαλίαις δαιμονίων," λέγοντες ὅτι "δεῖ ἡμᾶς, φησί, καὶ τὰ χαρίσματα δέχεσθαι." (5) καὶ ἡ ἁγία δὲ τοῦ θεοῦ ἐκκλησία ὁμοίως τὰ χαρίσματα δέχεται, ἀλλὰ τὰ ὄντως χαρίσματα καὶ ἤδη ἐν ἁγίᾳ θεοῦ ἐκκλησίᾳ διὰ πνεύματος ἁγίου δεδοκιμασμένα παρά τε προφητῶν καὶ ἀποστόλων καὶ αὐτοῦ τοῦ κυρίου, (6) φάσκοντος τοῦ ἀποστόλου Ἰωάννου ἐν τῇ ἐπιστολῇ ὅτι "δοκιμάζετε τὰ πνεύματα, εἰ ἔστιν ἐκ τοῦ θεοῦ" καὶ πάλιν δὲ λέγοντος ὅτι "ἠκούσατε ὅτι Ἀντίχριστος ἔρχεται καὶ νῦν Ἀντίχριστοι πολλοὶ γεγόνασιν. ἐξ ἡμῶν ἐξῆλθον, ἀλλ' οὐκ ἦσαν ἐξ ἡμῶν· εἰ γὰρ ἦσαν ἐξ ἡμῶν, μεμενήκεισαν ἂν μεθ' ἡμῶν· ἀλλ' ἵνα γνωσθῶσιν ὅτι οὐκ ἦσαν ἐξ ἡμῶν. τούτου χάριν γράφω ὑμῖν, τεκνία" καὶ τὰ ἑξῆς. (7) ἀληθῶς οὖν οὗτοι οὐκ εἰσὶν ἐξ αὐτῶν τῶν ἁγίων. ἐξέβησαν γὰρ τῇ αὐτῶν φιλονεικίᾳ, προσανέχοντες καὶ πνεύμασι πλάνης καὶ μυθολογίαις.
2. (1) ἰδοὺ γὰρ ἐξ αὐτῆς τῆς ὑποθέσεως ἐλέγχονται μὴ δυνάμενοι πληροῦν τὰ ὑπ' αὐτῶν ἐν φιλονεικίᾳ ὑπισχνούμενα. εἰ γὰρ δεῖ χαρίσματα δέχεσθαι καὶ δεῖ εἶναι ἐν ἐκκλησίᾳ χαρίσματα, πῶς οὐκέτι μετὰ Μοντανὸν καὶ Πρίσκιλλαν καὶ Μαξίμιλλαν ἔχουσι προφήτας; ἆρα ἤργησεν ἡ χάρις; οὐκ ἀργεῖ δὲ ἡ χάρις ἐν ἁγίᾳ ἐκκλησίᾳ· μὴ γένοιτο. (2) εἰ δὲ ἕως τινὸς προεφήτευσαν οἱ προφητεύσαντες καὶ * οὐκέτι προφητεύουσιν, ἆρα οὔτε Πρίσκιλλα οὔτε Μαξίμιλλα προεφήτευσαν, * μετὰ τὰς προφητείας τὰς διὰ τῶν ἁγίων ἀποστόλων ἐν τῇ ἁγίᾳ ἐκκλησίᾳ δοκιμασθείσας. (3) κατὰ δύο οὖν τρόπους ἐλεγχθήσεται ἡ αὐτῶν ἄνοια· ἢ γὰρ δείξωσιν εἶναι προφήτας μετὰ Μαξίμιλλαν, ἵνα μὴ ἀργήσῃ ἡ παρ' αὐτοῖς λεγομένη χάρις, ἢ οἱ περὶ Μαξίμιλλαν ψευδοπροφῆται εὑρεθήσονται, μετὰ τὸν ὅρον τῶν προφητικῶν χαρισμάτων τολμήσαντες οὐκ ἀπὸ ἁγίου πνεύματος, ἀλλ' ἀπὸ πλάνης δαιμονίων ἐνθουσιασθῆναι καὶ φαντασιάσαι τοὺς ἀκούοντας αὐτῶν.
(4) καὶ ὅρα πῶς ἐξ αὐτῶν τῶν παρ' αὐτοῖς λεγομένων ὁ ἔλεγχος πρὸς αὐτοὺς ῥηθήσεται. φάσκει γὰρ ἡ λεγομένη παρ' αὐτοῖς Μαξίμιλλα ἡ προφῆτις ὅτι, φησί· "μετ' ἐμὲ προφήτης οὐκέτι ἔσται, ἀλλὰ συντέλεια." (5) ἰδοὺ δὲ ἐκ πανταχόθεν φαίνεται τὸ ἅγιον πνεῦμα καὶ τὰ πνεύματα τῆς πλάνης· ὅσα γὰρ οἱ προφῆται εἰρήκασι καὶ μετὰ συνέσεως παρακο-

Montanus, and prophetesses named Priscilla and Maximilla. By giving attention to these, they have been diverted.][2]

(4) Now they hold the same view of the Father, Son, and Holy Spirit as the holy Catholic Church, but they have severed themselves, "devoting themselves to spirits of error and teachings of demons" (cf. 1 Tim 4:1) when they say that he says we too must receive the spiritual gifts.

(5) Now indeed, the holy Church of God likewise receives the spiritual gifts, but those which are truly spiritual gifts, and which have already been tested in the holy Church of God through the Holy Spirit, by both prophets and apostles, and the Lord himself, (6) since the apostle John declares in his epistle: "Test the spirits, if they are of God" (1 John 4:1). And he again says also: "You have heard that Antichrist comes; even now many Antichrists have come. They went out from us, but they were not of us, for if they had been of us, they would have remained with us; but that they might be known that they were not of us. For this reason I write to you, children," etc. (1 John 2:18-19). (7) They truly, therefore, are not of the saints themselves. For they have departed from them by their own contentiousness, devoting themselves to spirits that are both erring and fictions.

2. (1) For behold, they are refuted by the suggestion itself, since they cannot fulfill what they have contentiously promised. For if spiritual gifts must be received, and there is a need for spiritual gifts in the Church, how is it that they no longer have prophets after Montanus, Priscilla, and Maximilla? Has grace ceased? But grace is not ineffectual in the holy Church. God forbid! (2) And if those who prophesied prophesied up to a certain time, and no longer prophesy, then neither Priscilla nor Maximilla have prophesied after the prophecies which were approved by the holy apostles in the holy Church. (3) Their foolishness, then will be proven in two ways. For they will either prove that there are prophets after Maximilla, so that what they call grace may not be ineffectual, or the disciples of Maximilla will be found to be false prophets because they have had the audacity, after the limit for the prophetic gifts, to have been inspired, not by the Holy Spirit, but by demonic error, and to have duped their hearers.

(4) And notice how the argument against them will be spoken by their very own words. For the one they call Maximilla, the prophetess, declares: "After me there will no longer be a prophet, but the end." (5) Now behold, the Holy Spirit and the spirits of error appear from every side! For the prophets have uttered everything they have said in full possession of

---

[2]The bracketed sections (1-3) are not part of Epiphanius's source. The source, as identified by Voigt, begins with section 4.

λουθοῦντες ἐφθέγγοντο, καὶ ἐτελέσθη τὰ παρ' αὐτῶν εἰρημένα καὶ ἔτι πληροῦται. (6) αὕτη δὲ εἶπε μετ' αὐτὴν εἶναι συντέλειαν, καὶ οὔπω συνετελέσθη, μάλιστα τοσούτων βασιλέων γενομένων καὶ τοσούτου χρόνου ὑπερβεβηκότος. (7) ἔτη γάρ εἰσιν ἔκτοτε πλείω ἐλάσσω διακόσια ἐνενήκοντα ἕως τοῦ ἡμετέρου χρόνου, δωδεκάτου ἔτους Οὐαλεντινιανοῦ καὶ Οὐάλεντος καὶ [ὀγδόου] Γρατιανοῦ βασιλείας, καὶ οὔπω ἡ συντέλεια κατὰ τὴν αὐχήσασαν ἑαυτὴν προφήτιδα, μὴ γνοῦσαν μηδὲ τὴν ἡμέραν τῆς αὐτῆς τελευτῆς. (8) καὶ ἰδεῖν ἔστι πῶς πάντες οἱ ἀπὸ τῆς ἀληθείας ἑαυτοὺς ἀπαλλοτριώσαντες, ὅτι οὐκ ἐν εὐσταθείᾳ τινὶ λόγου μεμενήκασιν, ἀλλ' ὡς νήπιοι ὑπὸ τοῦ ἀεὶ πλανῶντος ὄφεως παραπεπλεγμένοι εἰς ἀπώλειαν ἑαυτοὺς ἐκδεδώκασι καὶ εἰς τὸ γενέσθαι κατάβρωμα τοῦ λύκου ἔξω τῆς μάνδρας εὑρεθέντες παρελκυσθῆναὶ [τε] καὶ οὕτως ἀπολέσθαι, μὴ κρατοῦντες τὴν ἀρχήν, ἀλλὰ καταλείψαντες τὴν ἀλήθειαν, ἐν ναυαγίῳ ἑαυτοὺς καὶ ἐν κλύδωνι τῆς πάσης πλάνης παραδεδώκασιν. (9) εἰ γὰρ λέγει Μαξίμιλλα ὅτι προφήτης οὐκέτι ἔσται, ἄρα ἀναιρεῖ τὸ εἶναι παρ' αὐτοῖς τὸ χάρισμα καὶ εἰς ἔτι δεῦρο φέρεσθαι. εἰ δὲ ἕως αὐτῆς μένει τὸ χάρισμα, ὡς προεῖπον ἄρα καὶ αὐτὴ οὐ μετέσχε τῶν χαρισμάτων.

3. (1) πεπλάνηται γάρ· ἐσφράγισε γὰρ ὁ κύριος τὴν ἐκκλησίαν καὶ ἐπλήρωσεν [ἐν] αὐτῇ τὰ χαρίσματα. ὅτε γὰρ ἦν χρεία προφητῶν, ἐν ἀληθινῷ πνεύματι καὶ ἐρρωμένῃ διανοίᾳ καὶ παρακολουθοῦντι νῷ οἱ αὐτοὶ ἅγιοι τὰ πάντα ἐπροφήτευον, ἐμπιπλώμενοι πνεύματος ἁγίου, κατὰ τὴν ἀναλογίαν [τῆς πίστεως] τῶν ἐκ πνεύματος χαρισμάτων ἑκάστῳ διδομένων καὶ κατὰ τὴν ἀναλογίαν τῆς πίστεως πρὸς τὸ συμφέρον.

(2) τί οὖν συμφέρον οὗτοι εἰρήκασιν ἢ ποῖον ἀνάλογον τῆς πίστεως; πῶς δὲ οὐχὶ μᾶλλον οὗτοί εἰσιν περὶ ὧν εἶπεν ὁ κύριος ὅτι "προσέχετε ἀπὸ τῶν ψευδοπροφητῶν, οἵτινες ἔρχονται πρὸς ὑμᾶς ἐν ἐνδύμασι προβάτων, ἔσω δέ εἰσι λύκοι ἅρπαγες." (3) συγκρίνοντες γὰρ τὰ παρ' αὐτῶν εἰρημένα καὶ [τὰ] κατὰ τὴν παλαιὰν διαθήκην καὶ καινὴν ἐν ἀληθείᾳ ὄντα καὶ ἐν ἀληθείᾳ γενόμενα καὶ πεπροφητευμένα δοκιμάσωμεν, ποία [ὄντως] προφητεία τυγχάνει, ποία δὲ ψευδοπροφητεία.

(4) ὁ προφήτης πάντα μετὰ καταστάσεως λογισμῶν καὶ παρακολουθήσεως ἐλάλει καὶ ἐφθέγγετο ἐκ πνεύματος ἁγίου, τὰ πάντα ἐρρωμένως λέγων ὡς Μωϋσῆς ὁ θεράπων τοῦ θεοῦ καὶ πιστὸς ἐν οἴκῳ ὁ βλέπων * ἐλέγετο ὁ προφήτης ἐν τῇ παλαιᾷ διαθήκῃ. (5) "ὅρασις, [γάρ] φησιν, ἣν εἶδεν Ἡσαΐας υἱὸς Ἀμὼς ὁ προφήτης"· "εἶδον [τὸν] κύριον, φησί, καθεζόμενον ἐπὶ θρόνου ὑψηλοῦ καὶ ἐπηρμένου· καὶ εἶδον Σεραφὶμ καὶ Χερουβίμ, καὶ

their understanding, and their words have been accomplished and are still being fulfilled. (6) But this woman said that after her the end would occur, and it has not happened yet, even though a very large number of kings have come and gone, and a large amount of time has elapsed. (7) For there have been approximately two-hundred-ninety years from then to our own time, the twelfth year of the reign of Valentinian, Valens, and (the eighth of) Gratian, and the end, according to the prophetess who boasted of herself, has not yet occurred; she did not even know the day of her own death (cf. Gen 27:2). (8) And it is possible to see how all who have alienated themselves from the truth have not continued with any stability of reason, but like infants made mad by the serpent who always misleads, they have delivered themselves to destruction, and having been found outside the fold, they have been drawn aside to become food for the wolf, and thus to perish. Because they do not grasp the principle (cf. Col 2:19), but have forsaken the truth, they have delivered themselves to shipwreck and the pounding waves of every error (cf. 1 Tim 1:19; Jas 1:6). (9) For if by Maximilla's word there will no longer be a prophet, then she destroys the existence of the spiritual gift among them and its continuing till now; and if, as I said before, the gift existed up to herself, then she too did not share in the spiritual gifts.

3. (1) She has erred. For the Lord has authenticated the Church and filled it with spiritual gifts. For when it needed prophecies, the same saints prophesied all things in the true Spirit, and with a powerful understanding, and in full possession of their intellect. They were filled with the Holy Spirit in proportion to the gifts of the Spirit given to each one (cf. 1 Cor 12:7), and in proportion to their faith (cf. Rom 12:6), for the common good (cf. 1 Cor 12:7).

(2) What, then, have these people said for the common good? Or what sort of proportion of faith do they have? And how is it not these, rather, of whom the Lord said: "Beware of false prophets who come to you in sheeps' clothing, but within are ravaging wolves" (Matt 7:15)? (3) For by comparing what they have said and the prophecies which exist in truth and came to be in truth in the Old and New Testaments, let us examine what constitutes prophecy and what constitutes false prophecy.

(4) The prophet used to speak in control of his powers of reasoning and understanding, and make his utterance from the Holy Spirit, saying all things vigorously. In this way Moses, who was God's servant, and faithful in his house (cf. Num 12:7), was called "the seer" (cf. 1 Kgs 9:9). The prophet says in the Old Testament: (5) "The vision which Isaiah, the prophet, son of Amos, saw: I saw the Lord," he says, "sitting upon a throne high and lifted up; and I saw Seraphim and Cherubim, and I heard the Lord

ἤκουσα κυρίου λέγοντος πρός με· Βάδιζε, εἰπὸν τῷ λαῷ τούτῳ ἀκοῇ ἀκούσητε καὶ οὐ μὴ συνῆτε, καὶ βλέποντες βλέψητε καὶ οὐ μὴ ἴδητε." καὶ ἀκούσας παρὰ τοῦ κυρίου ἐλθὼν πρὸς τὸν λαὸν ἔφη· "τάδε λέγει κύριος." (6) οὐχ ὁρᾷς ὅτι παρακολουθοῦντος ὁ λόγος καὶ οὐκ ἐξισταμένου, οὔτε ὡς ἐξισταμένης διανοίας ἡ φθογγὴ ἀπεδίδοτο; (7) ὡσαύτως δὲ καὶ Ἰεζε-κιὴλ ὁ προφήτης ἀκούων παρὰ κυρίου ὅτι "ποίησον σεαυτῷ ἄρτον ἐπὶ κόπρου ἀνθρωπείας," ἔλεγε "μηδαμῶς κύριε· οὐδέποτε κοινὸν ἢ ἀκάθαρτον εἰσῆλθεν εἰς τὸ στόμα μου." (8) γινώσκων γὰρ τὴν δι' ἀπειλὴν λεγομένην πρὸς αὐτὸν ῥῆσιν ὑπὸ κυρίου, [καὶ] οὐχ ὡς ἐν ἐκστάσει διανοίας φερό-μενος ἐπεβάλλετο τοῦτο πράττειν, ἀλλὰ ἠξίου, ἐρρωμένην ἔχων τὴν διάνοιαν καὶ παρακολουθοῦσαν, καὶ ἔλεγε "μηδαμῶς κύριε." ταῦτα γὰρ [τῶν] ἀληθῶς προφητῶν, ἐν ἁγίῳ πνεύματι ἐρρωμένην ἐχόντων τὴν διά-νοιαν, καὶ ἡ διδασκαλία καὶ ἡ διαλογή. (9) πῶς δὲ Δανιὴλ οὐχ εὑρί-σκεται πάσης συνέσεως ἔμπλεως καὶ τοῖς φρονήμασι παρακολουθῶν, ὃς τὰ αἰνίγματα τῷ Ναβουχοδονόσορ ἐπέλυσε καὶ ἃ ἐκεῖνος δι' ὀνειράτων ἐθεάσατο καὶ ἀπέστη ἀπ' αὐτοῦ τοῦ ἑωρακότος, (10) οὗτος ὑπεμίμνησκε καὶ τὴν ἐπίλυσιν εὐθὺς ἐπέφερεν ἐρρωμένῃ καταστάσει καὶ ὑπερβολῇ χαρίσματος, περιττοτέρως τὴν φρόνησιν ἔχων ὑπὲρ πάντα ἄνθρωπον διὰ τὸ χάρισμα τοῦ ἁγίου πνεύματος, τὸ σοφίζον ὄντως τὸν προφήτην καὶ τοὺς διὰ τοῦ προφήτου τῆς διδασκαλίας τῆς ἀληθείας καταξιωιμένους. (11) ἃ δὲ οὗτοι ἐπαγγέλλονται προφητεύειν, οὐδὲ εὐσταθοῦντες φα-νοῦνται οὔτε παρακολουθίαν λόγου ἔχοντες. λοξὰ γὰρ τὰ παρ' αὐτῶν ῥήματα καὶ σκαληνὰ καὶ οὐδεμιᾶς ὀρθότητος ἐχόμενα.

4. (1) Εὐθὺς γὰρ ὁ Μοντανός φησιν· "ἰδού, ὁ ἄνθρωπος ὡσεὶ λύρα κἀγὼ ἐφίπταμαι ὡσεὶ πλῆκτρον· ὁ ἄνθρωπος κοιμᾶται κἀγὼ γρηγορῶ. ἰδού, κύριός ἐστιν ὁ ἐξιστάνων καρδίας ἀνθρώπων καὶ διδοὺς καρδίαν ἀνθρώποις." (2) τίς τοίνυν τῶν παρακολουθούντων καὶ μετὰ συνέσεως δεχομένων τὸν τῆς ὠφελείας λόγον καὶ τῆς ἑαυτῶν ζωῆς ἐπιμελομένων οὐ καταγνώσεται τῆς τοιαύτης παραπεποιημένης ὑποθέσεως καὶ τοῦ λόγου τοῦ αὐχοῦντος ἑαυτὸν ἐν προφήταις καταλέγεσθαι, μὴ δυναμένου τὰ ὅμοια λέγειν προφήταις; (3) οὔτε γὰρ πνεῦμα ἅγιον ἐλάλησεν ἐν αὐτῷ. τὸ γὰρ εἰπεῖν "ἐφίπταμαι καὶ πλήσσω καὶ γρηγορῶ καὶ ἐξιστᾷ κύριος καρδίας," ἐκστα-τικοῦ ῥήματα ὑπάρχει ταῦτα καὶ οὐχὶ παρακολουθοῦντος, ἀλλὰ ἄλλον χαρακτῆρα ὑποδεικνύντος παρὰ τὸν χαρακτῆρα τοῦ ἁγίου πνεύματος τοῦ ἐν προφήταις λελαληκότος.

(4) Εἰ δὲ θελήσουσι παραπλέκειν τῇ ἀληθείᾳ τὸ ψεῦδος καὶ ἀνοητεῖν τὸν νοῦν τῶν τῆς ἀκριβείας ἐπιμελομένων, ἑαυτοῖς τε ἐπισωρεύουσι λόγους, δι' ὧν παραποιητεύονται τὴν ἑαυτῶν πλάνην, ὅμοιά τινα εἶναι

saying to me: Go, say to this people, hearing you will hear and not understand, and seeing you will see and will not perceive" (cf. Isa 1:1; 6:1,2,8,9). And when he had heard from the Lord, he went to the people and said: "Thus says the Lord." (6) Do you not see that the word comes from one who is in possession of his understanding, and not from one who has fallen into a trance? Nor was the voice offered up as from a mind which had been altered. (7) Likewise also Ezekiel, the prophet, when he heard from the Lord: "Make yourself bread on human dung" (cf. Ezek 4:12), said: "By no means, Lord, for never has anything common or unclean entered my mouth" (cf. Ezek 4:14; Acts 10:14). (8) For because he knew the word addressed to him by the Lord was spoken as a test, he also did not attempt to do it, as though he were carried along in ecstasy of understanding, but prayed, in possession of a mind that was sound and active and said: "By no means, Lord." For these words are the teaching and reasoning of those who are truly prophets, who possess a sound mind in the Holy Spirit.

(9) Daniel is surely found to be full of all understanding and in full possession of his thoughts. He solved the riddles for Nebuchadnezzar, and he suggested the things which Nebuchadnezzar had seen in dreams and which had eluded him who had seen them, (10) and he immediately added the explanation with forceful authority and by means of a superior spiritual gift. He possessed wisdom far beyond all men because of the gift of the Holy Spirit which makes the true prophet wise and, through the prophet, those men judged worthy of the true teaching.

(11) But these people set forth the things which they profess to prophesy neither with steadfastness nor in possession of the persuasion of reason. For their sayings are ambiguous, devious, and incorrect.

4. (1) For Montanus says, for instance: "Behold, man is like a lyre; and I flit about like a plectron; man sleeps, and I awaken him; behold it is the Lord who changes the hearts of men and gives men a heart."

(2) Who, then, of those who follow attentively and accept with understanding the profitable word, and care for their own life, will not condemn such a distorted assertion and the speech of the man who boasts that he is counted among the prophets, although he is unable to speak like the prophets? (3) For the Holy Spirit did not speak in him. For the expressions, "I flit about," and, "I strike," and "I awaken," and "the Lord changes hearts" are the words of one who is mentally deranged, and who is not in possession of his understanding, but demonstrates a character different than the character of the Holy Spirit who spoke in the prophets.

(4) Now if they wish to weave what is false in with the truth, and to be ignorant of the understanding of those concerned about accuracy, they accumulate arguments for themselves through which they disingenuously

λέγοντες, ἵνα δὴ παραστήσωσιν * ἀπὸ τοῦ τὴν ἁγίαν γραφὴν εἰρηκέναι "ἐπέβαλεν ὁ θεὸς ἔκστασιν ἐπὶ τὸν Ἀδὰμ καὶ ὕπνωσε," ἀλλὰ οὐκέτι ὅμοιον τοῦτο εἴη ἐκείνῳ. (5) οὐ γὰρ καὶ ἐνταῦθα σῶμα ἔμελλε πλάσσειν ὁ θεός, ἀφ' οὗ εἰς ἔκστασιν ἔφερεν, ἵνα τὰ ὅμοια ἐπενέγκῃ δι' ὑπερβολὴν τῆς φιλανθρωπίας. (6) τῷ γὰρ Ἀδὰμ ἐπήνεγκε τὴν ἔκστασιν τοῦ ὕπνου, οὐκ ἔκστασιν φρενῶν. ἔκστασις δὲ κατὰ διαφορὰς πολλὰς ἔχει τὸν τρόπον. ἔκστασις δι' ὑπερβολὴν θαύματος λέγεται καὶ ἔκστασις λέγεται ἡ μανία διὰ τὸ ἐκστῆναι τοῦ προκειμένου. (7) ἐκείνη δὲ ἡ τοῦ ὕπνου ἔκστασις κατ' ἄλλον τρόπον ἐρρέθη, κατὰ τὴν φυσικὴν ἐνέργειαν, μάλιστα διὰ τὸ βαθυτάτως αὐτὴν ἐπενηνέχθαι τῷ ἁγίῳ Ἀδὰμ καὶ χειρὶ θεοῦ πεπλασμένῳ.
5. (1) Καὶ γὰρ ἀληθῶς ἔστιν ἰδεῖν ὡς δικαίως ἔκστασιν ταύτην ἡ θεία γραφὴ κέκληκεν. ἐν τῷ γὰρ ὑπνοῦν τὸν ἄνθρωπον μεθίστανται πᾶσαι αἱ αἰσθήσεις, εἰς ἀνάπαυσιν τραπεῖσαι, ὡς οἷον εἰπεῖν παροῦσα ἡ διορατικὴ οὐχ ὁρᾷ· ἀποκέκλεισται γὰρ τὸ ὄμμα καὶ ἡσυχάζει τὸ κινοῦν ἐν τῷ ἀνθρώπῳ πνεῦμα εἴτ' οὖν [ἡ] ψυχή. (2) δυσοδμίας οὔσης ἐν οἴκῳ ἢ καὶ εὐοδμίας, καίτοι γε παρούσης τῆς ὀσφραντικῆς αἰσθήσεως, οὐκ ἀντιλαμβάνεται· ἐξέστη γὰρ ἡ τοιαύτη αἴσθησις εἰς ἀνάπαυσιν τραπεῖσα. (3) πικρῶν ὄντων χυμῶν ἐν τῷ στόματι ἢ ἁλμυρῶν ἢ γλυκέων τὸ γευστικὸν οὐκ αἰσθάνεται, ἐπειδὴ γὰρ ἐν ἐκστάσει τῆς ἀναπαύσεως κεῖται μὴ ἐνεργοῦν, ὅπερ ἐν τῷ ὕπαρ ὄντι ἐνήργει. (4) ἀκοὴ πάρεστιν, ἀλλὰ ἀργεῖ τὸ ἀκουστικὸν κατὰ τὴν αἴσθησιν. καὶ πολλάκις τινῶν λαλούντων ἐν οἴκῳ, εἰ μή τι διυπνισθῇ ὁ ἄνθρωπος, οὐκ ἐπακούει τῶν παρά τινων ῥηθέντων διὰ τὸ ἀποστῆναι τὴν ἐνέργειαν πρὸς τὴν ὥραν. (5) τινῶν κνωδάλων διερχομένων διὰ τοῦ ἡμετέρου σώματος οὐκ αἰσθανόμεθα τῆς αὐτῶν περὶ τὸ σῶμα ἡμῶν ἁφῆς, εἰ μή τι βαρέως ἡμῖν ἐπιθῶνται τὰ κνώδαλα, ὡς τοῦ παντὸς ὀργάνου διὰ τὴν ἀνάπαυσιν τοῦ ὕπνου ἐκστάντος ἀπὸ τῆς ἐνεργείας. (6) τὸ μὲν γὰρ ὄργανον, φύσεως ὂν γηΐνης καὶ περὶ τὴν ψυχὴν ἔχον, διὰ τὸ οὕτως ἐκ θεοῦ [τὸ] χρήσιμον ἡμῖν γεγενῆσθαι ἀποδίδοται αὐτῷ καιρὸς μεθιστῶν αὐτὸ ἀπὸ τῆς ἐναργεστάτης αἰσθήσεως εἰς κατάστασιν ἀναπαύσεως· αὐτὴ δὲ ἡ ψυχὴ οὐκ ἐξέστη τοῦ ἡγεμονικοῦ οὐδὲ τοῦ φρονήματος. (7) πολλάκις γὰρ φαντάζεται καὶ ὁρᾷ ἑαυτὴν ὡς ἐν ἐγρηγόρσει καὶ περιπατεῖ καὶ ἐργάζεται καὶ ποντοπορεῖ καὶ δημηγορεῖ, καὶ ἐν πλείοσι καὶ ἐν μείζοσι τούτων δι' ὀνειράτων ἑαυτὴν θεωμένη·

support their own error by saying that certain things are the same so that they present [their own falsehood as being][3] from the following words of Holy Scripture: "God cast a state of ecstasy on Adam, and he slept" (Gen 2:21). But this would never[4] be the same with that. (5) For God was not then about to form a body, which was the reason he brought Adam into ecstasy, that he might bring him beings similar to himself because of his great love for humanity. (6) For he brought the ecstasy of sleep on Adam, not an ecstasy of his wits. Now ecstasy has many different meanings. An excessive amount of amazement is termed ecstasy, and madness is called ecstasy because it stands outside what is prescribed. (7) But that ecstasy of sleep was mentioned in another sense, in relation to the natural activity, especially because it was brought very deeply on the holy Adam, even the man who was formed by the hand of God.

5. (1) And indeed it is actually possible to see how the divine Scripture has justly called this ecstasy. For when a man sleeps, all his senses are altered and give way to rest. For example, although his sense of sight is present, he does not see, for his eyes have been closed, and the spirit, or at least the soul, which moves in man is at rest. (2) If there should be a bad odor, or even a pleasant one, in the house, although his sense of smell is present, he does not perceive them, for such a sense has been altered and has given way to rest. (3) Should there be bitter flavors in his mouth, or salty, or sweet, his taste does not perceive them, since that which is active when he is awake lies inactive in the ecstasy of rest. (4) The sense of hearing is present, but the faculty of hearing in relation to the sense is at rest, and frequently, should people speak in the house, unless the man is awakened in some way, he does not listen to what they have said, because the activity is absent at the time. (5) If certain creatures pass over our body, we do not perceive their touch around our body, unless they put something on us heavily, because every organ is suspended from activity because of the rest of sleep. (6) For our physical body which is of an earthly nature and encircles the soul, because it has thus been made by God who is concerned for our interest, has been assigned a time for sleep, which alters the body from very distinct perception to a state of rest. But the soul itself has not retired from the governing faculty nor from the mind. (7) For it often makes its presence known and sees itself, as in wakefulness. It walks about, works, sails the open sea, makes popular speeches, and contemplates itself through dreams in situations more numerous and greater than these.

---

[3]My suggestion, based on the suggestion made by Holl.

[4]Emending οὐκέτι to οὐδέποτε.

(8) οὐ μὴν κατὰ τὸν ἀφραίνοντα καὶ ἐν ἐκστάσει γινόμενον ἐκστατικὸν ἄνθρωπον, τὸν τῷ σώματι καὶ τῇ ψυχῇ ἐγρηγορότα τὰ δεινὰ μεταχειριζόμενον καὶ πολλάκις ἑαυτῷ δεινῶς χρώμενον καὶ τοῖς πέλας· ἀγνοεῖ γὰρ ἃ φθέγγεται καὶ πράττει, ἐπειδήπερ ἐν ἐκστάσει γέγονεν ἀφροσύνης ὁ τοιοῦτος.

6. (1) Ταῦτα δὲ πάντα διὰ τὸ "ἐπέβαλε κύριος ἔκστασιν ἐπὶ τὸν Ἀδὰμ καὶ ὕπνωσεν" ἀνάγκην ἐσχήκαμεν, ὦ ἐπιπόθητοι, συναγαγεῖν [περὶ] τὰς διαφορὰς τῶν τρόπων τῆς ἐκστάσεως. (2) καὶ ἐφράσαμεν δι' ἣν αἰτίαν ἐκεῖ παρὰ κυρίου ἔκστασις εἴρηται ἡ τοῦ ὕπνου μετοχή, ὅτι διὰ τὴν τοῦ θεοῦ φειδὼ καὶ φιλανθρωπίαν, ἣν πᾶσι μὲν ἀνθρώποις ὁ αὐτὸς δεδώρηται εἰς τὸ μεταφέρεσθαι τὸν ἄνθρωπον ἀπὸ μερίμνης εἰς ἀνάπαυσιν ὕπνου καὶ τῶν ἐν τῷ βίῳ χρειωδῶν πραγμάτων· (3) ἐχεῖ δὲ περιττοτέρως ἐκείνην ἔκστασιν κέκληκε διὰ τὸ ποιῆσαι αὐτὸν πρὸς τὴν ὥραν μὴ αἰσθάνεσθαι πόνου, δι' ἣν ἔμελλε λαμβάνειν πλευρὰν ἀπ' αὐτοῦ καὶ πλάσσειν αὐτῷ αὐτὴν εἰς γυναῖκα. (4) ἀλλὰ οὐκ ἦν ἐν ἐκστάσει φρενῶν καὶ διανοημάτων. εὐθὺς γὰρ ἀναστὰς ἐπέγνω καὶ εἶπε "τοῦτο νῦν ὀστοῦν ἐκ τῶν ὀστῶν μου καὶ σὰρξ ἐκ τῆς σαρκός μου· αὕτη κληθήσεται γυνή, ὅτι ἐκ τοῦ ἀνδρὸς αὐτῆς ἐλήφθη αὐτή."

(5) καὶ ἐπίσταται γάρ, ὡς ὁρᾷς, καὶ τὰ πρῶτα καὶ τὰ παρόντα καὶ προφητεύει περὶ τῶν μελλόντων. ἰδοὺ γὰρ ἐλέγχω τὰ πρῶτα ὅτε ἦν ἐν ὕπνῳ, λέγων ὅτι "ὀστοῦν ἐκ τῶν ὀστῶν μου·" καὶ ἐπέγνω τὰ παρόντα, μετὰ τὸ πλασθῆναι τὴν γυναῖκα ἐπιγνοὺς αὐτὴν ἀπὸ τοῦ σώματος [αὐτοῦ] ἠρμένην· (6) καὶ ἐπροφήτευσε περὶ τῶν ἐσομένων, ὅτι "ἕνεκεν τούτου καταλείψει ἄνθρωπος τὸν πατέρα αὐτοῦ καὶ τὴν μητέρα αὐτοῦ καὶ προσκολληθήσεται τῇ γυναικὶ αὐτοῦ, καὶ ἔσονται οἱ δύο εἰς σάρκα μίαν." ταῦτα δὲ οὐκ ἐκστατικοῦ ἀνδρὸς οὐδὲ ἀπαρακολουθήτου, ἀλλὰ ἐρρωμένην ἔχοντος τὴν διάνοιαν.

7. (1) Εἰ δὲ καὶ περὶ τοῦ "ἐγὼ εἶπον ἐν τῇ ἐκστάσει μου, πᾶς ἄνθρωπος ψεύστης" λεκτέον, ἑτέρα πάλιν αὐτοῦ ἡ δύναμις, οὐχ ὃν τρόπον * τινὸς ἀφραίνοντος ἀνθρώπου καὶ ἐκστατικοῦ (μὴ γένοιτο), (2) ἀλλὰ ὑπερθαυμάζοντος καὶ διανοουμένου ὑπὲρ τὸν κατὰ τὴν συνήθειαν λογισμὸν [περὶ] τῶν [ἀ]συμμέτρως ὁρωμένων τε καὶ πραττομένων· ἐπειδὴ γὰρ ἐθαύμασεν ὁ προφήτης καὶ διὰ θαυμασμὸν ἐνταῦθα λέγει. (3) γεγόνασι δὲ ἐν ἐκστάσει οἱ προφῆται, οὐκ ἐν ἐκστάσει λογισμῶν. γέγονε γὰρ καὶ Πέτρος ἐν ἐκστάσει, οὐχὶ μὴ παρακολουθῶν τῷ λόγῳ, ἀλλὰ ὁρῶν ἀντὶ τῆς καθημερινῆς ἀκολουθίας ἕτερα παρὰ τὰ τοῖς ἀνθρώποις ὁρώμενα· (4) "εἶδε γὰρ ὀθόνην καθιεμένην τέσσαρσιν ἀρχαῖς δεδεμένην, καὶ πάντα τὰ τετράποδα καὶ ἑρπετὰ καὶ τοῦ οὐρανοῦ τὰ πετεινὰ ἐν αὐτῇ." (5) ὅρα δὲ ὅτι παρηκο-

(8) This, however, has no relation to the foolish and deranged man who has fallen into ecstasy, wide awake in body and soul, who undertakes things that are frightening, and often abuses himself and those near him in a frightening manner. For he is ignorant of what he utters and does, since such a man has fallen into an ecstasy of folly.

6. (1) Now we have said all these things because of the statement: "The Lord cast a state of ecstasy on Adam, and he slept" (cf. Gen 2:21). We have had, O dearly missed friends, to collect the different kinds of ecstasy, (2) and we have declared the reason participation in sleep is there said to be ecstasy from the Lord. It is because of God's consideration and love for humanity, which the same one has given to all men to transfer man from care and the necessary affairs of life to restful sleep. (3) In this passage he has with very good reason called that rest a state of ecstasy because it made him insensitive to pain for the time during which he was going to take a rib from him and form it into a woman for him. (4) But he did not experience an ecstasy of wits and thoughts. For as soon as he stood up he recognized her and said: "This now is bone of my bones and flesh of my flesh. She shall be called woman because she was taken from her man" (Gen 2:23).

(5) And indeed, as you see, he understands both what is past and present, and he prophecies concerning what is to come. For behold, he understood what was past, when he was asleep, when he said, "bone of my bones." And he understood the present things after the woman had been formed when he recognized that she had been taken from his body. (6) And he prophesied of things to come in the words: "For this reason a man shall leave his father and his mother and shall be joined to his wife, and the two shall be one flesh" (Gen 2:24). These were not the words of a man in ecstasy, nor of one not in full possession of his faculties, but the words of a man possessing a sound mind.

7. (1) And if we must also comment on the statement, "I said in my ecstasy, Every man is a liar" (Ps 115:2), its meaning, again is different. It is not at all like that of a man who is out of his senses and mentally deranged, (God forbid), (2) but of one who is greatly astonished and who thinks with the powers of reason customary to those who see and act in the proper way. For since the prophet was astonished, he also speaks here because of his astonishment. (3) Now the prophets have experienced ecstasy, but not an ecstasy of their powers of reasoning. Peter, for example, experienced ecstasy, not that he did not understand rationally, but that he saw phenomena different from the everyday order among men. (4) "For he saw a large piece of cloth being lowered, bound at its four corners, and in it all the four-footed beasts and creeping things and birds of heaven." (5) And

λούθει καὶ οὐκ ἦν ἐν ἐκστάσει φρενῶν ὁ ἅγιος Πέτρος. ὅτε γὰρ ἤκουσεν [τὸ] "ἀναστὰς θῦσον καὶ φάγε," οὐχ ὡς μὴ τὸν νοῦν ἐρρωμένος ἐπείσθη, ἀλλά φησι πρὸς τὸν κύριον "μηδαμῶς, κύριε· οὐδέποτε γὰρ κοινὸν ἢ ἀκάθαρτον εἰσῆλθεν εἰς τὸ στόμα μου." (6) καὶ Δαυὶδ δὲ ὁ ἅγιος εἶπεν ὅτι "[εἶπον ἐγώ·] πᾶς ἄνθρωπος ψεύστης." ὁ δὲ λέγων "εἶπον ἐγώ" ἰδίᾳ ἔλεγεν, καὶ περὶ τῶν ἀνθρώπων ὅτι, ἔλεγε, ψεύδονται· ἄρα αὐτὸς οὐκ ἐψεύδετο, ἐκπληττόμενος δὲ καὶ θαυμάζων τὴν τοῦ θεοῦ φιλανθρωπίαν καὶ τὰ αὐτῷ παρὰ τοῦ κυρίου κεκηρυγμένα ἐθαύμαζε καθ᾽ ὑπερβολὴν καὶ (7) ὁρῶν πάντα ἄνθρωπον ἐνδεόμενον τοῦ ἐλέους τοῦ θεοῦ μόνῳ κυρίῳ τὸ ἀληθεύειν ἐπέδωκε, πάντα δὲ ἄνθρωπον ὑπὸ ἐπιτίμιον ἔγνω, ἵνα δείξῃ τὸ ἀληθινὸν πνεῦμα. τὸ ἐν προφήταις λαλῆσαι καὶ τὰ βάθη αὐτοῖς ἀποκαλύψαν τῆς τοῦ θεοῦ γνώσεως ἀκριβείας.
(8) ἐγένετο δὲ καὶ Ἀβραὰμ ἐν ἐκστάσει, οὐκ ἐν ἐκστάσει φρενῶν ἀλλὰ ἐν ἐκστάσει φόβου. ἔβλεπεν γὰρ κλίβανον καὶ λαμπάδας περὶ τὴν τοῦ ἡλίου δύσιν * καὶ ἄλλοι προφῆται ὁρῶντες τὰ ὁράματα ἐν διανοίᾳ ἐρρωμένῃ ἔλεγον, ὡς ὁ Μωυσῆς φησιν "ἔμφοβός εἰμι καὶ ἔντρομος." (9) ἔγνω δὲ Ἀβραὰμ τὰ ὑπὸ τοῦ κυρίου λεγόμενα· "γινώσκων, γάρ [φησι], γνώσῃ ὅτι πάροικον ἔσται τὸ σπέρμα σου ἐν γῇ ἀλλοτρίᾳ ἔτη τετρακόσια." (10) καὶ ὁρᾷς ὡς ἔστιν ἰδεῖν τὰ πάντα ἐν ἀληθείᾳ παρὰ τοῖς προφήταις εἰρημένα καὶ ἐν ἐρρωμένῃ διανοίᾳ καὶ σώφρονι λογισμῷ, καὶ οὐκ ἐν παραπληξίᾳ.
8. (1) Εἰ δὲ καὶ πάλιν θελήσουσι λέγειν [ὅτι] "οὐχ ὅμοια τὰ πρῶτα χαρίσματα τοῖς ἐσχάτοις," πόθεν τοῦτο ἔχουσι δεῖξαι; ὁμοίως γὰρ ἀλλήλοις οἱ ἅγιοι προφῆται καὶ οἱ ἅγιοι ἀπόστολοι προεφήτευσαν. (2) πρῶτον μὲν οὖν ἀνερχομένου τοῦ σωτῆρος εἰς τὸν οὐρανὸν οἱ ἰδόντες τοὺς δύο τοὺς ἐν ἐσθήσεσι λευκαῖς οὐκ ἐν παραπληξίᾳ ὁρῶσιν, ἀλλὰ ἤκουον ἐρρωμένῃ τῇ διανοίᾳ ὅτι "ἄνδρες Γαλιλαῖοι, τί ἑστήκατε εἰς τὸν οὐρανὸν ἀτενίζοντες; οὗτος ὁ Ἰησοῦς ὁ ἀφ᾽ ὑμῶν εἰς τὸν οὐρανὸν ἀναληφθεὶς οὕτως ἐλεύσεται" καὶ τὰ ἑξῆς. (3) εἶτα δὲ καὶ Πέτρος, ὡς ἔφην, ὁρῶν καὶ ἀκούων καὶ ἀποκρινόμενος καὶ λέγων "μηδαμῶς, κύριε," εὐσταθῶν ἦν τῇ διανοίᾳ. (4) Ἄγαβος γὰρ προφητεύων ἔλεγεν καὶ μετὰ σχήματος θαυμαστοῦ αἰνιττόμενος, λαβὼν τὴν ζώνην τοῦ Παύλου καὶ δήσας τοῖς ἰδίοις ποσὶν φησίν "οὗτος οὗ ἐστιν ἡ ζώνη αὕτη, δήσουσιν αὐτὸν καὶ ἀποίσουσιν εἰς Ἱερουσαλήμ." (5) ἀλλὰ καὶ πάλιν ἐν Ἀντιοχείᾳ κατῆλθον προφῆται καὶ κατήγγελλον λιμὸν ἔσεσθαι καθ᾽ ὅλης τῆς οἰκουμένης. καὶ οὐ διέπεσεν ὁ τούτων λόγος· ἀλλ᾽ ἵνα δείξῃ αὐτοὺς ἀληθεῖς προφήτας, ἡ γραφὴ εὐθὺς ἐπιφέρει λέγουσα "ἥτις ἐγένετο ἐπὶ Κλαυδίου Καίσαρος." (6) Παῦλος δὲ ὁ ἁγιώτατος ἀπόστολος προφητεύων ἔλεγε "τὸ δὲ πνεῦμα ῥητῶς λέγει, ἐν ἐσχάταις ἡμέραις ἐνστήσονται

notice that the holy Peter understands, and was not in ecstasy of his wits. For when he heard: "Rise, kill, and eat," he did not obey as one not having a sound mind, but he says to the Lord: "By no means Lord; for never has anything common or unclean entered my mouth" (cf. Acts 10:10-14).

(6) And the holy David, too, said: "(I said), Every man is a liar" (Ps 115:2). But when he said, "I said," he spoke on his own, and he said of men that they lie. He himself, therefore, did not lie, but being amazed and astounded at God's love for mankind and the things which had been announced to him by the Lord, he marveled exceedingly, and (7) when he saw every man in need of God's mercy, and recognized that every man is subject to punishment, he ascribed truthfulness to the Lord alone, to make known the true Spirit which spoke in the prophets, and revealed to them the depths of the accurate knowledge of God.

(8) Now Abraham also experienced ecstasy, not an ecstasy of his wits, but an ecstasy of fear. For about sunset he saw a furnace and lamps (cf. Gen 15:17). And other prophets saw visions in their sound mind, and said, as Moses: "I am frightened and tremble" (Heb 12:21). (9) And Abraham knew those things which the Lord said: "For know assuredly," (he says), "that your seed will be a stranger in a foreign land four-hundred years" (Gen 15:13). (10) And you see that it is possible to see in truth that everything said by the prophets was said with sound understanding and a sober power of reasoning, and not in madness.

8. (1) And although they will again wish to say that the first spiritual gifts are not like the last, whence are they able to prove this? For the holy prophets and the holy apostles prophesied in a manner similar to one another. (2) First, then, when the Savior ascended into heaven, those who saw the two men in white garments did not see in madness, but with sound understanding they heard: "Men, Galileans, why do you stand gazing into heaven? This Jesus who has been taken up into heaven from you will come in the same way," etc. (Acts 1:11). (3) And then Peter too, as I said, was stable in his understanding when he saw, and heard, and answered, and said: "By no means, Lord" (Acts 10:14). (4) Agabus indeed spoke as a prophet and spoke in riddles in a marvelous fashion when he took Paul's girdle and bound his own feet, and said: "They will bind the man whose girdle this is, and carry him off to Jerusalem" (Acts 21:11). (5) But again in Antioch prophets came down and announced that there would be famine throughout the whole world (cf. Acts 11:27-28). And their word was not mistaken. But to prove them to have been true prophets, the Scripture immediately adds and says: "Which occurred in the time of Claudius Caesar" (cf. Acts 11:28). (6) And Paul, the most holy apostle, prophesied and said: "The Spirit expressly says, In the last days difficult times will arise,"

καιροὶ χαλεποί" καὶ τὰ ἑξῆς, (7) καὶ πάλιν ἄλλοτε ὅτι "ἀποστήσονταί τινες τῆς ὑγιαινούσης διδασκαλίας, προσέχοντες [πνεύμασι] πλάνοις καὶ διδασκαλίαις δαιμόνων, κωλυόντων γαμεῖν, ἀπέχεσθαι βρωμάτων, ἃ ὁ θεὸς ἔκτισεν εἰς μετάληψιν ἡμῖν τοῖς μετὰ εὐχαριστίας [λαμβάνουσιν]." (8) ὡς σαφῶς [τοῦτο] ἐφ' ὑμῖν καὶ τοῖς ὁμοίοις ὑμῖν πεπλήρωται, ἐξ αὐτῶν τῶν προκειμένων [δῆλον]· αἱ γὰρ πλείους τῶν αἱρέσεων τούτων τὸ γαμεῖν κωλύουσιν, ἀπέχεσθαι βρωμάτων παραγγέλλουσιν, οὐχ ἕνεκεν πολιτείας προτρεπόμενοι, οὐχ ἕνεκεν ἀρετῆς μείζονος καὶ βραβείων καὶ στεφάνων, ἀλλὰ βδελυκτὰ ταῦτα [τὰ] ὑπὸ τοῦ κυρίου γεγενημένα ἡγούμενοι.

9. (1) Ἡ δὲ ἁγία ἐκκλησία καὶ παρθενίαν δοξάζει καὶ μονότητα καὶ ἁγνείαν καὶ χηροσύνην ἐπαινεῖ καὶ γάμον σεμνὸν τιμᾷ καὶ δέχεται, πορνείαν δὲ καὶ μοιχείαν καὶ ἀσέλγειαν ἀπαγορεύει, (2) ὅθεν ἰδεῖν ἔστιν τὸν χαρακτῆρα τῆς ἁγίας καθολικῆς ἐκκλησίας καὶ τοὺς παραπεποιημένους τῶν ἄλλων τρόπους, [ὡς] καὶ τὸν δοκιμάσαντα ἀποδιδράσκειν ἀπὸ πάσης πλάνης καὶ σκολιᾶς ὁδοῦ καὶ τρίβου ἀνάντου διακειμένης. (3) ἔφην γὰρ ἄνω ὡς ἀπὸ τοῦ ἁγιωτάτου ἀποστόλου προείρηται καὶ πάλιν ἐρῶ, ὅτι ἀσφαλιζόμενος ἡμᾶς καὶ τὸν χαρακτῆρα τῆς ἁγίας ἐκκλησίας διαιρῶν ἀπὸ τῆς τῶν αἱρέσεων πλάνης ἔφη, ὡς τολμηρῶς τὰ ἐκ θεοῦ καλῶς τεταγμένα ἀπαγορεύοντες, νομοθετοῦσι, φήσας περὶ τῶν κωλυόντων γαμεῖν καὶ ἀπέχεσθαι βρωμάτων. (4) καὶ γὰρ συμμετρίᾳ τινὶ * ὁ θεὸς Λόγος ἐν τῷ εὐαγγελίῳ φήσας "θέλεις τέλειος γενέσθαι;" συγγνωμονῶν τῇ τῶν ἀνθρώπων πλάσει καὶ ἀσθενείᾳ χαίρει μὲν ἐπὶ τοῖς τὰ δοκίμια τῆς θεοσεβείας δυναμένοις ἐνδείκνυσθαι καὶ παρθενίαν ἀσκεῖν αἱρουμένοις καὶ ἁγνείαν καὶ ἐγκράτειαν, τὴν δὲ μονογαμίαν τιμᾷ· (5) εἰ καὶ μάλιστα τὰ χαρίσματα τῆς ἱερωσύνης διὰ τῶν ἀπὸ μονογαμίας ἐγκρατευομένων καὶ τῶν ἐν παρθενίᾳ διατελούντων τῷ κόσμῳ προδιετύπου, ὡς καὶ οἱ αὐτοῦ ἀπόστολοι τὸν ἐκκλησιαστικὸν κανόνα τῆς ἱερωσύνης εὐτάκτως καὶ ὁσίως διετάξαντο. (6) εἰ δέ τις κατὰ ἀσθένιαν ἐπιδεηθείη μετὰ τὴν τελευτὴν τῆς ἰδίας γαμετῆς συναφθῆναι δευτέρῳ γάμῳ, οὐκ ἀπαγορεύει τοῦτο ὁ κανὼν τῆς ἀληθείας, τουτέστιν τὸν μὴ ὄντα ἱερέα. (7) οὗτοι δὲ κωλύουσι κατὰ τὸ εἰρημένον "κωλυόντων γαμεῖν"· ἐκβάλλουσι γὰρ τὸν δευτέρῳ γάμῳ συναφθέντα καὶ ἀναγκάζουσι μὴ δευτέρῳ γάμῳ συνάπτεσθαι.

(8) ἡμεῖς δὲ οὐκ ἀνάγκην ἐπιτιθέαμεν, ἀλλὰ παραινοῦμεν μετὰ συμβουλίας ἀγαθῆς προτρεπόμενοι τὸν δυνάμενον, οὐκ ἀνάγκην δὲ ἐπιτιθέαμεν τῷ μὴ δυναμένῳ, ἀλλὰ οὐδὲ ἐκβάλλομεν αὐτὸν ἀπὸ τῆς ζωῆς. (9) ὁ γὰρ ἅγιος λόγος πάντη ἐκήρυξε τὴν ἀσθένειαν τῶν ἀσθενούντων βαστά-

etc. (cf. 1 Tim 4:1). (7) And again at another time: "Some will depart from sound teaching, giving heed to erring (spirits) and teachings of demons, forbidding to marry and commanding to abstain from foods which God created for us to receive with thanksgiving" (cf. 1 Tim 4:1,3). (8) How clearly (this) has been fulfilled in reference to you and those like you is (obvious) from these very words before us. For most of these heresies forbid marriage and command to abstain from foods, not to promote a way of life, nor for the sake of greater virtue, prizes, and crowns (cf. 1 Cor 9:24-25), but because they consider (these things) which the Lord has made to be abominable.

9. (1) And the holy Church glorifies virginity and celibacy, and praises chastity and widowhood, and honors and accepts holy marriage, but forbids prostitution, adultery, and disregard for sexual restraints. (2) In this way it is possible to see the character of the holy Catholic Church and the distorted tendencies of others, [so that] also the one who has put them to the test flees from every road which twists and turns, and from every overgrown path. (3) For I said above, and I shall repeat it, that the most holy apostle warned us and distinguished the character of the holy Church from the error of the heresies. Some, he said, enact laws by recklessly forbidding things God ordained to be good, when he spoke of those who forbid to marry and command to abstain from foods (cf. 1 Tim 4:3). (4) And indeed God the Word has said with a degree of moderation in the Gospel: "Do you wish to be perfect?" (cf. Matt 19:21). While the Word makes allowance for man's condition and weakness, he rejoices in those who are able to demonstrate the proofs of piety, and who choose to practice virginity, chastity, and self-control. He honors marrying only once, (5) since indeed he prefigured the gifts of the priesthood (cf. Lev 21:14) through those who live in chastity after a single marriage and those who continue in virginity in the world, as also his apostles ordained the ecclesiastical rule in an orderly and holy manner. (6) But if someone, because of weakness after the death of his wife, should need to be joined in a second marriage, the rule of truth does not forbid this, that is for one who is not a priest. (7) But these people forbid it according to the words, "forbidding to marry" (1 Tim 4:3). They cast out the one who has been joined in a second marriage, and compel them not to contract a second marriage.

(8) Now we do not impose any necessity (on such a person), but we advise with good counsel and encourage the one who is able (not to marry), but we impose no necessity on the one who is not able, nor do we cast him off from the life. (9) For the holy word proclaims in every way to bear the weakness of the weak (cf. Rom 15:1; Acts 20:35), as also the holy apostle will be found immediately saying and refuting such as are not of the same

ζειν, ὡς καὶ ὁ ἅγιος ἀπόστολος εὐθὺς εὑρεθήσεται λέγων καὶ ἐλέγχων τοὺς τοιούτους * μὴ ὄντας τοῦ αὐτοῦ χαρίσματος ὅτι "νεωτέρας χήρας παραιτοῦ· (10) μετὰ γὰρ τὸ καταστρηνιάσαι τοῦ Χριστοῦ γαμεῖν θέλουσιν, ἔχουσαι τὸ κρίμα, ὅτι τὴν πρώτην πίστιν ἠθέτησαν." αἱ γὰρ ἐπαγγειλάμεναι καὶ ἀθετήσασαι ἔχουσι κρίμα, αἱ δὲ μὴ ἐπαγγειλάμεναι, ἀλλὰ συναφθεῖσαι δι' ἀσθένειαν κρίμα οὐχ ἕξουσιν. εἰ δὲ κρίμα ἔμελλον ἔχειν, πῶς ἔλεγε "γαμείτωσαν, οἰκοδεσποτείτωσαν;"

10. (1) Πᾶς τοίνυν προφητεύων παρακολουθῶν εὑρίσκεται, κἄν τε ἐν τῇ παλαιᾷ διαθήκῃ κἄν τε ἐν τῇ καινῇ, ὡς καὶ ὁ ἅγιος Ἰωάννης ἐν τῇ Ἀποκαλύψει ἔλεγε "τάδε ἀπεκάλυψε κύριος." (2) ὁ ταῦτα δὲ λέγων ἐρρωμένην εἶχε τὴν διάνοιαν καὶ παρηκολούθει, ἰδοὺ τοίνυν * "τάδε λέγει κύριος" καὶ "ὅρασις ἣν εἶδεν."

(3) ὁ δὲ Μοντανὸς οὗτος ὁ αὐχῶν ἑαυτὸν εἶναι προφήτην καὶ πλανήσας τοὺς ὑπ' αὐτοῦ πεπλανημένους ἀσύστατα κατὰ τῆς θείας γραφῆς διηγεῖται. λέγει γὰρ ἐν τῇ ἑαυτοῦ λεγομένῃ προφητείᾳ "τί λέγεις τὸν ὑπὲρ ἄνθρωπον σῳζόμενον; λάμψει γὰρ (φησίν) ὁ δίκαιος ὑπὲρ τὸν ἥλιον ἑκατονταπλασίονα, οἱ δὲ μικροὶ ἐν ὑμῖν σῳζόμενοι λάμψουσιν ἑκατονταπλασίονα ὑπὲρ τὴν σελήνην." (4) ὁ δὲ κύριος ἐλέγχει τὸν τοιοῦτον, ὁ ἔχων τὴν ἐξουσίαν χαρίσασθαι τὸ λάμπειν τὰ πρόσωπα τῶν ἁγίων καὶ φαιδρύνας τὸ πρόσωπον τοῦ Μωϋσέως καὶ μεταβάλλων τοὺς ἁγίους αὐτοῦ ἐν τῇ μελλούσῃ ἀναστάσει τῶν σωμάτων, τοὺς σπειρομένους ἐν ἀτιμίᾳ καὶ ἐγειρομένους ἐν δόξῃ, (5) οὐκ ἄλλα σώματα παρὰ τὰ ὄντα, ἀλλὰ αὐτὰ τὰ ὄντα ἐγειρόμενα ὅλα, λαμβάνοντα δὲ δόξαν παρ' αὐτοῦ μετὰ [τὴν] ἀνάστασιν παρὰ τοῦ τὴν δόξαν ἀφθόνως παρέχοντος τοῖς ἑαυτοῦ ἁγίοις, ἐπειδὴ ἔχει τὴν ἐξουσίαν δοῦναι καὶ χαρίσασθαι ὡς θεὸς καὶ κύριος. (6) ἔχων δὲ τοῦ χαρίσασθαι [ἐξουσίαν] οὐκ ἐπηγγείλατο κατὰ τὸν Μοντανόν, ἀλλά φησι "λάμψει ὑμῶν τὰ πρόσωπα ὡς ὁ ἥλιος." εἰ τοίνυν ὁ ἔχων τὴν ἐξουσίαν καὶ ἀληθῶς ὑπάρχων δεσπότης καὶ κύριος ἡμῶν Ἰησοῦς Χριστὸς ὡς ὁ ἥλιος λέγει τὰ πρόσωπα τῶν δικαίων λάμψειν, πῶς ὁ Μοντανὸς ἐπαγγέλλεται περισσότερον ἑκατονταπλασίονα; (7) εἰ μὴ ἄρα ὅμοιος εἴη ἐκείνῳ τῷ ἐπαγγειλαμένῳ τοῖς περὶ τὸν Ἀδὰμ ὅτι ἔσεσθε ὡς θεοὶ [φήσαντι] καὶ ἀπὸ τῆς ὑπαρξούσης αὐτοῖς δόξης καὶ παραδείσου τρυφῆς παρασκευάσαντι αὐτοῖς τὴν ἐκβολὴν γενέσθαι καὶ εἰς φθορὰν θανάτου κατενεχθῆναι.

11. (1) Ἔτι δὲ προστίθησιν ὁ αὐτὸς Μοντανὸς οὕτως λέγων "ἐγὼ κύριος ὁ θεὸς ὁ παντοκράτωρ καταγινόμενος ἐν ἀνθρώπῳ." (2) ἄρα γοῦν καλῶς ἡμᾶς ἡ θεία γραφὴ ἐπασφαλίζεται καὶ ἡ ἀκολουθία τῆς τοῦ ἁγίου πνεύματος διδασκαλίας, νουθετοῦσα ἡμᾶς, ἵνα γινώσκωμεν ποῖά ἐστι τὰ μιμηλὰ

grace: "Refuse younger widows, (10) for after they have grown wanton against Christ, they wish to marry, having this judgment, that they have rejected their first faith" (1 Tim 5:11-12). For those who have taken vows and have rejected them have judgment, but those who have not taken vows, but have contracted a marriage because of their weakness will fall under no judgment. And if they were to fall under judgment, how could he say: "Let them marry; let them manage a household" (cf. 1 Tim 5:14).

10. (1) Everyone who prophesies, therefore, whether in the Old Testament or in the New, is found to be in full possession of his faculties, as also the holy John said in the Apocalypse: "The Lord revealed these things to his servants through his servant John" (cf. Rev 1:1), and: "Thus says the Lord." (2) Now he who speaks thus has a sound mind and is in possession of his understanding; behold, then, (the words): "thus says the Lord," and "the vision which he saw."

(3) But this Montanus, who boasts that he is a prophet, and has deceived those deceived by him, relates things that are inconsistent in relation to the divine Scriptures. For he says in his so-called prophecy: "Why do you call the more excellent man saved? For the just, he says, will shine a hundred times brighter than the sun, and the little ones among you who are saved will shine a hundred times brighter than the moon." (4) But the Lord refutes such an assertion. He is the one who possesses the power to grant that the faces of the saints shine, and who made Moses' face bright, and who, in the resurrection of bodies which will take place, transforms his saints who are sown in dishonor and raised in glory (cf. 1 Cor 15:43). (5) And they are not different bodies than those which existed, but the very bodies which existed are raised complete in all their parts. And after the resurrection they receive glory from him who grants glory to his saints in a bountiful manner, since he has the power to give and grant it, as God and Lord. (6) And having (the power) to grant the gift, he has made no promise after the fashion of Montanus, but says: "Your faces will shine like the sun" (cf. Matt 13:43). If, then, he who has the power, and who truly is our Master and Lord Jesus Christ, says the faces of the just will shine like the sun, how does Montanus promise that they will shine a hundred times more brightly? (7) Unless he happens to be like him who promised those around Adam: "You will be as gods" (cf. Gen 3:5), and prepared for them to be cast out of the glory and luxury of paradise which was theirs, and to be brought down into the corruption of death.

11. (1) But in addition, this same Montanus adds the following words: "I am the Lord God, the Almighty dwelling in man." (2) Appropriately, then, the divine Scripture puts us on our guard, and the deduction of the teaching of the Holy Spirit warns us that we might know what the imita-

τοῦ ἀλλοτρίου πνεύματος καὶ τὰ ἀντίθετα πρὸς τὴν ἀλήθειαν. (3) ὅτε γὰρ εὐθὺς τοῦτο εἶπε Μοντανός, ὑπόνοιαν ἡμῖν δέδωκεν ἀναμνησθῆναι τὰ ὑπὸ τοῦ κυρίου εἰρημένα. οὕτως γάρ φησιν ὁ κύριος ἐν τῷ εὐαγγελίῳ "ἐγὼ ἦλθον ἐν τῷ ὀνόματι τοῦ πατρός μου, καὶ οὐκ ἐδέξασθέ με. ἄλλος ἐλεύσεται ἐπὶ τῷ ἰδίῳ ὀνόματι, καὶ δέξονται τὸν τοιοῦτον." (4) ἀσύμφωνος τοίνυν παντάπασιν ὁ τοιοῦτος τῶν θείων γραφῶν ηὑρέθη, ὡς παντί τῳ σαφὲς εἴη [τῷ] νουνεχῶς ἐντυγχάνοντι. εἰ τοίνυν ἀσύμφωνος ὑπάρχει, ἀλλότριός ἐστι τῆς ἁγίας καθολικῆς ἐκκλησίας [αὐτὸς] καὶ ἡ κατ' αὐτὸν αὐχοῦσα αἵρεσις προφήτας ἔχειν καὶ χαρίσματα, ἃ μὴ εἴληφεν, ἀλλὰ ἐκ τούτων ἀπέστη. (5) τίς τοίνυν τολμήσειε παρακολουθῶν τούτους προφήτας καλεῖν καὶ μὴ μᾶλλον πλάνους εἶναι [φήσειεν] τοὺς τοιούτους; Χριστὸς γὰρ ἡμᾶς ἐδίδαξε λέγων ὅτι "τὸ πνεῦμα τὸ παράκλητον ἀποστέλλω ὑμῖν" καὶ τὰ σημεῖα διδοὺς ἔλεγεν ὅτι "ἐκεῖνός με δοξάσει" (6) ὡς τὰ ἀληθῆ ἔστιν ἰδεῖν ὅτι οἱ ἅγιοι ἀπόστολοι τὸ παράκλητον πνεῦμα λαβόντες κύριον ἐδόξασαν, οὗτος δὲ ὁ Μοντανὸς ἑαυτὸν δοξάζει· ὁ κύριος τὸν πατέρα αὐτοῦ ἐδόξασε καὶ ὁ κύριος πάλιν [ὁ] Χριστὸς τὸ πνεῦμα ἐδόξασε, λέγων αὐτὸ πνεῦμα ἀληθείας, Μοντανὸς δὲ ἑαυτὸν δοξάζει μόνον καὶ λέγει εἶναι πατέρα παντοκράτορα καὶ τὸ ἐν αὐτῷ ἐνοικῆσαν *, ἵνα πανταχόθεν δειχθῇ οὐκ αὐτὸς ὢν οὐδὲ ὑπ' ἐκείνου ἀπεσταλμένος οὐδέ παρ' αὐτοῦ λαμβάνων. (7) "ἐν τῷ γὰρ κυρίῳ ηὐδόκησε πᾶν τὸ πλήρωμα τῆς θεότητος κατοικῆσαι σωματικῶς" καὶ "ἀπὸ τοῦ πληρώματος αὐτοῦ πάντες οἱ προφῆται εἰλήφασι" κατὰ τὸν τοῦ ἁγίου Ἰωάννου λόγον. (8) καὶ ὅρα πῶς πάντες οἱ παλαιοὶ Χριστὸν κατήγγελλον καὶ οἱ μετέπειτα Χριστὸν ἐδόξασαν καὶ αὐτὸν ὡμολόγησαν, Μοντανὸς δὲ εἰσέφρησεν ἑαυτὸν τινὰ λέγων, ὅπως δειχθῇ ὅτι οὔτε αὐτὸς ἔστιν οὔτε αὐτὸς ἀπ' αὐτοῦ ἀπέσταλται οὔτε παρ' αὐτοῦ τι εἴληφεν.

(9) Εἶτα πάλιν φησὶ τὸ ἐλεεινὸν ἀνθρωπάριον Μοντανὸς ὅτι "οὔτε ἄγγελος οὔτε πρέσβυς, ἀλλ' ἐγὼ κύριος ὁ θεὸς πατὴρ ἦλθον." ταῦτα δὲ λέγων φωραθήσεται ἀλλότριος ὤν, Χριστὸν μὴ δοξάξων, ὃν πᾶν χάρισμα ἐκκλησιαστικὸν ἐν ἐκκλησίᾳ τῇ ἁγίᾳ δοθὲν ἐν ἀληθείᾳ ἐδόξασεν. (10) εὑρεθήσεται γὰρ ἐκτὸς εἶναι σώματος ἐκκλησίας καὶ κεφαλῆς τοῦ σύμπαντος καὶ "μὴ κρατῶν τὴν κεφαλήν, ἐξ ἧσπερ πᾶν τὸ σῶμα συναρμολογούμενον αὔξει" κατὰ τὸ γεγραμμένον. ὁ γὰρ κύριος ἡμῶν Ἰησοῦς Χριστὸς

tions of the alien spirit are like, and that they are antithetical to the truth. (3) For as soon as Montanus has said this it has prompted us to recall what the Lord said. For the Lord spoke as follows in the Gospel: "I have come in the name of my Father, and you did not receive me; another will come in his own name, and they will receive such a one" (cf. John 5:43).

(4) Such a man, therefore, is found to be at variance with the divine Scriptures on all points, as would be clear to everyone who reads them with a sound mind. If then he is at variance with Scripture, he (himself) is estranged from the holy Catholic Church, and so is the sect which boasts in relation to him that it possesses prophets and spiritual gifts, which it has not received, but has been deprived of them. (5) Who, then, in possession of his faculties would dare call these people prophets, and not rather (say) that such are deceivers? For Christ taught us, saying: "I am sending the Spirit, the Paraclete, to you" (cf. John 16:7). And after he indicated the signs, he said: "He will glorify me" (John 16:14). (6) In this way it is possible to see what is true, since the holy apostles glorified the Lord when they received the supporting Spirit, but this Montanus glorifies himself. The Lord glorified his Father, and again the Lord Christ glorified the Spirit, saying that he is the Spirit of truth. But Montanus glorifies only himself, and says that he is the Father Almighty, and that [the] (Spirit)[5] dwells in himself, so that it has been shown from every side that he is not (the Father),[6] and he has not been sent by him, and he does not receive anything from him. (7) "For the whole fulness of deity was pleased to dwell bodily in the Lord" (cf. Col 2:9), and, according to the word of the holy John, "all the prophets have received of his fulness" (cf. John 1:16). (8) Now observe how all the ancients announced Christ and afterwards glorified Christ and confessed him, but Montanus introduced himself claiming to be somebody. Consequently, it has been proven that he neither is (the Father), nor has he been sent by him, nor has he received anything from him.

(9) Then again this miserable little Montanus says: "Neither angel nor envoy, but I the Lord God the Father have come." But when he says these things he is exposed to be an alien, because he does not glorify Christ, whom every ecclesiastical gift given in the holy Church has glorified in truth. (10) For he will be found to be outside the body of the Church, and outside the head of the whole, and not to be grasping the head (cf. Col 2:19) from which the whole body being fitted together (cf. Eph 4:16) will grow (cf. Eph 2:21), according to what has been written. For our Lord Jesus

---

[5]My suggestion. Holl posits a lacuna here.

[6]There is no predicate in the text. The context seems to demand "the Father."

υἱὸν ἑαυτὸν ἔδειξεν, ὄντως ὢν υἱὸς ἐν ἀληθείᾳ, Μοντανὸς δ' ἑαυτὸν καὶ πατέρα λέγει.

12. (1) Πῶς τοίνυν, ὦ Φρύγες ἡμῖν πάλιν ἐπαναστάντες πολέμιοι καὶ μεμορφωμένοι εἰς Χριστιανικὴν ἐπίκλησιν, βαρβάρων δὲ ἐπανῃρημένοι μάχην καὶ τῶν Τρώων καὶ Φρυγῶν μιμούμενοι τὸ πολέμιον, πῶς πεισθῶμεν ὑμῖν λέγουσι διὰ χαρίσματα ἀφεστάναι τῆς ἐκκλησίας; (2) οὐκέτι γὰρ χαρίσματα εἴη τὰ ἀλλότρια χαρισμάτων ὄντα καὶ παρὰ τὸν χαρακτῆρα τὸν ὑπὸ κυρίου ὑπισχνούμενον, ὡς οἱ καθ' ὑμᾶς προφῆται λέγουσιν.

(3) εἰσάγετε δὲ ἡμῖν πάλιν καὶ Μαξίμιλλαν· καὶ γὰρ καὶ τὰ ὀνόματα ὑμῶν διηλλαγμένα καὶ φοβερώτατα καὶ οὔτε προσηνές τι καὶ γλυκύτατον ἔχοντα, ἀλλὰ ἄγριόν τι καὶ βαρβαρικόν. (4) εὐθὺς γὰρ αὕτη ἡ Μαξίμιλλα ἡ παρὰ τοῖς τοιούτοις κατὰ Φρύγας οὕτω καλουμένοις—ἀκούσατε, ὦ παῖδες Χριστοῦ, τί λέγει· "ἐμοῦ μὴ ἀκούσητε, ἀλλὰ Χριστοῦ ἀκούσατε." (5) καὶ ἐν οἷς ἔδοξε Χριστὸν δοξάζειν πεπλάνηται. εἰ γὰρ ἦν τοῦ Χριστοῦ, ἔλεγεν ἂν κατὰ τοὺς ἁγίους ἀποστόλους ὡς ἕκαστος [αὐτῶν] λέγει, Πέτρος μὲν πρῶτος λέγων ὅτι "ἡμεῖς παρ' αὐτοῦ ἠκούσαμεν" καὶ αὐτοῦ τοῦ κυρίου λέγοντος "ὁ ὑμῶν ἀκούων ἐμοῦ ἀκούει" καὶ τοῦ Παύλου λέγοντος "μιμηταί μου γίνεσθε, καθὼς κἀγὼ Χριστοῦ."

(6) αὕτη δὲ ἀληθεύει ψευδομένη, καὶ μὴ βουλομένη. καλῶς γὰρ λέγει φάσκουσα μὴ αὐτῆς ἀκούειν, ἀλλὰ Χριστοῦ. πολλάκις γὰρ τὰ ἀκάθαρτα πνεύματα ἀναγκάζεται ἑαυτὰ καθαιρεῖν, [ὡς] οὐκ ὄντα τῆς ἀληθείας, καὶ ὑποφαίνειν τὸν κύριον αὐτῶν, θέλοντα καὶ μὴ θέλοντα, δι' ἀνάγκην· (7) ὡς ἡ παιδίσκη ἡ ἔχουσα πνεῦμα Πύθωνος ἔλεγεν "οὗτοι οἱ ἄνθρωποι τοῦ θεοῦ δοῦλοι τοῦ ὑψίστου εἰσί," καὶ τὸ "τί ἦλθες πρὸ καιροῦ βασανίσαι ἡμᾶς; οἴδαμέν σε τίς εἶ, ὁ ἅγιος τοῦ θεοῦ," οὕτως καὶ αὕτη ἀναγκαζομένη ἔλεγεν αὐτῆς μὴ ἀκούειν ἀλλὰ Χριστοῦ. (8) πῶς οὖν τοῦτο οἱ παρ' αὐτῆς ἀκηκοότες καὶ αὐτῇ πεπιστευκότες βούλονται αὐτῆς ἀκούειν, παρ' αὐτῆς μαθόντες μὴ αὐτῆς ἀκούειν ἀλλὰ κυρίου; καὶ γὰρ ἀληθῶς ἐπίγεια φθεγγομένης αὐτῆς, εἰ παρῆν αὐτοῖς σύνεσις, οὐκ ἔδει αὐτὴν ἀκούεσθαι.

(9) καὶ μὴ λέγε ὅτι παρηκολούθει. οὐ γὰρ παρακολουθοῦντός ἐστιν τὸ διδάσκειν καὶ ἑαυτὸν ἀνατρέπειν. εἰ γὰρ ὅλως λέγει "μὴ ἀκούετέ μου," ποῖον ἦν τὸ πνεῦμα τὸ λαλοῦν ἐν αὐτῇ; (10) εἰ γὰρ αὐτὴ ἔλεγεν ἢ ἄνθρωπος, ἄρα οὐκ ἦν ἐν πνεύματι ἁγίῳ. ἡ γὰρ λέγουσα "μὴ ἀκούετέ μου" δῆλον ὅτι τὸ ἀνθρώπινον ἔλεγε καὶ οὐκ ἦν ἐν πνεύματι ἁγίῳ. εἰ δὲ μὴ

Christ showed himself to be the Son, really being the Son in truth, but Montanus says he himself is also the Father.

12. (1) How, then, O Phrygians, when you have again risen up against us like enemies even though you have modelled yourselves on the name Christian, but you have entered upon a battle of barbarians and are imitating the hostility of the Trojans and Phrygians, how can we believe you, when you say you have separated from the Church because of spiritual gifts? (2) For those would no longer be spiritual gifts which are alien to the spiritual gifts, and which profess things contrary to the character (indicated) by the Lord, as your prophets say.

(3) You introduce Maximilla to us again also; indeed even your names are different and most dreadful, possessing nothing that is soothing and pleasant, but having a wild and barbarous quality. (4) For hear, O children of Christ, what this Maximilla who belongs to such as are thus called Cataphrygians says in a straightforward manner: "Hear not me, but hear Christ." (5) She has gone astray even in these words in which she seemed to glorify Christ. For if she were of Christ, she would have spoken in accordance with the holy apostles, as each (of them) speaks. First there is Peter who says: "We have heard from him" (cf. 2 Pet 1:18); and the Lord himself says: "He who hears you hears me" (Luke 10:16); and Paul says: "Be imitators of me even as I am of Christ" (1 Cor 11:1).

(6) But Maximilla is telling the truth although she is deceived and does not wish to tell the truth. For she speaks correctly when she says not to hear herself, but Christ. For the unclean spirits are often compelled to condemn themselves although they are not of the truth, and to indicate their Lord, by necessity, whether they wish to or not. (7) For example, the maidservant who had the spirit of Python said: "These men are servants of the Most High God" (Acts 16:17). There is also the saying: "Why have you come to torment us before the time? We know who you are, the holy one of God" (cf. Matt 8:29; Mark 1:24). So too Maximilla, under compulsion said not to hear herself, but Christ. (8) How is it, then, that those who have heard this from her, and have believed in her wish to hear her when they have learned from her not to hear her, but the Lord? For indeed, there would truly be no necessity to listen to her when she utters earthly things if they possessed intelligence.

(9) And don't say that she understood (what she said). For it is not characteristic of one who understands to teach and to refute himself. For, in short, if she says, "Don't hear me," what kind of spirit was speaking in her? (10) For if she meant that man (was speaking) in her, then she was not in the Holy Spirit. For it is clear that she who says, "Don't hear me," made a human utterance, and was not in the Holy Spirit. And if she was

οὖσα ἐν πνεύματι ἁγίῳ ἄνωθεν, οὖσα δὲ τοῦ ἀνθρωπίνου φρονήματος, οὐδὲν ἐγίνωσκε καὶ οὐκ ἦν ἄρα προφῆτις, μὴ ἔχουσα πνεῦμα ἅγιον, ἀλλὰ ἀνθρωπίνῳ φρονήματι ἐλάλει καὶ ἐφθέγγετο. (11) εἰ δὲ πνεύματι ἁγίῳ ἐλάλει καὶ ἐπροφήτευε, ποῖον ἦν ἄρα τὸ πνεῦμα τὸ ἅγιον τὸ λέγον "ἐμοῦ μὴ ἀκούετε"; καὶ πολλή ἐστι τῆς ἀπάτης ἡ τύφλωσις καὶ μέγας ἐστὶν ὁ τοῦ θεοῦ λόγος, ὁ κατὰ πάντα τρόπον ἡμᾶς συνετίζων εἰς τὸ εἰδέναι ἡμᾶς ποῖα τὰ ἐκ τοῦ πνεύματος τοῦ ἁγίου λελαλημένα, πῇ μὲν ἐκ προσώπου πατρός, πῇ δὲ ἐκ προσώπου τοῦ υἱοῦ, πῇ δὲ ἐκ προσώπου τοῦ ἁγίου πνεύματος. (12) καὶ εἰ τὸ ἐν Μαξιμίλλῃ πνεῦμα [πνεῦμα] ἅγιον ἦν, οὐκ ἀπηγόρευε τὰ ἴδια ῥήματα· "ἓν γάρ ἐστι τὸ ἅγιον πνεῦμα, τὸ διαιροῦν ἑκάστῳ ὡς βούλεται." (13) εἰ δὲ ἔχει ἐξουσίαν διαιρεῖν ὡς βούλεται, λέγεται δὲ πνεῦμα γνώσεως καὶ πνεῦμα εὐσεβείας καὶ λέγεται πνεῦμα Χριστοῦ [εἶναι] καὶ πνεῦμα πατρός, τὸ ἐκ τοῦ πατρὸς ἐκπορευόμενον καὶ τοῦ υἱοῦ λαμβάνον, οὐκ ἀλλότριον πατρὸς καὶ υἱοῦ ὄν, ἄρα οὐκ ἔλεγε "μὴ ἀκούετέ μου." (14) τὰ γὰρ Χριστοῦ τὸ πνεῦμα ἐλάλει καὶ ὁ Χριστὸς τὸ πνεῦμα ἀποστέλλει καὶ ἐν πνεύματι ἁγίῳ ἐκβάλλει τὰ δαιμόνια, καὶ ὁ υἱὸς τὰ τοῦ πατρὸς λέγει καὶ ὁ πατὴρ τὸν υἱὸν ἡγίασε καὶ ἀπέστειλεν εἰς τὸν κόσμον, ἵνα γινώσκωσιν αὐτὸν καὶ δοξάσωσι, καθὼς δοξάζουσι τὸν πατέρα. (15) καὶ διέπεσε κατὰ πάντα τρόπον ἡ τῶν ἀπαλλοτριούντων ἑαυτοὺς διάνοια ἀπὸ τῆς τοῦ Χριστοῦ ἀκολουθίας.

13. (1) Φάσκει δὲ πάλιν ἡ αὐτὴ Μαξιμίλλα, ἡ τῆς παρακολουθίας γνῶσις καὶ διδασκαλία, ἵνα καὶ χλευαστικῶς εἴπω, ὅτι "ἀπέστειλέ με κύριος τούτου τοῦ πόνου καὶ τῆς συνθήκης καὶ τῆς ἐπαγγελίας αἱρετιστὴν μηνυτὴν ἑρμηνευτήν, ἠναγκασμένον, θέλοντα καὶ μὴ θέλοντα, γνωθεῖν γνῶσιν θεοῦ." (2) σκοπήσωμεν οὖν τῆς ἡμῶν ζωῆς τὴν εὐσταθῆ βάσιν καὶ τὴν ὁδὸν τοῦ φωτός, ὦ ἀγαπητοί, καὶ μὴ σφαλῶμεν διὰ τῶν λόγων τοῦ δι' ἐναντίας καὶ τοῦ βοσκήματος τοῦ ἀλλοτρίου πνεύματος. (3) ὅρα γὰρ ἐνταῦθα τὸν οὕτω λαλήσαντα, ἀναγκασμένον ἑαυτὸν ἀποφήναντα, οὐχ ἑκουσίᾳ γνώμῃ. ὁ δὲ κύριος ἡμῶν οὐκ ἄκων ἦλθεν εἰς τὸν κόσμον οὐδὲ μετὰ ἀνάγκης ὑπὸ πατρὸς ἀπεστάλη, ἀλλὰ ἅμα σὺν πατρὶ ἔχων τὸ θέλειν καὶ σὺν ἁγίῳ πνεύματι τὸ παρέχειν· (4) καὶ ὡς αὐτὸς ἅμα σὺν πατρὶ τὸ θέλειν ἔχει καὶ τὸ οὐχὶ μετὰ ἀνάγκης καὶ τὴν χάριν πᾶσι διδόναι, ἀλλὰ δι' ὑπερβολὴν φιλανθρωπίας, οὕτω καὶ οὓς ἐκάλεσε μετὰ προαιρέσεως κέκληκεν, οὐκ ἀνάγκην ἐπιβάλλων, οὐ κλοιὸν ἐπιτιθέμενος. (5) φάσκει γὰρ ὅτι "οἱ διψῶντες ἔλθατε πρός με" καὶ πάλιν "εἴ τις θέλει ἔρχεσθαι πρός με, ἀρνησάσθω ἑαυτὸν καὶ ἀκολουθείτω μοι" καὶ διὰ Ἡσαΐου τὸ αὐτὸ φθεγ-

not in the Holy Spirit from above, but was under the influence of human thought, she knew nothing, and was not, then, a prophetess, nor did she possess the Holy Spirit, but she spoke and uttered her words under the influence of human thought. (11) But if she did not speak and prophesy in the Holy Spirit, of what sort, then, was the Holy Spirit which said: "Don't hear me"? Great is the blindness of deceit, and great is the Word of God who instructs us in every way so that we know what has been said by the Holy Spirit, sometimes in the person of the Father, sometimes in that of the Son, and at other times in the person of the Holy Spirit. (12) And if the spirit in Maximilla had been holy, she would not have rejected her own words, for "it is one and the same Holy Spirit which distributes to each as he wills" (1 Cor 12:11). (13) And if he has the authority to distribute as he wills, and is said to be the Spirit of knowledge and the Spirit of piety, and is said to be the Spirit of Christ, and the Spirit of the Father which proceeds from the Father and receives from the Son, not being estranged from the Father and the Son, then he did not say: "Don't hear me." (14) For the Spirit speaks the words of Christ, and Christ sends the Spirit and casts out demons by the Holy Spirit, and the Son speaks the words of the Father, and the Father has sanctified the Son and sent him into the world, that they might know him and glorify him as they glorify the Father. (15) And the understanding of those who alienate themselves from following Christ has erred in every way.

13. (1) And again the same Maximilla, who claims to be the gnosis of persuasion and doctrine, to speak derisively, declares: "The Lord has sent me as partisan, revealer, and interpreter of this suffering, covenant, and promise. I am compelled to come to understand the knowledge of God whether I want to or not." (2) Let us, therefore, brothers, contemplate the firm foundation of our life and the way of light, and let us not be tripped up by the arguments of this adversary and the herd of followers of an alien spirit. (3) For consider here the one who has spoken in this way, who has revealed that she has been compelled and has not acted on her own free will. Now our Lord did not come into the world unwillingly, nor was he sent by the Father under compulsion. He possessed a will in harmony with the Father, and his largess was in harmony with the Holy Spirit, (4) and just as he has a will in harmony with the Father, he also gives grace to all, not under compulsion, but because of his exceedingly great love for mankind. And so also those whom he has called, he has called with their free choice, casting no necessity on them, nor placing a collar on them. (5) For he declares: "Come to me, you who thirst" (cf. John 7:37); and again: "If anyone wishes to come to me, let him deny himself and follow me" (cf. Luke 9:23). And he uttered the same thing through Isaiah and said: "If you

γόμενος ἔλεγεν "ἐὰν θέλητε καὶ εἰσακούσητέ μου" καὶ ὕστερον, ἵνα δείξῃ ὁ προφήτης [ὅτι] τίς ἐστιν ὁ λέγων, ἔφη "τὸ γὰρ στόμα κυρίου ἐλάλησε ταῦτα." (6) καὶ ὁρᾷς κατὰ πάντα τρόπον τὴν πρὸς τὸ θεῖον γράμμα τούτων διαφωνίαν καὶ τὴν ἀλλοίαν ὑπόνοιάν τε καὶ ὑπόληψιν παρὰ τὴν τοῦ θεοῦ πίστιν καὶ ἀκολουθίαν; (7) καὶ γὰρ καὶ Μαξίμιλλα τοὺς θέλοντας καὶ μὴ θέλοντας ἔλεγεν ἀναγκάζειν, ὡς καὶ ἐξ αὐτοῦ τοῦ ῥητοῦ ψεύσεται ἡ τοιαύτη. οὔτε γὰρ θέλοντας ἐδίδαξε γνῶσιν θεοῦ ἣν οὐκ ᾔδει οὐδὲ τοὺς μὴ θέλοντας ἠνάγκασεν. (8) αὐτίκα [γοῦν] οὐ πάντες οἱ ἐν τῷ κόσμῳ οἴδασι τί ἐστιν ὄνομα Μαξιμίλλης οὐδὲ τῶν αὐτῆς λόγων τὸ παράφθεγμα. καὶ κατὰ πάντα τρόπον διέπεσεν ἡ τούτων πεπλανημένη ἐπίνοια, οὐκ οὖσα τῆς τοῦ θεοῦ ἀληθείας.

are willing, and you hearken to me'' (Isa 1:19). And later, that the prophet might show who the speaker was, he said: ''For the mouth of the Lord has spoken these words'' (Isa 58:14). (6) Do you see the disagreement of these people with the divine Scripture in every way, and that both their opinion and assumption are different from the faith in God and what follows from it? (7) For indeed even Maximilla said she compelled those who were willing and those who were not, so that such a woman will be lying even on the basis of her own word. For neither did she teach the willing the knowledge of God, which she did not know, nor did she compel those who were not willing. (8) To begin with, all who are in the world do not know what the name of Maximilla is, nor do they know the deception of her words. The erring thought of these people has fallen apart in every way because it is not of God's truth.

Testimonia Concerning Montanism in Rome

Irenaeus

27. *Sancti Irenaei libros quinque adversus haereses* 3.11.12 (ed. Harvey, Tom. II, pp. 50-52).

Τούτων δὲ οὕτως ἐχόντων, μάταιοι πάντες καὶ ἀμαθεῖς, προσέτι δὲ καὶ τολμηροί, οἱ ἀθετοῦντες τὴν ἰδέαν τοῦ Εὐαγγελίου, καὶ εἴτε πλείονα, εἴτε ἐλάττονα τῶν εἰρημένων παρεισφέροντες Εὐαγγελίων πρόσωπα· οἱ μὲν, ἵνα πλείονα δόξωσι τῆς ἀληθείας ἐξευρηκέναι· οἱ δὲ, ἵνα τὰς οἰκονομίας τοῦ θεοῦ ἀθετήσωσιν.

His igitur sic se habentibus, vani omnes, et indocti, et insuper audaces, qui frustrantur speciem Evangelii, et vel plures quam dictae sunt, vel rursus pauciores inferunt personas Evangelii: quidam ut plus videantur quam est veritatis adinvenisse: quidam vero, ut reprobent dispositiones Dei. etenim Marcion totum rejiciens Evangelium, imo vero seipsum abscindens ab Evangelio, partem gloriatur se habere Evangelii. Alii vero ut donum Spiritus frustrentur, quod in novissimis temporibus secundum placitum Patris effusum est in humanum genus, illam speciem non admittunt, quae est secundum Johannis Evangelium, in qua Paracletum se missurum Dominus promisit; sed simul et Evangelium, et propheticum repellunt Spiritum. Infelices vere, qui pseudoprophetas quidem esse nolunt, prophetiae vero gratiam repellunt ab Ecclesia: similia patientes his, qui propter eos qui in hypocrisi veniunt, etiam a fratrum communicatione se abstinent. Datur autem intelligi, quod hujusmodi neque Apostolum Paulum recipiant. In ea enim Epistola quae est ad Corinthios, de propheticis charismatibus diligenter locutus est, et scit viros et mulieres in Ecclesia

Testimonia Concerning Montanism in Rome[7]

Irenaeus

27. *The Five Books of Irenaeus against Heresies* 3.11.12.

But since these things are so,[8] all those who disregard the form of the gospel and introduce either more types of Gospels than those mentioned, or less, are vain and ignorant, and in addition, also shameless. Some do it to appear to have discovered more than the truth; others to disregard the plan of God.

For while Marcion rejects the whole gospel, or rather separates himself from the gospel, he boasts that he has a part in the gospel.

Others, to be sure, to nullify the gift of the Spirit which has been poured out on the human race in accordance with the Father's good pleasure in the last times (cf. Joel 2:28-29; Acts 2:17-18), do not receive that form [of the gospel] which is the Gospel according to John, in which the Lord promised to send the Paraclete (cf. John 14:16; 16:13-14). These reject, at the same time, the Gospel and the prophetic Spirit. They are miserable indeed, since they certainly do not wish[9] that there be false prophets, but they remove the prophetic gift from the Church.[10] They suffer the same things as those who cut themselves off also from participation in community life with their brothers because of those who are hypocrites. Moreover it is to be taken for granted that such men also would not accept the apostle Paul. For in that epistle which is to the Corinthians he has spoken diligently about prophetic gifts (cf. 1 Cor 11:4-5; 12-14), and he knows men and women who

---

[7]See also below, no. 63.

[8]Irenaeus has just argued that there can be no more nor less than the four Gospels recognized by the Church.

[9]Labriolle has correctly emended volunt to nolunt. For his reasoning see *La crise montaniste*, 233-35.

[10]Irenaeus refers to a group in *Proof of the Apostolic Preaching* 99 who "do not admit the gifts of the Holy Spirit, and reject from themselves the charism of prophecy" (J. P. Smith, *St. Irenaeus: Proof of the Apostolic Preaching*, ACW 16 [New York: Newman Press, 1952] 108-109).

54   THE MONTANIST ORACLES AND TESTIMONIA

prophetantes. Per haec igitur omnia peccantes in Spiritum Dei, in irremissibile incidunt peccatum.

Gaius

28. Eusebius, H.E. 2.25.5-7 (GCS, ed. Schwartz, pp. 176-78).

Παῦλος δὴ οὖν ἐπ᾽ αὐτῆς Ῥώμης τὴν κεφαλὴν ἀποτμηθῆναι καὶ Πέτρος ὡσαύτως ἀνασκολοπισθῆναι κατ᾽ αὐτὸν ἱστοροῦνται, καὶ πιστοῦταί γε τὴν ἱστορίαν ἡ Πέτρου καὶ Παύλου εἰς δεῦρο κρατήσασα ἐπὶ τῶν αὐτόθι κοιμητηρίων πρόσρησις, οὐδὲν δὲ ἧττον καὶ ἐκκλησιαστικὸς ἀνήρ, Γάϊος ὄνομα, κατὰ Ζεφυρῖνον Ῥωμαίων γεγονὼς ἐπίσκοπον· ὃς δὴ Πρόκλῳ τῆς κατὰ Φρύγας προϊσταμένῳ γνώμης ἐγγράφως διαλεχθείς, αὐτὰ δὴ ταῦτα περὶ τῶν τόπων, ἔνθα τῶν εἰρημένων ἀποστόλων τὰ ἱερὰ σκηνώματα κατατέθειται, φησίν· "ἐγὼ δὲ τὰ τρόπαια τῶν ἀποστόλων ἔχω δεῖξαι. ἐὰν γὰρ θελήσῃς ἀπελθεῖν ἐπὶ τὸν Βασικανὸν ἢ ἐπὶ τὴν ὁδὸν τὴν Ὠστίαν, εὑρήσεις τὰ τρόπαια τῶν ταύτην ἱδρυσαμένων τὴν ἐκκλησίαν."

29. Ibid. 6.20.3 (Schwartz, p. 566).

ἦλθεν δὲ εἰς ἡμᾶς καὶ Γαΐου, λογιωτάτου ἀνδρός, διάλογος, ἐπὶ Ῥώμης κατὰ Ζεφυρῖνον πρὸς Πρόκλον τῆς κατὰ Φρύγας αἱρέσεως ὑπερμαχοῦντα κεκινημένος· ἐν ᾧ τῶν δι᾽ ἐναντίας τὴν περὶ συντάττειν καινὰς γραφὰς προπέτειάν τε καὶ τόλμαν ἐπιστομίζων, τῶν τοῦ ἱεροῦ ἀποστόλου δεκατριῶν μόνων ἐπιστολῶν μνημονεύει, τὴν πρὸς Ἑβραίους μὴ συναριθμήσας ταῖς λοιπαῖς, ἐπεὶ καὶ εἰς δεῦρο παρὰ Ῥωμαίων τισὶν οὐ νομίζεται τοῦ ἀποστόλου τυγχάνειν.

The Muratorian Canon

30. Ed. Rauschen, *Florilegium patristicum,* fasc. 3, p. 35.

Arsinoi autem seu Valentini vel Miltiadis nihil in totum recipimus; quin etiam nouum psalmorum librum Marciani conscripserunt una cum Basilide Asiano Cataphrygum constitutore.

Hippolytus

31. Εἰς τὸν Δανιήλ 4.20 (GCS, ed. Bonwetsch, p. 230.).

Ταῦτα συμβαίνει τοῖς ἰδιώταις καὶ ἐλαφροῖς ἀνθρώποις, ὅσοι ταῖς μὲν γραφαῖς ἀκριβῶς οὐ προσέχουσιν, ταῖς δὲ ἀνθρωπίναις παραδόσεσιν καὶ ταῖς ἑαυτῶν πλάναις καὶ τοῖς ἑαυτῶν ἐνυπνίοις καὶ μυθολογίαις καὶ λόγοις γραώδεσι μᾶλλον [ἡδέως] πείθονται. . . . Καὶ [γὰρ] νῦν δέ τινες τὰ ὅμοια τολμῶσιν "προσέχοντες" ὁράμασι ματαίοις "καὶ διδα-

prophesy in the Church. Sinning against the Spirit of God, therefore, in all these respects, they fall into the unforgivable sin (cf. Luke 12:10; Mark 3:29).

Gaius

28. Eusebius, *Ecclesiastical History* 2.25.5-7.

It is stated that during Nero's reign Paul was beheaded in Rome itself and that Peter likewise was impaled, and the designation "of Peter and Paul" which has prevailed over the burial places at the place until the present confirms the story. And also no less a Churchman named Gaius, a bishop of the Romans in the time of Zephyrinus, who had a written discussion with Proclus, a leader of the Cataphrygian doctrine, speaks in these very words of the places where the sacred bodies of the apostles under discussion have been placed. "But I can point out the trophies of the apostles. For if you wish to go to the Vatican or to the Ostian Way you will find the trophies of those who established this Church."

29. Ibid., 6.20.3.

Now we have also received a dialogue of Gaius, a most eloquent man, with Proclus, a defender of the Cataphrygian heresy. The dialogue took place at Rome in the time of Zephyrinus. In it, while curbing the rashness and daring of his opponents in composing new scriptures, he mentions only thirteen epistles of the holy apostle, since he did not count the epistle to the Hebrews with the rest, because even till now it is not thought to belong to the apostle by some of the Romans.

The Muratorian Canon

30. *A Collection of Patristic Texts*, fasc. 3, p. 35.

But we accept nothing at all of Arsinoes, or of Valentinus or Miltiades; indeed also the Marcionites have drawn up a new book of psalms together with the Asian Basilides, founder of the Cataphrygians.

Hippolytus

31. *Commentary on Daniel* 4.20.

These things happen to uneducated and simple people who do not give careful attention to the Scriptures, but rather [gladly] listen to human traditions, their own errors and dreams, fables, and silly tales (cf. 1 Tim 4:7). . . . And even now some undergo the same things "by giving heed" to vain visions "and teachings of demons" (cf. 1 Tim 4:1), and by frequently

56	THE MONTANIST ORACLES AND TESTIMONIA

σκαλίαις δαιμονίων" καὶ ἐν σαββάτῳ καὶ κυριακῇ πολλάκις νηστείαν ὁρίζοντες, ἥνπερ ὁ Χριστὸς οὐχ ὥρισεν, ἵνα τὸ τοῦ Χριστοῦ εὐαγγέλιον ἀτιμάσωσιν.

32. *Refutatio Omnium Haeresium*, 8.19 (GCS, ed. Wendland).

Ἕτεροι δὲ καὶ αὐτοὶ αἱρετικώτεροι τὴν φύσιν, Φρύγες τὸ γένος, προληφθέντες ὑπὸ γυναίων ἠπάτηνται, Πρισκίλλης τινὸς καὶ Μαξιμίλλης καλουμένων, ἃς προφήτιδας νομίζουσιν, ἐν ταύταις τὸ παράκλητον πνεῦμα κεχωρηκέναι λέγοντες, καὶ τινὰ πρὸ αὐτῶν Μοντανὸν ὁμοίως δο-ξάζουσιν ὡς προφήτην, ὧν βίβλους ἀπείρους ἔχοντες πλανῶνται, μήτε τὰ ὑπ' αὐτῶν λελαλημένα λόγῳ κρίναντες, μήτε τοῖς κρῖναι δυναμένοις προσέχοντες, ἀλλ' ἀκρίτως τῇ πρὸς αὐτοὺς πίστει προφέρονται, πλεῖόν τι δι' αὐτῶν φάσκοντες [ὡς] μεμαθηκέναι ἢ ἐκ νόμου καὶ προφητῶν καὶ τῶν εὐαγγελίων. ὑπὲρ δὲ ἀποστόλους καὶ πᾶν χάρισμα ταῦτα τὰ γύναια δοξάζουσιν, ὡς τολμᾶν πλεῖόν τι Χριστοῦ ἐν τούτοις λέγειν τινὰς αὐτῶν γεγονέναι. οὗτοι τὸν μὲν πατέρα τῶν ὅλων θεὸν καὶ πάντων κτίστην ὁμοίως τῇ ἐκκλησίᾳ ὁμολογοῦσι καὶ ὅσα τὸ εὐαγγέλιον περὶ τοῦ Χριστοῦ μαρτυρεῖ, καινίζουσι δὲ νηστείας, καὶ ἑορτὰς, καὶ ξηροφαγίας, καὶ ῥαφανοφαγίας, φάσκοντες ὑπὸ τῶν γυναίων δεδιδάχθαι. τινὲς δὲ αὐτῶν τῇ τῶν Νοητιανῶν αἱρέσει συντιθέμενοι τὸν πατέρα αὐτὸν εἶναι τὸν υἱὸν λέγουσι, καὶ τοῦτον ὑπὸ γένεσιν καὶ πάθος καὶ θάνατον ἐληλυθέναι. περὶ τούτων αὖθις λεπτομερέστερον ἐκθήσομαι· πολλοῖς γὰρ ἀφορμὴ κακῶν γεγένηται ἡ τούτων αἵρεσις. ἱκανὰ μὲν οὖν καὶ τὰ περὶ τούτων εἰρημένα κρίνομεν, δι' ὀλίγων τὰ πολλὰ φλύαρα αὐτῶν βιβλία τε καὶ ἐπιχειρήματα πᾶσιν ἐπιδείξαντες ἀσθενῆ ὄντα καὶ μηδενὸς λόγου ἄξια, οἷς οὐ χρὴ προσέχειν τοὺς ὑγιαίνοντα νοῦν κεκτημένους.

33. Ibid. 10.25-26 (Wendland).

25. Οἱ δὲ Φρύγες ἐκ Μοντανοῦ τινος καὶ Πρισκίλλης καὶ Μαξιμίλλης τὰς ἀρχὰς τῆς αἱρέσεως λαβόντες, προφήτιδας τὰ γύναια νομίζοντες καὶ προφήτην τὸν Μοντανόν, τὰ δὲ περὶ τῆς τοῦ παντὸς ἀρχῆς καὶ δημιουργίας ὀρθῶς [λέγειν] νομίζουσι, καὶ τὰ περὶ τὸν Χριστόν οὐκ ἀλλοτρίως προσειλήφασιν, ἐν δὲ τοῖς προειρημένοις σφάλλονται, ὧν τοῖς λόγοις ὑπὲρ τὰ εὐαγγέλια προσέχοντες πλανῶνται, νηστείας καινὰς καὶ παραδόξους ὁρίζοντες.

26. Ἕτεροι δὲ αὐτῶν τῇ τῶν Νοητιανῶν αἱρέσει προσκείμενοι τὰ μὲν περὶ τὰ γύναια καὶ Μοντανὸν ὁμοίως δοκοῦσι, τὰ δὲ περὶ [τὸν] τῶν ὅλων πατέρα δυσφημοῦσιν, αὐτὸν εἶναι υἱὸν καὶ πατέρα λέγοντες, ὁρατὸν καὶ ἀόρατον, γεννητὸν καὶ ἀγέννητον, θνητὸν καὶ ἀθάνατον· οὗτοι τὰς ἀφορμὰς ἀπὸ Νοητοῦ τινος λαβόντες.

appointing a fast on the Sabbath and the Lord's day, which Christ did not appoint, so that they dishonor the gospel of Christ.

32. *Refutation of all Heresies* 8.19.

But there are others who themselves are even more heretical in nature, Phrygians by race. Having been prejudiced by women named Priscilla and Maximilla, whom they take to be prophetesses, they have been deceived in that they say the Spirit, as the Paraclete, has gone forth in these women. And likewise they magnify a certain Montanus before them as a prophet. Since they have countless books of these people they go astray, because they neither apply the critique of reason to what they have said nor do they pay attention to those who can apply such a critique, but are swept away by their uncritical faith in them. They say that they have learned something more through them than from the Law and the Prophets and the Gospels. And they magnify these weak females above the apostles and every divine gift, so that some of them dare say that something greater has occurred in them than in Christ. They, like the Church, confess that God is the Father of the universe and the creator of all things, and they accept all that the gospel testifies about Christ. But they devise new fasts, feasts, and the eating of dry food and cabbage, declaring that these things have been taught by those females. But some of them, agreeing with the heresy of the Noetians, say that the Father himself is the Son, and that he has experienced birth, suffering, and death. I will present a more detailed treatment of these matters later, for their heresy has become an occasion of evil to many. Therefore, we consider what we have said on these matters to be sufficient. In a few words we have demonstrated to all that their many books and undertakings are nonsense, being weak and deserving of no argument. Those who possess a sound mind need not pay any attention to them.

33. Ibid., 10.25-26.

(25) Now the Phrygians received the beginnings of their heresy from a certain Montanus, and from Priscilla and Maximilla. They take those females to be prophetesses, and Montanus to be a prophet. They are thought to speak correctly concerning the origin and creation of the universe, and they have not accepted strange teachings about Christ. But they err with those previously mentioned, and go astray by paying more attention to their words than to the Gospels when they appoint new and unusual fasts.

(26) But others of them, although they are devoted to the heresy of the Noetians, hold the same views concerning those females and Montanus. They blaspheme, however, the Father of the universe, by saying that he is Son and Father, visible and invisible, begotten and unbegotten, mortal and immortal. These received their starting-point from a certain Noetus.

Pseudo-Tertullian

34. *Adversus Omnes Haereses,* 7 (CSEL 47, ed. Kroymann, p. 224).

Accesserunt alii haeretici, qui dicuntur secundum Phrygas, sed horum non una doctrina est. Sunt enim qui kata Proclum dicuntur, sunt alii, qui secundum Aeschinen pronuntiantur. Hi habent aliam communem blasphemiam, aliam blasphemiam non communem, sed peculiarem et suam: et communem quidem illam, qua in apostolis quidem dicant Spiritum sanctun fuisse, paracletum non fuisse, et qua dicant paracletum plura in Montano dixisse quam Christum in Evangelium protulisse, nec tantum plura, sed etiam meliora atque maiora. Priuatem autem blasphemiam illi qui sunt kata Aeschinen, hanc habent qua adiciunt etiam hoc, uti dicant Christum ipsum esse Filium et Patrem.

Pseudo-Tertullian

34. *Against All Heresies* 7.

There are other heretics in addition who are called Cataphrygians, but their teaching is not uniform. For there are some who are called followers of Proclus, and others who are designated followers of Aeschinus. These have one blasphemy which is common to them all and another which is not, but is particular and individual. Now that which is common to them all is that they say that the Holy Spirit indeed was in the apostles, not the Paraclete; and they say that the Paraclete said more in Montanus than Christ revealed in the gospel, and they say he has said not only more, but things that are better and greater. Those, however, who are followers of Aeschinus have this blasphemy which is peculiar to themselves in that they add this also, that Christ himself is Son and Father.

Testimonia Concerning Montanism in North Africa

The Passion of Perpetua and Felicitas

35. *Passio SS. Felicitatis et Perpetuae* 1 (Krüger, Ruhbach, pp. 35-36).

1. (1) Si uetera fidei exempla, et Dei gratiam testificantia et aedificationem hominis operantia, propterea in litteris sunt digesta, ut lectione eorum quasi repraesentatione rerum et Deus honoretur et homo confortetur; cur non et noua documenta aeque utrique causae conuenientia et digerantur? uel quia proinde et haec uetera futura quandoque sunt et necessaria posteris, se in praesenti suo tempore minori deputantur auctoritati, propter praesumptam uenerationem antiquitatis. (2) sed viderint qui unam virtutem Spiritus unius Sancti pro aetatibus iudicent temporum: cum maiora reputanda sunt nouitiora quaeque ut nouissimiora, secundum exuperationem gratiae in ultima saeculi spatia decretam. (3) In nouissimis enim diebus, dicit Dominus, effundam de Spiritu meo super omnem carnem, et prophetabunt filii filiaeque eorum: et super seruos et ancillas meas de meo Spiritu effundam: et iuuenes visiones videbunt, et senes somnia somniabunt. (4) itaque et nos, qui sicut prophetias ita et uisiones nouas pariter repromissas et agnoscimus et honoramus, ceterasque virtutes Spiritus Sancti ad instrumentum Ecclesiae deputamus (cui et missus est idem omnia donatiua administrans in omnibus prout unicuique distribuit Dominus) necessario et digerimus et ad gloriam Dei lectione celebramus; ut ne qua aut imbecillitas aut desperatio fidei apud ueteres tantum aestimet gratiam diuinitatis conuersatam, siue in martyrum siue in reuelationum dignatione: cum semper Deus operetur quae repromisit, non credentibus in testimonium, credentibus in beneficium. (5) et nos itaque quod audiuimus [et vidimus] et contrectauimus, annuntiamus et uobis, fratres et filioli, ut et uos qui interfuistis

Testimonia Concerning Montanism in North Africa

The Passion of Perpetua and Felicitas

35. *The Passion of Saints Felicitas and Perpetua* 1.

(1) The ancient examples of faith both testify to God's grace and edify human beings. For this reason they have been described in writing so that by reading them as if the things were made present, God might be honored and man comforted. If this is so, why should not recent examples equally suited for each of these two concerns also be described? Indeed these too, in the same way, will be ancient some day and useful for future generations, even if they are accorded less authority in the present because of the presumed greater respect of antiquity.

(2) But let those who would declare that the one power of the one Holy Spirit is for periods of time consider the following: the examples which are more recent ought to be reckoned superior, as being the most recent, in accordance with the decreed superiority of grace in the final periods of the world. (3) "For in the last days says the Lord, I will pour out of my Spirit upon all flesh, and their sons and daughters will prophesy; and I will pour out of my Spirit upon my servants and maid-servants; and the young men will see visions, and the old men will dream dreams" (Acts 2:17; cf. Joel 2:28). (4) Consequently we too of necessity both describe these events and celebrate them when they are read to the glory of God, for just as we recognize and honor new prophecies, so also we recognize and honor new visions as promised in equal measure, and we esteem the other manifestations of the Holy Spirit for the assistance of the Church, to which the same Spirit has been sent to administer all the gifts among all as the Lord distributes to each one (cf. Rom 12:3; 1 Cor 7:17). Let no feebleness or despair of faith think that the grace of deity dwelt only with the ancients, whether in the grandeur of martyrdoms or of revelations, since God always accomplishes what he has promised, for testimony to the unbelievers, for benefit to the believers. (5) And consequently we announce also to you, brothers and little children, that which we have heard [and seen] and have touched (cf. 1 John 1:1,3), that you who were participants may recall the glory of

rememoremini gloriae Domini, et qui nunc congnoscitis per auditum communionem habeatis cum sanctis martyribus, et per illos cum Domino Iesu Christo, cui est claritas et honor in saecula saeculorum. amen.

Tertullian

36. *De virginibus velandis* 1 (CSEL 76, ed. Bulhart, pp. 79-81).

1. . . . (3) Haereses non tam nouitas quam ueritas reuincit. Quodcumque aduersus ueritatem sapit, hoc erit haeresis, etiam uetus consuetudo. Ceterum suo vitio quis quid ignorat. Quod autem ignoratur, fuit tam requirendum quam recipiendum, quod agnoscitur.

(4) Regula quidem fidei una omnino est, sola immobilis et irreformabilis, credendi scilicet in unicum Deum omnipotentem, mundi conditorem, et filium eius Iesum Christum, natum ex virgine Maria, crucifixum sub Pontio Pilato, tertia die resuscitatum a mortuis, receptum in caelis, sedentem nunc ad dexteram patris, venturum iudicare uiuos et mortuos per carnis etiam resurrectionem.

(5) Hoc lege fidei manente cetera iam disciplinae et conuersationis admitunt nouitatem correctionis, operante scilicet et proficiente usque in finem gratia dei. Quale est enim, ut diabolo semper opperante et adiciente cottidie ad iniquitatis ingenia opus dei aut cessauerit aut proficere destiterit? (6) cum propterea paraclitum miserit dominus, ut, quoniam humana mediocritas omnia semel capere non poterat, paulatim dirigeretur et ordinaretur et ad perfectum perduceretur disciplina ab illo uicario domini, spiritu sancto. (7) "Adhuc multa habeo loqui ad vos, sed nondum potestis ea baiulare; cum uenerit ille spiritus ueritatis, deducet uos in omnem ueritatem et superuenientia renuntiabit uobis." Sed et supra de hoc eius opere pronuntiauit. (8) Quae est ergo paracliti administratio, nisi haec, quod disciplina dirigitur, quod scripturae revelantur, quod intellectus reformatur, quod ad meliora proficitur? Nihil sine aetate est, omnia tempus expectant; denique Ecclesiastes, "Tempus, inquit, omni rei." (9) Aspice ipsam creaturam paulatim ad fructum promoueri: granum est primo et de grano frutex oritur et de frutice arbuscula enititur, deinde rami et frondes invalescunt et totum arboris nomen expanditur, inde germinis tumor et flos de germine soluitur, et de flore fructus aperitur: is quoque rudis aliquamdiu et informis paulatim aetatem suam dirigens eruditur in mansuetudinem saporis. (10) Sic et iustitia—nam idem deus iustitiae et creaturae—primo fuit in rudi-

the Lord, and you who learn about it now by hearing may have communion with the holy martyrs, and through them with the Lord Jesus Christ, to whom belongs glory and honor for ever and ever. Amen.

Tertullian

36. *On the Veiling of Virgins* 1.

(3) It is not so much novelty as truth which refutes heresies. Whatever smacks of opposition to the truth will be heresy, even if it is an ancient custom. On the other hand, he who is ignorant of something has himself to blame. For what is not known was to be inquired after in the same way as what is well known was to be received.

(4) The rule of faith, indeed, is completely one, alone unalterable and irreformable, that is, of believing in one God alone, omnipotent, creator of the world, and in his son Jesus Christ, born of the virgin Mary, crucified under Pontius Pilate, resurrected from the dead on the third day, received into heaven, now seated at the Father's right hand, who will come to judge the living and the dead by the resurrection of their flesh also.

(5) While this law of faith is permanent, the other articles, indeed, of discipline and life admit new revisions, since the grace of God continues to operate, of course, and advance until the end. For how is it that while the devil is always operating and adds daily to the inventions of iniquity, the work of God has either ceased or desisted from advancing? (6) It was indeed for this reason that the Lord sent the Paraclete, that, since human mediocrity could not grasp everything at once, discipline could, little by little, be directed and regulated, and brought to perfection by that vicar of the Lord, the Holy Spirit. (7) "I still have many things to say to you," he said, "but you cannot yet bear them; when that Spirit of truth has come, he will lead you into all truth, and will announce to you things to come" (cf. John 16:12-13). But he also made a declaration about this work of his above (see John 14:26). (8) What then is the Paraclete's assistance if not this: to direct discipline, to reveal the Scriptures, to reform the understanding, to advance the understanding to better things? There is nothing without its time; all things await their moment. For the Preacher says: "There is a time for everything" (cf. Eccl 3:1). (9) Behold, creation itself is advanced to fruit gradually. First there is the grain, and from the grain the sprout appears, and from the sprout the bush grows up, then branches and leaves increase, and the whole, called a tree, expands, then the bud swells and blossoms, and from the blossom the fruit is revealed. The fruit too, rough and shapeless for a while, gradually, in the course of its season, ripens into a mellow taste. (10) So also righteousness (for the God of righ-

mentis, natura deum metuens, dehinc per legem et prophetas promouit in infantiam, dehinc per euangelium efferbuit in iuuentutem, nunc per paraclitum componitur in maturitatem. (11) Hic erit solus a Christo magister et dicendus et uerendus; non enim ab se loquitur, sed quae mandantur a Christo; hic solus antecessor, quia solus post Christum; hunc qui receperunt, ueritatem consuetudini anteponunt; hunc qui audierunt usque non olim prophetantem, uirgines contegunt.

37. *De exhortatione castitatis* 10 (CSEL 70, ed. Kroymann, pp. 144-46).

Rape occasionem, etsi non exoptatissimam, attamen opportunam, non habere cui debitum solueres et a quo exsolueris. Desisti esse debitor. O te felicem! Dimisisti debitorem: sustine damnum. Quid si, quod diximus damnum, lucrum senties? Per continentiam enim negotiaberis magnum substantiam sanctitatis, parsimonia carnis spiritum adquires. Recogitemus enim ipsam conscientiam nostram, quam alium se homo sentiat, cum forte a sua femina cessat. Spiritaliter sapit. Si orationem facit ad Dominum prope est caelo; si scripturis incumbit, totus illic est. Si psalmum canit, placet sibi; si daemonem adiurat, confidet sibi. Ideo apostolus temporalem purificationem orationum commendandarum causa adiecit, ut sciremus, quod ad tempus prodest semper nobis exercere esse, ut semper prosit. Si quotidie, omni momento oratio hominibus necessaria est, utique et continentia, post quam oratio, necessaria est. Oratio de conscientia procedit: si conscientia erubescat, erubescit oratio. Spiritus deducit orationem ad deum: si spiritus reus apud se sit conscientiae erubescentis, quomodo audebit orationem deducere ab alia re[a], qua erubescente et ipse suffunditur? Sanctus minister etenim est, et prophetica vox veteris testamenti: "Sancti eritis, quia deus sanctus," et rursus: "Cum sancto sanctificaberis, et cum uiro innocenti innocuus eris et cum electo electus." Debemus enim ita ingredi in disciplina Domini, ut deo dignum fructum, non secundum carnis squalentes concupiscentias. Ita enim et apostolus dicit, quod sapere secundum carnem mors sit, secundum spiritum uero sapere uita aeterna sit in Christo

teousness and the God of the creation is the same) was first in a crude state, fearing God by nature; hence it progressed through the law and the prophets to a state of infancy; from there through the gospel it knew the vigor of youth; now, through the Paraclete it is being brought to maturity. (11) He alone will be the teacher after Christ (cf. John 14:26); he is to be both so designated and honored. For he does not speak from himself, but speaks what he is commanded by Christ (cf. John 16:13). He alone is our forerunner, for he alone comes after Christ. Those who have received him have preferred truth to custom. Those who have heard him prophesying even to the present, veil virgins. . . .

37. *On Exhortation to Chastity* 10.

Seize the opportunity not to be obligated to anyone in conjugal matters (cf. 1 Cor 7:3) nor to have anyone who is obligated to you, for this is advantageous even if you do not greatly desire it. You have ceased to be a debtor. How fortunate you are! You have released the debtor; endure the loss. What if you shall experience that which we called a loss as a gain? For by continence you will gain a great store of holiness; by frugality of the flesh you will amass the Spirit. For let us reflect on our own conscience. Does a man not perceive himself to be a different man when, by chance, he abstains from his wife? He has a taste for spiritual things. If he offers prayer to the Lord, he is near heaven. If he devotes himself to the Scriptures, he is totally involved. If he sings a psalm, he is satisfied. If he adjures a demon, he does so confidently. This is why the apostle added a temporary period of purification for the sake of making the most of our prayers (cf. 1 Cor 7:5), that we might know that we ought always practice that which is profitable for a time, that it might be profitable always. If prayer is necessary for men daily, at every moment, continence, to be sure, which prayer follows, is also necessary.

Prayer proceeds from the conscience. If the conscience should be ashamed, the prayer is ashamed. The Spirit leads the prayer to God. If the Spirit should be a debtor on its part to a conscience which is ashamed, how will he dare lead prayer from another debtor, since when conscience is ashamed, the holy minister himself is also tinged. For the prophetic voice of the Old Testament says: "You shall be holy, because God is holy" (cf. Lev 11:44-45; 19:2; 20:7). And again: "You shall be sanctified with the saint, and you shall be innocent with the innocent, and elect with the elect" (cf. Ps 18:25-26). For we ought thus to walk in the discipline of the Lord that our fruit might be worthy of God (cf. Eph 4:1; Col 1:10; 1 Thes 2:12); not according to the squalid desires of the flesh. For thus the apostle also says that to have a taste for that which is according to the flesh is death, but to have a taste for that which is according to the spirit is eternal life in

Iesu domino nostro. Item per sanctam prophetidem Priscam ita euangelizatur, quod sanctus minister sanctimoniam nouerit ministrare. "Purificantia enim concordat, ait, et uisiones uident et ponentes faciem deorsum etiam uoces audiunt salutares, tam manifestas quam et occultas." Si haec obfusio, etiam cum in unis nuptiis res carnis exercetur, spiritum sanctum auertit, quanto magis, cum in secundo matrimonio agitur?

38. *Adversus Marcionem* 1.29 (CSEL 47, ed. Kroymann, pp. 331-32).

. . . Sed et si nubendi iam modus ponitur, quem quidem apud nos spiritalis ratio pracleto auctore defendit, unum in fide matrimonium praescribens, eiusdem erit modum figere, qui modum aliquando diffuderat; is colliget qui sparsit; is caedet siluam, qui plantauit; is metet segetem qui seminauit; is dicet: "Superest, ut et qui uxores habent sic sint quasi non habeant," cuius et retro fuit: "Crescite et multiplicamini": eiusdem finis, cuius et initium. Non tamen ut accusanda caeditur silua, nec ut damnanda secatur seges, sed ut tempori suo parens. Sic et conubii res non ut mala securem et falcem admittit sanctitatis, sed ut matura defungi, ut ipsi sanctitati reseruata, cui cedendo praestaret esse. Unde iam dicam deum Marcionis, cum matrimonium ut malum et impudicitiae negotium reprobat, aduersus ipsam facere sanctitatem, cui uidetur studere.

39. Ibid. 3.24 (Kroymann, pp. 419-20).

De restitutione uero Iudaeae, quam et ipsi Iudaei ita ut describitur sperant, locorum et regionum nominibus inducti, quomodo allegorica interpretatio in Christum et in ecclesiam et habitum et fructum eius spiritaliter competat, et longum est persequi et in alio opere digestum, quod inscribimus *de spe fidelium,* et in praesenti vel eo otiosum, quia non de terrena, sed de caelesti promissione sit quaestio. Nam et confitemur in terra nobis regnum promissum, sed ante caelum, sed alio statu, utpote post resurrectionem in mille annos in ciuitate diuini operis Hierusalem caelo delatum,

Christ Jesus our Lord (cf. Rom 8:5-6). Likewise the holy prophetess Prisca preaches that the holy minister should know how to administer purity of life. "For purification produces harmony,"[11] she says, "and they see visions, and when they turn their faces downward they also hear salutary voices, as clear as they are secret." If this dullness averts the Holy Spirit even when the act of the flesh is exercised in a single marriage, how much more is this the case when it is performed in a second marriage?

38. *Against Marcion* 1.29.

But if a limit is now placed on marrying, which indeed for our part a spiritual principle maintains by the authority of the Paraclete, which prescribes one marriage in the faith, it will be his to set the limit, who at one time diffused the limit. He who scattered shall gather; he who planted the forest shall fell it; he who sowed shall reap the crop; he whose former word was: "Increase and multiply" (Gen 1:22), shall say: "It remains that also those who have wives should be as those who have not" (cf. 1 Cor 7:29). The end belongs to him whose was also the beginning.

Nevertheless, the forest is not felled to be called to account, nor is the crop cut to be punished, but because their time has come. So also the matter of marriage receives the ax and scythe of sanctity not because it is evil, but because it has reached the age to die, because it has been preserved for sanctity itself, in that by being cut down for sanctity it demonstrates that sanctity exists. On this basis I shall now say that when Marcion's god condemns marriage as evil and a lewd affair, he acts contrary to sanctity itself, for which he gives the appearance of being zealous.

39. Ibid. 3.24.

On the restoration of Judea, however, which also the Jews themselves hope for in the literal sense, misled by the names of places and regions, it would take a long time to pursue how the allegorical interpretation applies spiritually to Christ and the Church both in respect to its nature and fruit. We have treated this in another work which we entitled *On the Hope of the Faithful*. In the present discussion it would also be unprofitable to pursue this matter because the question at issue does not concern an earthly, but an heavenly promise. Now we also acknowledge that a kingdom on earth has been promised to us, but prior to heaven, and in another state, inasmuch as after the resurrection Jerusalem, which the apostle also designates as "our mother from on high" (cf. Gal 4:26), is to be brought down from heaven for a thousand years in a city of divine workmanship. When the

---

[11]I read *concordat* with Labriolle. Kroymann prints *cum cor dat*.

quam et apostolus "matrem nostram sursum" designat, et politeuma nostrum, id est municipatum, in caelis esse pronuntians, alicui utique caelesti ciuitati eum deputat. Hanc et Ezechiel nouit et apostolus Iohannes uidit et qui apud fidem nostram est nouae prophetiae sermo testatur, ut etiam effigiem ciuitatis ante repraesentationem eius conspectui futuram in signum praedicarit. Denique proxime expunctum est orientali expeditione. Constat enim ethnicis quoque testibus in Iudaea per dies quadraginta matutinis momentis ciuitatem de caelo pependisse, omni moeniorum habitu euanescente de profectu diei, et alias de proximo nullam. Hanc dicimus excipiendis [de] resurrectione sanctis et refouendis omnium bonorum, utique spiritalium, copia in compensationem eorum, quae in saeculo vel despeximus vel amisimus, a deo prospectam, siquidem et iustum et deo dignum illic quoque exultare famulos eius, ubi sunt et adflicti in nomine ipsius. Haec ratio regni [sub]caelestis. Post cuius mille annos, intra quam aetatem concluditur sanctorum resurrectio pro meritis maturius vel tardius resurgentium, tunc, et mundi destructione et iudicii conflagratione commissa, demutati in atomo in angelicam substantiam, scilicet per illud incorruptelae superindumentum, transferemur in caeleste regnum. . . .

10. Ibid. 4.22 (Kroymann, pp. 492-93).

Igitur et Petrus, meritum contubernium Christi sui agnoscens, [in] indiuiduitatem eius suggerit consilium: "bonum est hic nos esse,"—bonum plane, ubi Moyses scilicet et Helias—et "faciamus hic tria tabernacula, unum tibi et Moysi unum et Heliae unum." Sed "nesciens, quid diceret." Quomodo nesciens? Utrumne simplici errore an ratione, qua defendimus in causa nouae prophetiae gratiae exstasin, id est amentiam, conuenire? In spiritu enim homo constitutus, praesertim cum gloriam dei conspicit uel cum per ipsum deus loquitur, necesse est excidat sensu, obumbratus scilicet uirtute diuina. De quo cum inter nos et psychicos quaestio est, interim facile est amentiam Petri probare.

apostle also announces that our *politeuma,* that is our citizenship, is in heaven (cf. Phil 3:20), he assigns it undoubtedly to some heavenly city. Ezekiel knew this city (cf. Ezek 48:30-35); the apostle John saw it (cf. Rev 21:2); and the word, which, as we believe, belongs to the new prophecy, testifies to it. It has predicted that an image of the city will appear as a sign before the manifestation of its presence. This, in fact, was recently fulfilled in an expedition to the East. For it is established by pagan witnesses too that for a period of forty days a city was suspended from the sky for a brief time in the mornings, every appearance of its walls vanishing with the advance of day; at other times there was no city near. We say that God has provided this city to receive the saints after the resurrection and to refresh them with an abundance of all good things, spiritual of course, as compensation for those things which we either disdained or lost in the world, since it is both just and worthy of God that his servants also revel where they have been afflicted in his name. This is the reason for the subcelestial kingdom. After its thousand years, during which time the resurrection of the saints is concluded, who arise earlier or later on the basis of their merits, then, when the destruction of the world has commenced and the conflagration of judgment, having been changed in a moment into the substance of angels, that is by means of that outer garment of incorruptibility, we shall be transferred to the heavenly kingdom.

40. Ibid. 4.22.

And Peter, therefore, justly recognizing the companions of his Christ in their indivisibility from him, suggests a plan: "It is good that we are here" ("good" clearly refers to being where Moses and Elias are), and "Let us make three tabernacles; one for you, one for Moses, and one for Elias." But "he did not know what he said" (cf. Luke 9:33). How was it that he did not know? Was it because of a simple error, or the principle which we maintain in the cause of the new prophecy, that ecstasy, that is being out of one's senses, accompanies the divine gift? For since man has been formed in the Spirit, he must be deprived of sense perception particularly when he beholds the glory of God, or when God speaks through him, since he has been manifestly overshadowed by the divine power. Although there is a dispute about this between us and the unspiritual men (cf. 1 Cor 2:14), meanwhile it is easy to prove that Peter was out of his senses.[12]

---

[12]Tertullian argues that the fact that Peter recognized the other two men to be Moses and Elijah proves that he was speaking under the influence of the Spirit, for he had no other basis on which to recognize them.

41. *De anima* 9.4 (ed. Waszink, p. 11).

Est hodie soror apud nos reuelationum charismata sortita, quas in ecclesia inter dominica sollemnia per ecstasin in spiritu patitur; conuersatur cum angelis, aliquando etiam cum domino, et uidet et audit sacramenta et quorundam corda dinoscit et medicinas desiderantibus sumit. Iamuero prout scripturae leguntur aut psalmi canuntur aut allocutiones proferuntur aut petitiones delegantur, ita inde materiae uisionibus subministrantur. Forte nescio quid de anima disserueramus, cum ea soror in spiritu esset. Post transacta sollemnia dimissa plebe, quo usu solet nobis renuntiare quae uiderit (nam et diligentissime digeruntur, ut etiam probentur), ''inter cetera,'' inquit, ''ostensa est mihi anima corporaliter, et spiritus uidebatur, sed non inanis et uacuae qualitatis, immo quae etiam teneri repromitteret, tenera et lucida et aerii coloris, et forma per omnia humana. Hoc visio.'' Et deus testis et apostolus charismatum in ecclesia futurorum idoneus sponsor; tunc et si res ipsa de singulis persuaserit, credas.

42. Ibid. 55.4-5 (Waszink, p. 74).

(4) . . . Et quomodo Iohanni in spiritu paradisi regio revelata, quae subicitur altari, nullas alias animas apud se praeter martyrum ostendit? Quomodo Perpetua, fortissima martyr, sub die passionis in reuelatione paradisi solos illic martyras uidit, nisi quia nullis romphaea paradisi ianitrix cedit nisi qui in Christo decesserint, non in Adam? (5) Nova mors pro deo et extraordinaria pro Christo alio et priuato excipitur hospitio. Agnosce itaque differentiam ethnici et fidelis in morte, si pro deo occumbas, ut paracletus monet, non in mollibus febribus et in lectulis, sed in martyriis, se crucem tuam tollas et sequaris dominum, ut ipse praecepit. Tota paradisi clauis tuus sanguis est. Habes etiam de paradiso a nobis libellum, quo constituimus omnem animam apud inferos sequestrari in diem domini.

41. *On the Soul* 9.4.

There is a sister among us at this time who has received gifts of revelations which she experiences by ecstasy in the Spirit in the Church at the
Sunday service. She converses with angels, sometimes even with the Lord;
she both sees and hears secret things; she discerns the hearts of some, and
she obtains instructions for healing for those who want them. Now to be
sure, just as Scriptures are read, or Psalms sung, or addresses delivered,
or prayers offered, so themes are furnished from these for her visions. By
chance I do not know what we had been discussing about the soul when
that sister was in the Spirit. After the religious service was completed, when
the people had been dismissed, according to her custom of reporting what
she has seen to us (for her visions are also described very carefully that
they may also be tested), she said, among other things: "A soul was ex-
hibited to me in bodily form, and a spirit appeared, but it was not of an
empty and vacuous quality, but rather of a quality that would suggest it
could be grasped, being soft and bright and of the color of the air, and resembling the human form in all respects. This is the vision." God is wit-
ness, and the apostle is a sufficient guarantor of future gifts in the church.
At such a time you would believe too if the vision itself were persuasive
at each point.

42. Ibid. 55.4-5.

(4) . . . And how does the region of Paradise which lies under the altar
(cf. Rev 6:9) which was revealed to John in the Spirit display no souls in
it other than those of the martyrs? How did Perpetua, that bravest of martyrs, see only martyrs there in the revelation of Paradise on the day of her
passion,[13] unless it is that the sword, the door-keeper of Paradise, with-
draws for none but those who have died in Christ, not in Adam? (5) A new
death for God, and an extraordinary death for Christ is received in the grave
for each person individually. Notice, therefore, the difference between the
pagan and faithful man in death! If you should die for God, as the Paraclete
instructs, not in mild fevers and on your beds, but in martyrdoms, if you
take up your cross and follow the Lord as he himself commands (cf. Matt
10:38; 16:34), your blood is the complete key of Paradise. You also have
a little book about Paradise by us in which we have established that every
soul is sequestered in Hades until the day of the Lord.

---

[13]Labriolle, *Sources,* 22, notes that this vision was seen by Saturus rather than Perpetua.
See the *Passio SS. Felicitatis et Perpetuae* 11.

43. Ibid. 58.8 (Waszink, pp. 79-80).

(8) In summa, cum carcerem illum, quem euangelium demonstrat, inferos intellegimus et nouissimum quadrantem modicum quoque delictum mora resurrectionis illic luendum interpretamur, nemo dubitabit animam aliquid pensare penes inferos salua resurrectionis plenitudine per carnem quoque. Hoc etiam paracletus frequentissime commendauit, si qui sermones eius ex agnitione promissorum charismatum admiserit.

44. *De corona* 1 (CSEL 70, ed. Kroymann, pp. 154-55).

Exinde sententiae super illo,—nescio an Christianorum; non enim aliae ethnicorum,—ut de abrupto et praecipiti et mori cupido, qui de habitu interrogatus nomini negotium fecerit, solus scilicet fortis inter tot fratres commilitones, solus Christianus. * * Plane superest, ut etiam martyria recusare meditentur qui prophetias eiusdem spiritus sancti respuerunt.

45. *De fuga in persecutione* 1.1 (CSEL 76, ed. Bulhart, p. 17).

Quanto enim frequentiores imminent persecutiones, tanta examinatio procuranda est, quomodo eas excipere fides debeat. Procuranda autem examinatio penes [s]uos [qui] si forte Paraclitum non recipiendo, deductorem omnis ueritatis, merito adhuc etiam aliis quaestionibus obnoxii estis.

46. Ibid. 9.4 (Bulhart, p. 32).

Spiritum uero si consulas, quid magis sermone illo Spiritus probat? Namque omnes paene ad martyrium exhortantur, non ad fugam, ut et illius commemoremur: ''Publicaris?'' inquit, ''bonum tibi est; qui enim non publicatur in hominibus, publicatur in domino. Ne confundaris: iustitia te producit in medium; quid confunderis laudem ferens? Potestas fit, cum conspiceris ab hominibus.'' Sic et alibi: ''Nolite in lectulis nec in aborsibus et febribus mollibus optare exire, sed in martyriis, uti glorificetur, qui est passus pro uobis.''

47. Ibid. 11.3 (Bulhart, p. 35).

Si et spiritum quis agnouerit, audiet fugitiuos denotantem.

43. Ibid. 58.8.

In short, since we understand that "prison" which the Gospel indicates (cf. Matt 5:25) to be Hades, and we interpret the "last farthing" (cf. Matt 5:26) to mean that even a modest offence is to be expiated there in the interval before the resurrection, no one will doubt that the soul pays some penalty in Hades, without violation of the fullness of the resurrection through the flesh also. The Paraclete has also frequently made this manifest, if one grants access to his words by a recognition of the promised gifts.

44. *On the Crown* 1.

Then there were judgments against that soldier[14]—I do not know if they originated from Christians, since their judgments are not different from those of the pagans—that he was rash and hasty and desirous of death, since when he was interrogated about his attire, he made trouble for the name, he alone, of course, being brave among so many brothers who were his fellow-soldiers, he alone being a Christian. As for the rest, it is evident that those who have refused the prophesies of the same Holy Spirit intend to reject the martyrdoms too.

45. *On Flight* 1.1.

For inasmuch as persecutions are threatening more frequently, we ought to give attention to a consideration of how faith ought to receive them. Moreover you ought to give attention to the consideration, since perhaps by not receiving the Paraclete, the leader of all truth, you are justly subject to yet additional problems.

46. Ibid. 9.4.

But if you consult the Spirit, what does he approve more than that word of the Spirit? For nearly all his words exhort to martyrdom, not to flight, as we are also reminded by his saying: "It is good for you to be publicly exposed. For he who is not exposed among men is exposed in the Lord. Do not be disturbed; righteousness brings you before the public. Why are you disturbed when you are receiving praise? There is opportunity when you are observed by men." So he also says elsewhere: "Wish not to die in your beds, nor in miscarriages and mild fevers, but in martyrdoms, that he who has suffered for you may be glorified."

47. Ibid. 11.3.

And if anyone recognizes the Spirit, he will hear him stigmatizing the deserters.

---

[14]Tertullian has been relating the story of a Christian soldier who was imprisoned for his refusal to wear the laurel crown.

48. Ibid. 14.3 (Bulhart, p. 43).

Non potest, qui pati timet, ei esse, qui passus est, at qui pati non timet, iste erit perfectus in dilectione, utique dei; "perfecta enim dilectio foras mittit timorem." Et ideo "multi uocati, pauci electi"; non quaeritur, qui latam uiam sequi paratus sit, sed qui angustam; et ideo paraclitus necessarius, deductor omnium ueritatum, exhortator omnium tolerantiarum. Quem qui receperunt, neque fugere persecutionem neque redimere nouerunt, habentes ipsum, qui pro nobis erit, sicut locuturus in interrogatione, ita iuuaturus in passione.

49. *De carnis resurrectione* 11 (CSEL 47, ed Kroymann, p. 39).

Hucusque de praeconio carnis adversus inimicos et nihilominus amicissimos eius. Nemo enim tam carnaliter uiuit quam qui negant carnis resurrectionem. Negantes enim poenam despiciunt et disciplinam. De quibus luculente et paracletus per prophetidem Priscam: "Carnes sunt, et carnem oderunt."

50. Ibid. 63 (Kroymann, pp. 124-25).

At enim deus omnipotens aduersus haec incredulitatis et peruersitatis ingenia prouidentissima gratia sua effundens in nouissimis diebus de suo spiritu in omnem carnem, in seruos suos et ancillas, et fidem laborantem resurrectionis carnalis animauit et pristina instrumenta manifestis uerborum et sensuum luminibus ab omni ambiguitatis obscuritate purgauit. Nam quia haereses esse oportuerat, ut probabiles quique manifestarentur, hae autem sine aliquibus occasionibus scripturarum audere non poterant, idcirco pristina instrumenta quasdam materias illis uidentur subministrasse, et ipsas quidem isdem litteris reuincibiles. Sed quoniam nec dissimulare spiritum sanctum oportebat, quominus et huiusmodi eloquiis superinundaret, quae nullis haereticorum uersutiis semina subspargerent, immo et ueteres eorum cespites uellerent, idcirco iam omnes retro ambiguitates et quas uolunt parabolas aperta atque perspicua totius sacramenti praedicatione discussit per nouam prophetiam de paracleto inundantem. Cuius si hauseris fontes nullam poteris sitire doctrinam, nullus te ardor exuret quaestionum: resurrectionem quoque carnis usquequaque potando refrigerabis.

48. Ibid. 14.3.

He who is afraid to suffer cannot belong to him who suffered. But he who is not afraid to suffer will be perfected in love, meaning God's love, of course. "But perfect love casts out fear" (1 John 4:18). And for that reason "many are called, but few are chosen" (Matt 22:14). He who is prepared to follow the broad way is not sought, but he who is prepared to follow the narrow (cf. Matt 7:13). And for that reason the Paraclete is the indispensable teacher of all truth (cf. John 16:13), the encourager of all who persevere. Those who have received him practice neither flight in persecution nor bribery to avoid it, since they possess him who will aid us in suffering, just as he will speak for us in the interrogation (cf. Luke 12:11-12).

49. *On the Resurrection of the Flesh* 11.

So much for the praise of the flesh against its enemies who are also, nonetheless, its dearest friends. For no one lives in such a fleshly manner as those who deny the resurrection of the flesh. For by denying the penalty they despise also the discipline. The Paraclete has also said well of them through the prophetess Prisca: "They are flesh, and they hate the flesh."

50. Ibid. 63.

But indeed Almighty God, in his most providential grace, "by pouring out of his Spirit in the last days on all flesh, on his servants and his maidservants" (cf. Acts 2:17-18; Joel 2:28-29) against these inventions of disbelief and perversity, has both animated the struggling faith in the resurrection of the flesh and has purged the primitive instruments from all their obscurity of ambiguity by the clear illuminations of their words and meanings. For there had to be heresies that those who are worthy of approval might become manifest (cf. 1 Cor 11:19). The heresies, however, could not be bold without some occasions from the Scriptures. The primitive instruments, therefore, seemed to furnish them certain themes, and yet the themes themselves may be refuted from the same literature. But since it is not necessary that the Holy Spirit not appear, and that he should not overflow in declarations of this kind which scatter seeds with none of the deceits of the heretics, but on the contrary pluck out their ancient tares, therefore, he has now dispersed all the former ambiguities, even the parables which they like, with the plain and clean proclamation of the complete mystery by the new prophecy which is overflowing from the Paraclete. If you draw water from his fountains you will not be able to thirst for any doctrine; no burning heat of questions will consume you. By continuing to drink the resurrection of the flesh also, you will experience refreshment.

51. *Do monogamia* 1.1-6 (CSEL 76, ed. Bulhart, pp. 44-45).

(1) Haeretici nuptias auferunt, psychici ingerunt; illi nec semel, isti non semel nubunt. Quid agis, lex creatoris? Inter alienos spadones et aurigas tuos tantundem quereris de domestico obsequio quantum de fastidio extraneo; proinde te laedunt qui abutuntur quemadmodum qui non utuntur. (2) Uerum neque continentia eiusmodi laudanda, quia haeretica est, neque licentia defendenda, quia psychica est; illa blasphemat, ista luxuriat; illa destruit nuptiarum deum, ista confundit. (3) Penes nos autem, quos Spiritales merito dici facit agnitio spiritalium charismatum, continentia tam religiosa est cum licentia uerecunda; ambae cum creatore sunt: continentia legem nuptiarum honorat, licentia temperat; illa non cogitur, ista regitur; illa arbitrium habet, haec modum. (4) Unum matrimonium nouimus sicut unum deum. Magis honorem refert lex nuptiarum, ubi habet et pudorem. (5) Sed psychicis non recipientibus Spiritum ea quae sunt Spiritus non placent. Ita, dum quae sunt spiritus non placent, ea quae sunt carnis placebunt ut contraria spiritus. "Caro," inquit, "aduersus spiritum concupiscit et spiritus aduersus carnem" (6) Quid autem concupiscet caro quam quae magis carnis sunt? Propter quod et in primordio extranea spiritus facta est; "non," inquit, "permanebit spiritus meus in istis hominibus in aeuum, eo quod caro sint."

52. Ibid. 2.1-4 (Bulhart, pp. 45-56).

(1) Itaque monogamiae disciplinam in haeresim exprobrant nec ulla magis ex causa paraclitum negare coguntur, quam dum existimant nouae disciplinae institutorem et quidem dirissimae illis, ut iam de hoc primum consistendum sit in generali retractatu, an capiat paraclitum aliquid tale docuisse, quod aut nouum deputari possit aduersus catholicam traditionem aut onerosum aduersus leuem sarcinam. (2) De utroque autem ipse dominus pronuntiauit; dicens enim: "Adhuc multa habeo quae loquar ad uos, sed nondum potestis portare ea; cum uenerit spiritus sanctus, ille uos ducet in omnem ueritatem," satis utique praetendit edocturum illum, quae et noua existimari possint ut numquam retro edita, et aliquanto onerosa ut idcirco non edita.

51. *On Monogamy* 1.1-6.

(1) The heretics desist from marriages; the psychics heap them up. The former do not marry even once; the later do not stop with one marriage. What do you do, Law of the Creator? Between the alien eunuchs and your own charioteers, you will complain just as much about the indulgence of those who belong to your household as about the aversion of those outside it. Those who abuse marriage wound you just as those who do not use it. (2) But neither is continence of that kind to be praised, because it belongs to the heretics, nor is licentiousness to be defended, because it belongs to the psychics. The one blasphemes, the other indulges to excess; the one destroys the God of marriage, the other puts him to shame. (3) But with us, who are justly called ''spiritual'' because we recognize spiritual gifts, continence is the more religious because the freedom to marry is diffident; both are in harmony with the Creator. Continence honors the law of marriage; the freedom to marry moderates it. The former is not compelled; the latter is controlled. The first has choice; the latter a limit. (4) We recognize one marriage as we recognize one God. The law of marriage yields more honor when it also possesses modesty. (5) But the things which are of the Spirit are not pleasing to the psychics who do not receive the Spirit (cf. 1 Cor 2:14). So, as long as the things which are of the Spirit are not pleasing, the things which are of the flesh will be pleasing, as contrary to the Spirit. ''The flesh,'' he says, ''lusts against the spirit, and the spirit against the flesh'' (Gal 5:17). (6) But what will the flesh lust for than those things which are more completely of the flesh? This is also why the flesh became estranged from the Spirit originally. ''My Spirit,'' God said, ''will not continue in those men forever, because they are flesh'' (cf. Gen 6:3).

52. Ibid. 2.1-4.

(1) They reproach the discipline of monogamy with heresy in the following way. They are compelled to deny the Paraclete for no other reason than that they consider him to be the instigator of a new discipline, and one that is too harsh indeed for them. Consequently, the first thing to be discussed in this general examination is whether one should assume that the Paraclete has taught any such thing that could either be considered new compared to the catholic tradition, or burdensome compared to the ''light burden'' (cf. Matt 11:30). (2) Now the Lord himself has addressed each issue. For when he says: ''I still have many things which I would say to you, but you cannot bear them yet; when the Holy Spirit has come, he will lead you into all truth'' (cf. John 16:12-13), he asserts sufficiently indeed that the Spirit will inform fully of things which can both be considered to be new, in that they have never been made known before, and sometimes burdensome, in that they had not been made known for that very reason.

(3) "Ergo," inquis, "hac argumentatione quiduis nouum et onerosum paraclito adscribi poterit, etsi ab aduersario spiritu fuerit." Non utique; adversarius enim spiritus ex diuersitate praedicationis appareret, primo regulam adulterans fidei, et ita ordinem adulterans disciplinae, quia cuius gradus prior est, eius corrupteia antecedit, id est fidei, quae prior est disciplina: ante quis de deo haereticus sit necesse [e]st et tunc de instituto; (4) paraclitus autem multa habens edocere, quae in illum distulit dominus secundum praefinitionem ipsum primo Christum contestabitur qualem credimus cum toto ordine dei creatoris et ipsum glorificabit et de ipso commemorabit et sic de principali regula illa multa, quae sunt disciplinarum, reuelabit fidem dicente pro eis integritate praedicationis, [licet] nouuis, quia nunc reuelantur, licet onerosis, quia nec nunc sustinentur, non alterius tamen Christi quam qui habere se dixit et alia multa quae a paraclito edocerentur, non minus istis onerosa quam illis, a quibus nondum tunc sustinebantur.

53. Ibid. 3.1, 10-12 (Bulhart, pp. 46-49).

(1) . . . Illud enim amplius dicimus: etiamsi totam et solidam uirginitatem siue continentiam paraclitus hodie determinasset, ut ne unis quidem nuptiis feruorem carnis despumare permitteret, sic quoque nihil noui in ducere uideretur, ipso domino spadonibus aperiente regna caelorum ut et ipso spadone, quem spectans et apostolus propterea et ipse castratus continentiam mauult.

. . . (10) Igitur si omnia ista oblitterant licentia[m] nubendi et conditione licentiae inspecta et praelatione continentiae imposita, cur non potuerit post apostolos idem spiritus superueniens ad deducendam disciplinam in omnem ueritatem per gradus temporum—secundun quod Ecclesiastes: "Tempus omnis rei," inquit—supremam iam carni fibulam imponere, iam non oblique a nuptiis auocans, sed exerte, cum magis nunc tempus in collecto factum sit annis circiter CLX exinde productis?

(3) Therefore, you say, following this line of argumentation, whatever is new and burdensome will be able to be ascribed to the Paraclete, even if it should be from the rival spirit. By no means! For the rival spirit would become apparent from the difference in the preaching, first falsifying the rule of faith, and thus falsifying the order of discipline, for the corruption of that whose position stands first, that is faith, which is prior to discipline, occurs first. One must first be heretical about God, and then about his design.

(4) But the Paraclete, having many things to teach fully, which the Lord, according to his previous determination, conferred upon him, will in the first place, bear testimony to Christ himself, that he is such as we believe, together with the whole order of God the Creator, and he will glorify Christ (cf. John 16:14), and will cause things to be remembered about him. And when he has thus taught those things about the primitive rule of faith, he will reveal "many things" belonging to the discipline. The integrity of his preaching will be the guarantee for them (even if) they be new, because they are now being revealed; even if they be burdensome, because even now they cannot be endured. Nevertheless, these revelations come from no other Christ than him who said he had also many other things which the Paraclete would teach fully (cf. John 16:12-13). These teachings are no less burdensome to the present men than they were to those who at that time could not yet endure them (cf. John 16:12).

53. Ibid. 3.1, 10-12.

(1) . . . For we make the following statement which is even broader: Even if the Paraclete had prescribed virginity in our time, or total and complete continence, so that he did not even permit the raging heat of the flesh to cool down in a single marriage, even so he would appear to introduce nothing new, since the Lord himself opens the kingdom of heaven to eunuchs (cf. Matt 19:12), as also being a eunuch himself. The apostle also, looking to him, because he too was himself castrated, prefers continence (cf. 1 Cor 7.7). . . .

(10) If, therefore, all these considerations obliterate the freedom to marry, both when the creation of the freedom has been considered and when the preference of continence has been imposed, why could not the same Spirit which follows the apostles to lead the discipline gradually into all truth (as Ecclesiastes says: "There is a time for everything" [Eccl 3:1]) now impose the final restraint on the flesh, no longer indirectly, but openly calling us away from marriage, since now the time has become even more "compressed" (cf. 1 Cor 7:29), as about one hundred sixty years have passed since then?

(11) Nonne ipse apud te retractares, uetus haec disciplina sit, praemon-
strata iam tunc in carne domini et uoluntate, dehinc in apostolorum eius
tam consiliis quam exemplis? "Olim sanctitati huic destinabamur; nihil noui
paraclitus inducit, quod praemonuit, definit, quod sustinuit, exposcit." Et
nunc recogitans ista facile tibi persuadebis multo magis unicas nuptias
competisse paraclito praedicare, qui potuit et nullas, magisque credendum
temperasse illum, quod et abstulisse decuisset. (12) Si quae velit Christus
intelligas, in hoc quoque paraclitum agnoscere debes aduocatum, quod a
tota continentia infirmitatem tuam excusat.

54. Ibid. 4.1 (Bulhart, p. 49).

Secedat nunc mentio paracliti, ut nostri alicuius auctoris; euoluamus
communia instrumenta scripturarum pristinarum. Hoc ipsum demonstra-
tur a nobis neque nouam, neque extraneam esse monogamiae disciplinam,
immo et antiquam et propriam Christianorum, ut paraclitum restitutorem
potius sentias eius quam institutorem.

55. Ibid. 14.3-7 (Bulhart, pp. 73-74).

(3) Si enim Christus abstulit, quod Moyses praecepit, quia ab initio non
fuit sic, nec sic ideo ab alia uirtute uenisse reputabitur Christus, cur non et
paraclitus abstulerit quod Paulus indulsit, quia et secundum matrimonium
ab initio non fuit, nec ideo suspectus habendus sit quasi spiritus alienus,
tantum ut deo et Christo dignum sit, quod superducitur? (4) Se deo et
Christo dignum fuit duritiam cordis tempore expleto compescere, cur non
dignius sit et deo et Christo infirmitatem carnis tempore iam collectiore
discutere? Si iam iustum est matrimonium non separari, utique et non ite-
rari honestum est. Denique apud saeculum utrumque in bona disciplina de-
putatur, aliud concordiae nomine, aliud pudicitiae. (5) Regnauit duritia
cordis usque ad Christum, regnauerit et infirmitas carnis usque ad paraclitum; noua lex abstulit repudium—habuit et, quod auferret—et noua prophetia secundum matrimonium, non minus repudium prioris. (6) Sed
facilius duritia cordis Christo cessit quam infirmitas carnis; plus haec sibi

(11) Would you not yourself reconsider? This discipline is ancient. It was predicted as early as the time of the Lord in his flesh and will. Since then it has been presented as much in the counsels as in the examples of his apostles. "Long ago we were destined for this holiness. The Paraclete has introduced nothing new. What he admonished beforehand he has defined; what he has held back he has set forth." And now as you reflect on these things you will easily persuade yourself how much more suitable it was for the Paraclete to proclaim one marriage and no more. He could also have proclaimed no marriage. And you must be even more convinced that he has tempered that which it would have been proper for him to have abolished. (12) If you understand what Christ wishes, in this also you ought to acknowledge the Paraclete to be your "advocate" (1 John 2:1) since he excuses your weakness from complete continence.

54. Ibid. 4.1.

Let consideration of the Paraclete as an authority belonging to us pass into the background for the present. Let us unroll and read the instruments of the ancient Scriptures which we have in common. This is our point: the discipline of monogamy is neither novel nor foreign. On the contrary it is both ancient and the special possession of Christians. Consequently, you should perceive that the Paraclete is its restorer rather than its initiator.

55. Ibid. 14.3-7.

(3) If Christ removed what Moses ordered, because "from the beginning it was not so" (Matt 19:8), nor on that account will Christ thus be thought to have come from another power, why should the Paraclete also not have removed what Paul allowed, because a second marriage too was not from the beginning, nor on that account be considered suspect as if he were an alien spirit, so long as what is added is worthy of God and Christ? (4) If it was worthy of God and Christ to restrain "hardness of heart" (Matt 19:8) when the time was fulfilled, why is it not worthy also of God and Christ to dispel the weakness of the flesh now that the time has become shorter? If now it is right that a marriage not be severed, it is also undoubtedly honorable that it not be repeated. For in the case of the world both are considered in the realm of good discipline, the one under the name of harmony, the other under the name of modesty. (5)Hardness of heart reigned until Christ, and weakness of the flesh will have reigned until the Paraclete. The new law removed divorce—it knew what it was removing—; the new prophecy has removed second marriage, which is no less than a divorce of the former one. (6) But hardness of heart has ceased with Christ more easily than the weakness of the flesh. The latter defends Paul more in its own interest that the former does Moses. Despite the fact that it de-

Paulum defendit quam illa Moysen, si tamen defendit, cum indulgentem eum captat, praescribentem recusat, quae potiores sententias et perpetuas uoluntates eius eludit, quae non sinit nos hoc apostolo praestare quod mauult.

(7) Et quousque infirmitas ista impudentissima in expugnando meliora pereseuerabit? Tempus eius donec paraclitus operaretur, fuit, in quem dilata sunt a domino, quae tunc sustineri non poterant, quae iam nemini competit portare non posse, quia, per quem datur portare posse, non deest.

56. Ibid. 15.1-3 (Bulhart, p. 74).

(1) Quae igitur hic duritia nostra, si non facientibus uoluntatem dei renuntiamus? Quae haeresis, si secundas nuptias ut illicitas iuxta adulterium iudicamus? Quid est enim adulterium quam matrimonium illicitum? (2) Notat apostolus eos, qui in totum nubere prohibebant, qui et de cibis interdicebant, quos deus condidit. Nos uero non magis nuptias auferimus, si secundas recusamus, quam cibos reprobamus, si saepius ieiunamus. Aliud est auferre, alius temperare, aliud est legem non nubendi ponere, aliud est modum nubendi statuere. (3) Plane, qui exprobrant nobis duritiam uel haeresim in hac causa aestimant, si in tantum fouent carnis mei [in]firmitatem, ut in nubendo frequenter sustinendam putant, cur illam in alia causa neque sustinent neque uenia fouent, cum tormentis expugnata est in negationem?

57. *De ieiunio adversum psychicos* 1 (CSEL 20, ed. Reiffershceid and Wissowa, pp. 274-75).

Piget iam cum talibus congredi, pudet etiam de eis altercari quorum nec defensio uerecunda est. Quomodo enim protegam castitatem et sobrietatem sine taxatione aduersariorum? Quinam isti sint, semel nominabo: exteriores et interiores botuli psychicorum. Hi paracleto controuersiam faciunt; propter hoc nouae prophetiae recusantur; non quod alium deum praedicent Montanus et Priscilla et Maximilla, nec quod Iesum Christum soluant, nec quod aliquam fidei aut spei regulam euertant, sed quod plane doceant sacpius ieiunare quam nubere. . . . Arguunt nos, quod ieiunia propria custodiamus, quod stationes plerumque in uesperam producamus, quod etiam xerophagias obseruemus siccantes cibum ab omni carne et omni iurulentia et uuidioribus quibusque pomis nec quid uinositatis uel edamus uel potemus; lauacri quoque abstinentiam, congruentem arido uictui. . . .

fends Paul when it longs for him granting a concession, it rejects him when he gives a command; it avoids his stronger judgments and his constant desires, it does not permit us to offer to this apostle what he prefers. (7) And how long will that most shameless weakness persist in subduing better things? Its time continued to that time when the Paraclete became active, to whom the Lord deferred those things which could not be borne at that time (cf. John 16:12-13). Anyone can bear them now, since he who gives power to bear them is present.

56. Ibid. 15.1-3.

(1) What then is our oppresiveness in this instance, if we renounce those who do not do the will of God? What is our heresy if we condemn second marriage as illicit, on a par with adultery? For what is adultery but illicit marriage? (2) The apostle censures those who forbid marriage completely, who also forbid some foods which God made (cf. 1 Tim 4:3). But we no more remove marriage if we reject second marriage than we condemn food if we fast more often. It is one thing to remove something, another to regulate it. It is one thing to make a law forbidding marriage; it is another to establish a limit to marrying. (3) To be sure, if those who accuse us of oppressiveness, or think there is heresy in this matter, cherish the weakness[15] of the flesh so much that they think it should be sustained by frequent marriages, why, in a different matter, do they neither sustain it nor cherish it with indulgence when it has been brought down to denial by torments.?

57. *On Fasting* 1.

Moreover it is disgusting to contend with such people; it is also embarrassing to quarrel about those subjects which cannot even be defended modestly. For how shall I defend moral purity and moderation without an appraisal of their antagonists? What those are I shall mention only once: they are the genitals and guts of the Psychics. These cause controversies with the Paraclete; for this reason the new prophecies are rejected. They are not rejected because Montanus, Priscilla, and Maximilla preach another God, nor because they dismiss Jesus Christ, nor because they overturn some rule of faith or hope, but simply because they teach that our fasts ought to be more numerous than our marriages. . . . They censure us because we keep our own special fasts, because we frequently extend fast-days into the evening, because we also practice the eating of dry food, stripping our diet of all flesh and all juice, and every succulent fruit, nor do we eat or drink anything that has the flavor of wine. We also abstain from the bath in keeping with our dry diet.

---

[15]I follow Labriolle in omitting mei.

58. Ibid. 10 (Reifferscheid and Wissowa, p. 287).

Haec autem propter illos qui se putant ex forma Petri agere, quam ignorant; non quasi respuamus nonam, cui et quarta sabbati et sexta plurimum fungimur, sed quia eorum quae ex traditione obseruantur tanto magis dignam rationem adferre debemus, quanto carent scripturae auctoritate, donec aliquo caelesti charismate aut confirmentur aut corrigantur. "Et si qua," inquit, "ignoratis, dominus uobis reuelabit." Itaque seposito confirmatore omnium istorum paracleto, duce uniuersae ueritatis, an dignior apud nos ratio adferatur nonam obseruandi require, ut etiam Petro ea ratio deputanda sit, si statione tunc functus est.

59. Ibid. 11 (Reifferscheid and Wissowa, p. 289).

Spiritus diaboli est, dicis, o psychice. Et quomodo dei nostri officia indicit nec alii offerenda quam deo nostro? Aut contende diabolum cum deo facere nostro aut satanas paracletus habeatur. Sed hominem antichristum adfirmas; hoc enim uocantur haeretici homine penes Iohannem. Et quomodo, quisquis ille est, in Christo nostro haec erga dominum nostrum officia disposuit, cum et antichristi erga deum, aduersum nostrum processerint Christum? Quo itaque putas laterum confirmatum apud nos spiritum, cum imperat an cum probat, quae deus noster et imperauit semper et probauit? Sed rursus palos terminales figitis deo, sicut de gratia, ita de disciplina, sicut de charismatibus, ita et de solemnibus, ut perinde officia cessauerint, quemadmodum et beneficia eius, atque ita negetis usque adhuc eum munia imponere, quia et hic "lex et prophetae usque ad Iohannem." Superest ut totum auferatis, quantum in uobis, tam otiosum.

60. Ibid. 12 (Reifferscheid and Wissowa, p. 291).

Ideo sobrietatis disciplinam qui praedicant, pseudoprophetae, ideo haeretici, qui obseruant. Quid ergo cessatis paracletum, quem in Montano negatis, in Apicio credere?

61. Ibid. 13 (Reifferscheid and Wissowa, pp. 291-92).

Bene autem, quod et episcopi uniuersae plebi mandare ieiunia adsolent, non dico de industria stipium conferendarum, ut uestrae capturae est, sed

58. Ibid. 10.

We have said these things because of those who think they are acting on the basis of Peter's model, of which they are ignorant. It is not as though we reject the ninth hour, which we usually observe on the forth and sixth days of the week, but that we ought to offer a reason that is all the more worthy of those matters which are observed on the basis of tradition, in so far as they lack the authority of Scripture, until they are either confirmed or corrected by some heavenly gift. "And if you are ignorant of anything," he says, "the Lord will reveal it to you" (cf. Phil 3:15). Therefore, the Paraclete, the leader of all truth (cf. John 16:13), aside, who confirms all such things, inquire whether a more worthy reason for observing the ninth hour is offered in our case so that that reason ought also to be credited to Peter if he observed a fast at that time.

59. Ibid. 11.

"It is the spirit of the devil," you say, O Psychic. And how is it that he enjoins duties to our God, and duties that are to be offered to no other than our God? Either assert that the devil sides with our God, or let the Paraclete be regarded as Satan. But you maintain he is a human antichrist, for heretics are so named in John (cf. 1 John 2:18). And how is it that, whoever he is, in the name of our Christ he has determined these duties in relation to our Lord, since indeed the antichrists, being against God, have proceeded in opposition to our Christ. In which way, then do you think the Spirit has been confirmed to be among us, when he commands or when he approves those things which our God has always commanded and approved? But again you fix boundaries for God, as concerning grace, so concerning discipline, as concerning gifts, so also concerning religious rites, so that just as our duties have ceased, in the same manner have God's blessings ceased. And in this way you deny that he continues to impose duties to the present, because in this case too, "the law and the prophets were until John" (Luke 16:16). It remains for you to suppress him completely, so far as you are able, since he is so superfluous.

60. Ibid. 12.

Therefore, those who preach the discipline of moderation are false prophets; consequently those who practice it are heretics. Why, then, do you hesitate to believe that the Paraclete, whom you deny to be in Montanus, is in Apicius?

61. Ibid. 13.

But it is well that the bishops too customarily enjoin fasts on all the faithful, I do not mean for the purpose of collecting donations as your un-

interdum et ex aliqua sollicitudinis ecclesiasticae causa. Itaque si et ex hominis edicto et in unum omnes ταπεινοφρόνησιν agitatis, quomodo in nobis ipsam quoque unitatem ieiunationum et xerophagiarum et stationum denotatis? Nisi forte in senatus consulta et in principum mandata coitionibus opposita delinquimus. Spiritus sanctus, cum in quibus uellet terris et per quos uellet praedicaret, ex prouidentia imminentium siue ecclesiasticarum temptationum siue mundialium plagarum, qua paracletus id est aduocatus ad exorandum iudicem dicitur, huiusmodi officiorum remedia mandabat, puta, nunc ad exercendam sobrietatis et abstinentiae disciplinam; hunc qui recipimus, necessario etiam quae tunc constituit obseruamus. Aspice ad Iudaicos fastos et inuenies nihil nouum, si, quae patribus sunt praecepta, omnis deinceps posteritas hereditaria religione custodit. Aguntur praeterea per Graecias illa certis in locis concilia ex uniuersis ecclesiis, per quae et altiora quaeque in commune tractantur, et ipsa repraesentatio totius nominis Christiani magna ueneratione celebratur. Et hoc quam dignum fide auspicante congregari undique ad Christum! Uide, "quam bonum et quam iucundum habitare fratres in unum!" Hoc tu psallere non facile nosti, nisi quo tempore cum compluribus cenas. Conuentus autem illi stationibus prius et ieiunationibus operati dolere cum dolentibus et ita demum congaudere gaudentibus norunt. Si et ista sollemnia, quibus tunc praesens patrocinatus est sermo, nos quoque in diuersis prouinciis fungimur in spiritu inuicem repraesentati, lex est sacramenti.

62. Ibid. 15 (Reifferscheid and Wissowa, p. 293).

Reprobat etiam illos qui iubeant cibis abstinere, sed de prouidentia spiritus sancti, praedamnans iam haereticos perpetuam abstinentiam praecepturos ad destruenda et despicienda opera creatoris, quales inueniam apud Marcionem, apud Tatianum, apud Iouem, hodiernum de Pythagora haereticum, non apud paracletum. Quantula est enim apud nos interdictio ciborum? Duas inanno hedomadas xerophagiarum nec totas exceptis scilicet sabbatis et dominicis, offerimus deo abstinentes ab eis quae non reicimus, sed differimus.

derstanding has it, but occasionally also from some motive that arises from ecclesiastical responsibility. Therefore, if you also, on the basis of a human edict, practice *tapeinophronesis* (i.e. humility) and are all together, how do you denounce the same unity of fasting and eating dry food and stations among us? Unless perhaps we are transgressing the decrees of the senate and the mandates of the princes which oppose meetings. When the Holy Spirit used to preach in the lands in which he wished and through those whom he wished, on the basis of his foreknowledge of trials threatening the Church or of plagues threatening the world (on which basis he is said to be the Paraclete, that is the advocate to prevail upon the judge), he used to command remedies consisting of duties of this kind, for example now to exercise the discipline of moderation and abstinence. We who receive him necessarily also observe those things which he appointed then. Consider the Jewish festival-calender and you will discover nothing new. All posterity subsequently in their hereditary religion guards those things which were taught to the fathers. Moreover throughout Greece those councils of all the Churches are held in certain places. It is by means of these councils that deeper issues, whatever they be, are treated for the common good, and the representation itself of the whole Christian name is celebrated with great reverence. And how worthy a thing this is, that men from everywhere are brought together to Christ under the auspices of the faith! Behold, "how good and how pleasant it is for brothers to dwell in unity" (Ps 133:1/132:1). You do not know how to sing this psalm well except when you are dining with many people. Those assemblies, however, which have labored first in stations and fastings know how to grieve with those who are grieving and thus, at length, to rejoice with those who are rejoicing (cf. Rom 12:15). If indeed we also, in our diverse provinces, having been mutually rendered present in spirit (cf. 1 Cor 5:3; Col 2:5), observe those religious rites which the present discourse has accordingly defended, it is a law of the divine order.

62. Ibid. 15.

[The apostle] also condemns those who command to abstain from foods (cf. 1 Tim 4:3), but he does so from the foreknowledge of the Holy Spirit, condemning in advance the heretics who would teach perpetual abstinence to destroy and despise the works of the Creator. I find such in Marcion, in Tatian, in Jupiter the present heretic of the school of Pythagoras; not in the Paraclete. For how trifling is the prohibition of foods with us? We offer God two weeks of eating dry food a year, and these are not two complete weeks, for the sabbaths and Lord's Days are excepted, of course. In this time we abstain from those things which we do not reject, but whose usage we postpone.

63. *Aduersus Praxean* 1 (CSEL 47, ed. Kroymann, pp. 227-28).

Nam iste primus ex Asia hoc genus peruersitatis intulit Romanae humo, [homo] et alias inquietus, insuper de iactatione martyrii inflatus ob solum et simplex et breue carceris taedium; quando, et si corpus suum tradidisset exurendum, nihil profecisset, dilectionem dei non habens, cuius charismata quoque expugnauit. Nam idem tunc episcopum Romanum, agnoscentem iam prophetias Montani Priscae Maximilae et ex ea agnitione pacem ecclesiis Asiae et Phrygiae inferentem, falsa de ipsis prophetis et ecclesiis eorum adseuerando et praecessorum eius auctoritates defendendo coegit et litteras pacis reuocare iam emissas et a proposito recipiendorum charismatum concessare. Ita duo negotia diaboli Praxeas Romae procurauit: prophetiam expulit et haeresim intulit, paracletum fugauit et Patrem crucifixit.

Fructificauerant auenae Praxeanae hic quoque, superseminatae dormientibus multis in simplicitate doctrinae; traductae dehinc per quem deus voluit, etiam euulsae uidebantur. Denique cauerat pristinum doctor de emendatione sua, et manet chirographum apud phychicos, apud quos tunc gesta res est. Exinde silentium. Et nos quidem postea agnitio paracleti atque defensio disiunxit a psychicis. Auenae vero illae ubique tunc semen excusscrant. Id aliquamdiu per hypocrisin subdola uiuacitate latitauit et nunc denuo erupit. Sed et denuo eradicabitur, si uoluerit dominus, in isto commeatu; si quo minus, die suo colligentur omnes adulterae fruges et cum ceteris scandalis igni inextinguibili cremabuntur.

64. Ibid. 2 (Kroymann, pp. 228-29).

Nos uero et semper et nunc magis, ut instructiores per paracletum, deductorem scilicet omnis ueritatis, unicum quidem deum credimus, sub hac tamen dispensatione, quam oikonomiam dicimus, ut unici dei sit et filius, sermo ipsius, qui ex ipso processerit, per quem omnia facta sunt et sine quo factum est nihil.

65. Ibid. 8 (Kroymann, p. 238).

Sermo ergo et in patre semper, sicut dixit: "Ego in patre," et apud deum semper, sicut scriptum est: "Et sermo erat apud deum," et nunquam se-

63. Against Praxeas, 1.

For Praxeas first brought this kind of perversity from Asia to Rome, a man troubled also in other matters. He was haughty in addition from the ostentation of martyrdom on account of a single, simple, brief nuisance of imprisonment, at which time even if he had delivered his body to be burned he would have profited nothing, since he did not have the love of God (cf. 1 Cor 13:3), whose gifts he also attacked. For the same man, when the bishop of Rome at that time had already acknowledged the prophecies of Montanus, Prisca, and Maximilla, and on the basis of that acknowledgment had brought peace to the Churches of Asia and Phrygia, by making false assertions about the prophets themselves and their Churches, and by bringing forward the views of his predecessors, forced him both to recall the letter of peace which had already been sent and to desist from his intention of admitting the gifts. In this way Praxeas attended to two matters of the devil at Rome: he expelled prophecy and introduced heresy; he put the Paraclete to flight and crucified the Father.

Praxeas' tares have produced fruit here too, having been sown over many who are asleep in doctrinal simplicity (cf. Matt 13:25-26). These appear indeed to have been eradicated, having been removed from here by him whom God chose. At length the teacher decreed his earlier position on the basis of his own amendment, and a document in his own handwriting remains among the Psychics, among whom the affair occurred at that time. After that, silence. And afterwards our acknowledgment and defence of the Paraclete separated us indeed from the Psychics. But those tares had sent their seed forth everywhere at that time. For a while it lay hidden through hypocrisy with cunning vital force, and now it has burst forth again. But it will also be eradicated again, if the Lord should wish, in this time, otherwise in its own day all corrupt fruits will be gathered and will be burned in unquenchable fire together with the other causes of offence (cf. Matt 13:30; 41-42).

64. Ibid. 2.

But we both always and even more now as we have been further instructed by the Paraclete, who is the leader, of course, of all truth (cf. John 16:13), believe that God is unique. Nevertheless, under this dispensation, which we call an economy, we believe that there is also a son of this unique God, his Word, who has proceeded from him, by whom all things were made and without whom nothing was made (cf. John 1:1,3).

65. Ibid. 8.

The Word, therefore, is always in the Father, as he said: "I am in the Father" (John 14:11), and is always with God, as it has been written: "And

paratus a patre, aut alius a patre, quia: "Ego et pater unum sumus." Haec erit probola ueritatis, custos unitatis, qua prolatum dicimus filium a patre, sed non separatum. Protulit enim deus sermonem, quemadmodum etiam paracletus docet, sicut radix fructicem et fons fluuium et sol radium. Nam et istae species probolae sunt earum substantiarum, ex quibus prodeunt.

66. Ibid. 13 (Kroymann, p. 248).

"Ergo," inquis, "prouocabo te, ut hodie quoque ex auctoritate istarum scripturarum constanter duos deos et duos dominos praedices." Absit! Nos enim, qui et tempora et causas scripturarum per dei gratiam inspicimus, maxime paracleti, non hominum discipuli, duos quidem definimus, patrem et filium, et iam tres cum spiritu sancto,—secundum rationem oikonomiae, quae facit numerum, ne, ut uestra peruersitas infert, pater ipse credatur natus et passus, quod non licet credi, quoniam non ita traditum est—duos tamen deos et duos dominos numquam ex ore nostro proferimus, non quasi non et pater deus et filius deus et spiritus deus et dominus unusquisque, sed quoniam [ideo] retro et duo dei et duo domini praedicabantur, ut, ubi uenisset Christus, et deus agnosceretur et dominus uocaretur, quia filius dei et domini.

67. Ibid. 30 (Kroymann, p. 288).

Hic interim acceptum a patre munus effudit, spiritum sanctum, tertium nomen diuinitatis et tertium gradum maiestatis, unius praedicatorem monarchiae, sed et oikonomiae interpretatorem, si quis sermones nouae prophetiae eius admiserit et deductorem omnis ueritatis, quae est in patre et filio et spiritu sancto secundum Christianum sacramentum.

68. *De pudicitia* 1 (CSEL 20, ed. Reifferscheid and Wissowa, p. 222).

Nobis autem maxima aut summa sic quoque praecauentur, dum nec secundas quidem post fidem nuptias permittitur nosse, nuptialibus et dotalibus, si forte, tabulis a moechiae et fornicationis opere diuersas, et ideo durissime nos infamantes paracletum disciplinae enormitate digamos foris

the Word was with God'' (John 1:1), and is never separated from the Father or different from the Father, because: ''I and the Father are one'' (John 10:30). This will be the procession of the truth, the guard of the unity, by which we say that the son has been brought forth from the Father, but not separated. For God brought forth the Word, as the Paraclete also teaches, as the root brings forth a tree, and a fountain a stream, and the sun a ray. For these spectacles too are processions of those substances from which they proceed.

66. Ibid. 13.

You say, ''therefore, I will challenge you today also to proclaim consistently two Gods and two Lords on the authority of those Scriptures.'' By no means. For we, who by the grace of God perceive the times and principles of the Scriptures, who above all are disciples not of men, but of the Paraclete, declare that there are two indeed, the Father and the Son, and now three with the Holy Spirit,—according to the principle of the economy which effects the number, lest, as your perversity introduces, the Father himself be thought to have been born and to have suffered. This belief is inadmissible since it has not been so handed down. Nevertheless, we never bring forth from our mouth that there are two Gods and two Lords. It is not as though the father is not God, and the Son is not God, and the Spirit is not God, and each one is not Lord, but because formerly two Gods and two Lords were proclaimed so that when the Christ had come he might both be recognized as God and called Lord, because he is the Son of God and the Lord.

67. Ibid. 30.

Meanwhile the Son has poured forth the gift which he received from the Father, the Holy Spirit (cf. Acts 2:33). The Spirit is the third name of the divinity, and the third grade of the majesty, the proclaimer of the one monarchy but also the interpreter of the economy, if one receives the word of his new prophecy, and he is the leader of all truth (cf. John 16:13) which resides in the Father and in the son and in the Holy Spirit according to the Christian religion.

68. *On Modesty* 1.

But we also seek to avert the greatest or most serious faults in this manner, since it is not permitted to have known a second marriage after becoming a believer, if by chance such is differentiated from adultery and fornication by a contract pertaining to the marriage and dowry. For this reason we very sternly exclude those who have been married twice because they dishonor the Paraclete by the irregularity of their discipline. We

sistimus. Eundem limitem liminis moechis quoque et fornicationibus fi-
gimus, ieiunas pacis lacrimas profusuris, nec amplius ab ecclesia quam
publicationem dedecoris relaturis.

69. Ibid. 12 (Reifferscheid and Wissowa, p. 241).

Itaque isti, qui alium paracletum in apostolis et per apostolos receperunt, quem nec in prophetis propriis agnitum iam nec in apostolis possi-
dent, age nunc uel de apostolico instrumento doceant maculas carnis post
baptisma respersae paenitentia dilui posse.

70. Ibid. 21 (Reifferscheid and Wissowa, pp. 269-71).

Exhibe igitur et nunc mihi, apostolice, prophetica exempla, ut agno-
scam diuinitatem, et uindica tibi delictorum eiusmodi remittendorum potestatem. Quod si disciplinae solius officia sortitus es, nec imperio
praesidere, sed ministerio, quis aut quantus es indulgere, qui neque prophetam nec apostolum exhibens cares ea uirtute cuius est indulgere? Sed
habet, inquis, potestatem ecclesia delicta donandi. Hoc ego magis et agnosco et dispono, qui ipsum paracletum in prophetis nouis habeo dicentem: "Potest ecclesia donare delictum, sed non faciam, ne et alia
delinquant." Quid, si pseudoproheticus spiritus pronuntiauit? Atqui magis
euersoris fuisset et semetipsum de clementia commendare et ceteros ad de-
linquentiam temptare. Aut si et hoc secundum spiritum ueritatis adfectare
gestiuit, ergo spiritus ueritatis potest quidem indulgere fornicationibus
ueniam, sed cum plurium malo non uult. De tua nunc sententia quaero,
unde hoc ius ecclesiae usurpes. . . .

Secundum enim Petri personam spiritalibus potestas ista conueniet aut
apostolo aut prophetae. Nam et ipsa ecclesia proprie et principaliter ipse
est spiritus, in quo est trinitas unius diuinitatis, pater et filius et spiritus
sanctus. Illam ecclesiam congregat, quam dominus in tribus posuit. Atque
ita exinde etiam numerus omnis qui in hanc fidem conspirauerint, ecclesia
ab auctore et consecratore censetur. Et ideo ecclesia quidem delicta dona-
bit, sed ecclesia spiritus per spiritalem hominem, non ecclesia numerus
episcoporum. Domini enim, non famuli est ius et arbitrium; dei ipsius, non
sacerdotis.

fix the same limit also for adulterers and fornicators, who will pour forth tears devoid of peace, nor will they bring anything more from the church than the publication of their disgrace.

69. Ibid. 12.

Accordingly, come now, let those who have received another Paraclete in the apostles and by the apostles, a Paraclete who is not recognized among his own prophets, teach indeed from the apostolic instrument that the stains of the flesh which has been defiled after baptism can be washed away by penitence.

70. Ibid. 21.

Then show me, even now, O apostolic man, prophetic examples, that I may recognize your divinity, and appropriate for yourself the power to forgive sins of this kind. But if you have been allotted the duties of discipline alone, to preside not by supreme power, but by the functions of a minister, who are you or what is your greatness to grant pardon? Since you present yourself neither as a prophet nor an apostle, do you not lack that power to which granting pardon belongs? "But," you say, "the Church has the right to pardon sins." This I recognize and will more than you, for I have the Paraclete himself who says in the new prophets: "The Church can pardon sin, but I will not do it, lest they also commit other offences." What if a pseudo-prophetic spirit has made the pronouncement? But certainly he would have been more of a subverter both by commending himself concerning clemency and by tempting others to transgress. Or even if he has eagerly wished to feign this in accordance with the Spirit of truth, the Spirit of truth, as I was saying, is able to grant forgiveness to fornicators, but he does not wish to do so because he has the consequent calamity for the multitudes in mind. Now I inquire concerning your viewpoint. On what basis do you make use of this right in the Church? . . .

For according to the person of Peter, this right will pertain to those who are spiritual, either to an apostle or prophet. For indeed the Church itself is properly and principally the Spirit himself, in whom is the trinity of the one divinity, the Father, the Son, and the Holy Spirit. He unites that Church which the Lord has placed in three (cf. Matt 18:20). And consequently since then and still, the whole number who are in accord in this faith are considered to be a Church by its author and consecrator. And for this reason the Church indeed will pardon transgressions; but it is the Church of the Spirit, done by means of a spiritual man, not the Church which consists of a number of bishops. For the right and the decision belongs to the Lord, not to the servant; it belongs to God himself, not to the priest.

Other Testimonia from the Third Century

Clement of Alexandria

71. *Stromata* 4.13.93.1 (GCS, ed. Stählin 2, p. 89).

Μὴ τοίνυν ψυχικοὺς ἐν ὀνείδους μέρει λεγόντων ἡμᾶς οἱ προειρημέ-
νοι, ἀλλὰ καὶ οἱ Φρύγες· ἤδη γὰρ καὶ οὗτοι τοὺς τῇ νέᾳ προφητείᾳ μὴ
προσέχοντας ψυχικοὺς καλοῦσιν, πρὸς οὓς ἐν τοῖς Περὶ προφητείας
διαλεξόμεθα.

72. Ibid. 7.17.108.1 (Stählin 3, p. 76).

Τῶν δ' αἱρέσεων αἱ μὲν ἀπὸ ὀνόματος προσαγορεύονται, ὡς ἡ ἀπὸ Οὐα-
λεντίνου καὶ Μαρκίωνος καὶ Βασιλείδου . . . αἱ δὲ ἀπὸ τόπου, ὡς οἱ
Περατικοί, αἱ δὲ ἀπὸ ἔθνους, ὡς ἡ τῶν Φρυγῶν.

Origen

73. *De principiis* 2.7.3 (GCS, ed. Koetschau, pp. 150-51).

Sicut autem multi sunt intellectus de Christo, qui utique quamuis "sapientia" sit, non tamen in omnibus sapientiae agit aut obtinet, uim nisi in
his, qui in ipso sapientiae student . . . : ita arbitror etiam de spiritu sancto,
in quo omnis est natura donorum. "aliis" namque praebetur "per spiritum
sermo sapientia, aliis sermo scientiae, aliis fides"; et ita per singulos, qui
eum capere possunt, hoc efficitur uel hoc intellegitur ipse spiritus, quo in-
diget ille, qui eum participare meruerit. Quas diuisiones ac differentias non
aduertentes hi, qui "paracletum" eum in euangelio audiunt nominari, ne-

Other Testimonia from the Third Century[16]

Clement of Alexandria

71. *Stromata* 4.13.93.1.

Therefore, let not the previously mentioned Valentineans call us psychics in a reproachful manner. This holds for the Phrygians too, for they as well call those psychics who do not heed the new prophecy. We will argue with them in our discussions *Concerning Prophecy.*

72. Ibid. 7.17.108.1.

Some of the heresies get their title from a name, as that from Valentinus, and that from Marcion, and that from Basilides. . . . Others are named from a place, as the Peratici; still others from a race, as the Phrygians.

Origen

73. *On First Principles* 2.7.3.

But just as there are many ways of understanding Christ, who although he is wisdom to be sure, does not, nevertheless, exert or demonstrate the power of wisdom in all men, but only in those who strive after wisdom in him . . , so too, I think, it is of the Holy Spirit, in whom lies the total essence of the gifts. For "to some a word of wisdom" is offered "by the Spirit, to others a word of knowledge, to others faith" (cf. 1 Cor 12:8-9). In this way, through each of those who are able to receive him the same Spirit is demonstrated in this way, or is understood in that way, which that person needs who has been considered worthy to participate in him.

Some, who hear him called "Paraclete" in the Gospel, since they do not observe these distinctions and differences, nor do they consider for what

---

[16]The sources included in this category either (1) cannot be identified with any particular place; (2) are, as with Firmilian in Cappadocia and Clement in Alexandria, identified with some other area than the three previously considered; or (3) as in the case of Origen's later writings, may reflect information about Montanism gained from contact with people from all of the above areas.

que considerantes ex quo opere uel actu ''paracletus'' nominetur, uilibus eum nescio quibus spiritibus compararunt et per hoc conturbare conati sunt ecclesias Christi, ita ut dissensiones fratribus non modicas generarent. Euangelium uero tantae eum potentiae ac maiestatis ostendit, ut dicat apostolos ''non posse capere'' adhuc ea, quae uolebat eos docere saluator, nisi ''cum aduenerit spiritus sanctus,'' qui se eorum animabus infundens inluminare eos possit de ratione ac fide trinitatis. Isti uero pro imperitia intellectus sui, qua non solum ipsi quod rectum est consequenter non ualent exponere, sed ne his quidem quae a nobis dicuntur possunt audientiam commodare, minora de eius deitate quam dignum est sentientes, erroribus se ac deceptionibus tradiderunt, erratico magis spiritu deprauati quam sancti spiritus institutionibus eruditi, secundum quod apostolus dixit: ''Doctrinam spirituum daemoniorum sequentes, prohibentium nubere'' ''ad interitum et ruinam multorum'' ''et inportune se abstinere a cibis,'' ut per ostentationem acrioris obseruantiae seducant animas innocentum.

74. *In Matthaeum* 15.30 (GCS, ed. Klostermann, p. 441).

Καὶ εἰ τοιαῦτά γε ἐζήτουν . . . πάντες οἱ τὸ κατὰ 'Ιωάννην Εὐαγγέλιον ἀναγινώσκοντες, οὐκ ἂν προσέσχον τινές, ὡς παρακλήτῳ ''πνεύμασι πλάνης καὶ διδασκαλίαις δαιμονίων, ἐν ὑποκρίσει ψευδολόγων, κεκαυτηριασμένων τὴν ἰδίαν συνείδευιν'' ὥστε τὰ τῆς πλάνης πνεύματα καὶ τὰ δαιμόνια ἀναγορεῦσαι τῷ μεγάλῳ τοῦ παρακλήτου ὀνόματι, ὅπερ ὁ σωτὴρ τοῖς ἀποστόλοις, καὶ εἴ τις τοῖς ἀποστόλοις παραπλήσιός ἐστιν, ἐπηγγείλατο.

75. Ibid. Comm. ser. 28 (Klostermann, p. 52).

Adhuc autem quaeramus quod scriptum est in Luca, dicente domino: ''quia non capit prophetam perire extra Hierusalem.'' si ergo ''non capit perire prophetam extra Hierusalem,'' id est interfici, quaeres si post destructionem Hierusalem iam nemo propheta est, ne forte qui interficitur ''extra Hierusalem'' propheta falsum uerbum Christi demonstret. si autem cogunt nos scripturae propter Agabum et filias Philippi euangelistae (non propter falsos Phrygiae prophetas), quaeramus, ne forte omnis iustus sit [in] Hierusalem et non ''extra Hierusalem,'' quoniam ''non capit'' eum qui est extra Hierusalem passionibus adfici propter uerbum.

work or activity he is named "Paraclete," have compared him to some common spirits, of what sort I do not know, and by this means have tried to throw the Churches of Christ into confusion, with the result that they have produced some rather significant dissensions among brothers. But the Gospel shows him to be of such power and majesty that it says the apostles could not yet receive those things which the Savior wished to teach them, except at that time when the Holy Spirit had come, who, by pouring himself into their souls, could illuminate them concerning the logic and faith of the Trinity (cf. John 16:12-13). But those men, by the inexperience of their understanding in which they not only consequently cannot themselves set forth what is correct, but neither can they give their attention to these matters indeed which are discussed by us, by holding opinions that are less than worthy of his deity, have delivered themselves to errors and deceptions, seduced by some erring spirit more than informed by the instructions of the Holy Spirit, in relation to which the apostle said: "Following the teaching of demonic spirits, which forbid marriage" "to the destruction and ruin of many," and urge unsuitably "to abstain from foods" (cf. 1 Tim 4:1,3; Luke 2:34), so as to lead astray the souls of the innocent by the display of their more zealous observance of religious duties.

74. *Commentary on Matthew* 15.30.

And if all who read the Gospel according to John would inquire into such things, . . . some would not devote themselves, as to the Paraclete, "to spirits of error and teachings of demons, speaking lies in hypocricy, having their conscience seared" (1 Tim 4:1-2). As a result they have proclaimed the spirits of error and the demons in the great name of the Paraclete which the Savior promised to the apostles and to anyone nearly equal to the apostles.

75. Ibid. 28.

But now let us investigate what has been written in Luke, when the Lord says: "Because it is inconceivable that a prophet perish outside Jerusalem" (Luke 13:33). If then "it is inconceivable that a prophet perish outside Jerusalem," that is to be killed, you will ask if there is no prophet since the destruction of Jerusalem, lest by chance a prophet who is killed "outside Jerusalem" should show the saying of Christ to be false. But if the Scriptures compel us because of Agabus (see Acts 11:28; 21:10) and the daughters of Philip the evangelist (see Acts 21:8-9)—not because of the false prophets of Phrygia— , let us ask whether perhaps every just man is in Jerusalem and not "outside Jerusalem" since it is inconceivable for him who is "outside Jerusalem" to be afflicted with sufferings because of the Word.

76. Ibid. Comm. ser. 47 (Klostermann, p. 96).

Sola autem ecclesia neque subtrahit huius fulguris uerbum et sensum, neque addit quasi prophetiam aliud aliquid.

77. *Catenae in sancti Pauli epistolas ad Corinthios* 14.36 (ed. Jenkins, JTS 10 [1909]: 41-42).

Ὡς γὰρ πάντων λεγόντων καὶ δυναμένων λέγειν, ἐὰν ἀποκάλυψις αὐτοῖς γένηται, φησὶν "Αἱ γυναῖκες ἐν ταῖς ἐκκλησίαις σιγάτωσαν." ταύτης δὲ τῆς ἐντολῆς οὐκ ἦσαν οἱ τῶν γυναικῶν μαθηταί, οἱ μαθητευθέντες Πρισκίλλῃ καὶ Μαξιμίλλῃ, οὐ Χριστοῦ τοῦ ἀνδρὸς τῆς νύμφης. ἀλλ᾽ ὅμως εὐγνωμονῶμεν καὶ πρὸς τὰ πιθανὰ ἐκείνων ἀπαντῶντες. τέσσαρές φασι θυγατέρες ἦσαν Φιλίππου τοῦ εὐαγγελιστοῦ καὶ προεφήτευον. εἰ δὲ προεφήτευον, τί ἄτοπόν ἐστι καὶ τὰς ἡμετέρας, ὡς φασὶν ἐκεῖνοι, προφήτιδας προφητεύειν; ταῦτα δὲ λύσομεν. πρῶτον μὲν λέγοντες ὅτι Αἱ ἡμέτεραι προεφήτευον, δείξατε τὰ σημεῖα τῆς προφητείας ἐν αὐταῖς· δεύτερον δὲ Εἰ καὶ προεφήτευον αἱ θυγατέρες Φιλίππου, ἀλλ᾽ οὐκ ἐν ταῖς ἐκκλησίαις ἔλεγον· οὐ γὰρ ἔχομεν τοῦτο ἐν ταῖς Πράξεσι τῶν Ἀποστόλων. ἀλλ᾽ οὐδ᾽ ἐν τῇ παλαιᾷ· Δεββῶρα μεμαρτύρηται προφῆτις εἶναι, "λαβοῦσα δὲ Μαριὰμ ἡ ἀδελφὴ Ἀαρὼν τὸ τύμπανον ἐξῆρχε" τῶν γυναικῶν. ἀλλ᾽ οὐκ ἂν εὕροις ὅτι Δεββῶρα ἐδημηγόρησεν εἰς τὸν λαὸν ὥσπερ Ἱερεμίας καὶ Ἡσαΐας· οὐκ ἂν εὕροις ὅτι Ὀλδὰ προφῆτις οὖσα ἐλάλησε τῷ λαῷ ἀλλ᾽ ἑνί τινι ἐλθόντι πρὸς αὐτήν. ἀλλὰ καὶ ἐν τῷ εὐαγγελίῳ ἀναγέγραπται· "Ἄννα προφῆτις, θυγάτηρ Φανουήλ, ἐκ φυλῆς Ἀσήρ·" ἀλλ᾽ οὐκ ἐν ἐκκλησίᾳ ἐλάλησεν. ἵνα οὖν καὶ δοθῇ ἐκσημείου προφητικοῦ εἶναι προφῆτις γυνή, ἀλλ᾽ οὐκ ἐπιτρέπεται ταύτῃ λαλεῖν ἐν ἐκκλησίᾳ. ὅτε ἐλάλησε Μαριὰμ ἡ προφῆτις ἄρχουσα ἦν τινων γυναικῶν· "αἰσχρὸν γὰρ γυναικὶ λαλεῖν ἐν ἐκκλησίᾳ," καὶ "διδάσκειν δὲ γυναικὶ οὐκ ἐπιτρέπω" ἁπλῶς ἀλλ᾽ "οὐδὲ αὐθεντεῖν ἀνδρός."

The Martyrdom of Pionius

78. *Martyrium Pionii* 11.1-2 (ed. Krüger, Ruhbach, p. 51).

(1) ταῦτα εἰπόντος αὐτοῦ μόλις ἐκ τοῦ ὄχλου ἐσφιγμένους ὥστε συμπνίγεσθαι ἐνέβαλον αὐτοὺς εἰς τὴν φυλακὴν παραδόντες τοῖς δεσμοφύλαξιν. (2) εἰσελθόντες δὲ εὗρον κατακεκλεισμένον πρεσβύτερον τῆς

76. Ibid. 47.

But the Church alone neither takes away the word and meaning of his lightning (cf. Matt 24:27), nor adds one thing or another, as if it were a prophecy.

77. *Catenae on Paul's Epistles to the Corinthians* 14.36.

For insofar as all speak and can speak if a revelation should come to them (cf. 1 Cor 14:30-31), he says: "Let the women be silent in the Churches" (1 Cor 14:34). But the disciples of the women, who were instructed by Priscilla and Maximilla, not by Christ the husband of the bride[17] (cf. John 3:29), were not obedient to this command. But nevertheless let us be reasonable also as we reply to the arguments they find plausible. "Philip the evangelist had four daughters," they say, "and they prophesied (cf. Acts 21:9). And if they prophesied, why is it strange that our prophetesses also prophesy?" as they say. But we shall put an end to these arguments. First, when you say that your prophetesses have prophesied, demonstrate the signs of prophecy among them. And second, even if Philip's daughters prophesied, they did not speak in the churches, for we do not have this in the Acts of the Apostles; nor do we find it even in the Old Testament. It is attested that Deborah was a prophetess (cf. Judg 4:4). And Mariam, the sister of Aaron, took the timbrel and led the women (cf. Exod 15:20). But you would not find that Deborah addressed the people as Jeremiah and Isaiah did; you would not find that Huldah spoke to the people, although she was a prophetess; she spoke to a certain individual who came to her (cf. 2 Kgs 22:14). And Anna, a prophetess, the daughter of Phanuel of the tribe of Asher has been mentioned in the Gospel (cf. Luke 2:36), but she did not speak in the church. Therefore, even though a woman be granted to be a prophetess by a prophetic sign, nevertheless she is not permitted to speak in church. When Mariam the prophetess spoke she was leading some women. "For it is shameful for a woman to speak in church" (1 Cor 14:35), and: "I do not permit a woman to teach in general, nor to have authority over a man" (cf. 1 Tim 2:12).

The Martyrdom of Pionius

78. *The Martyrdom of Pionius* 11.1-2.

When he had said these things, they were pressed by the crowd to the extent that they were choked; with difficulty they threw them into prison, having delivered them over to the jailor. And when they entered the prison

---

[17]Jenkins suggests reading χριστῷ τῷ ἀνδρί in place of the genitives.

καθολικῆς ἐκκλησίας ὀνόματι Λίμνον καὶ γυναῖκα Μακεδονίαν ἀπὸ κώμης Καρίνης καὶ ἕνα ἐκ τῆς αἱρέσεως τῶν Φρυγῶν ὀνόματι Εὐτυχιανόν.

The Acts of Acacius

79. *Acta disputationis s. Achatii* 4.8 (ed. Krüger and Ruhbach, p. 59).
    Cataphrygas aspice homines religionis antiquae [et] ad mea sacra con-
    uersos reliquisse quod fuerant.

Firmilian of Caesarea

80. Epistula 75.7 in *S. Thasci Caecili Cypriani Opera Omnia* (CSEL 3.2, ed. Hartel,
    pp. 814-15).
    Sed et ad illam partem bene a uobis responsum est, ubi Stephanus in
    epistola sua dixit haereticos quoque ipsos in baptismo conuenire et quod
    alterutrum ad se uenientes non baptizent, sed communicent tantum, quasi
    et nos hoc facere debeamus. Quo in loco, etsi uos iam probastis satis ri-
    diculum esse ut quis sequatur errantes, illud tamen ex abundanti addimus
    non esse mirum si sic haeretici agant, qui etsi in quibusdam minoribus dis-
    crepant, in eo tamen quod est maximum unum et eumdem consensum te-
    nent, ut blasphement creatorem, quadam domnia sibi et fantasma ignoti
    dei confingentes, quo utique consequens est sic consentire in baptismi sui
    uanitate ut consentiunt in repudianda diuinitatis ueritate.
    De quibus quoniam longum est ad singula eorum uei scelesta uei su-
    peruacua respondere, satis est breuiter illud in compendio dicere eos qui
    non teneant uerum Dominum patrem tenere non posse nec filii nec spiritus
    sancti ueritatem, secundum quod etiam illi qui Cataphrygas appellantur et
    nouas prophetias usurpare conantur nec patrem possunt habere nec filium
    quia nec spiritum sanctum: a quibus si quaeramus quem Christum prae-
    dicent, respondebunt eum se praedicare qui miseret spiritum per Mon-
    tanum et Priscam locutum. In quibus cum animaduertamus non ueritatis
    spiritum sed erroris fuisse, cognoscimus eos qui falsam illorum prohetiam
    contra Christi fidem uindicant Christum habere non posse. Sed et ceteri
    quique haeretici, si se ab ecclesia dei sciderint, nihil habere potestatis aut
    gratiae possunt, quando omnis potestas et gratia in ecclesia constituta sit,
    ubi praesident maiores natu qui et baptizandi et manum imponendi et or-
    dinandi possident potestatem. Haereticum enim sicut ordinare non licet nec

they found imprisoned a presbyter of the Catholic Church named Limnus, and a Macedonian woman from the village of Karinê, and a man named Eutychian from the Phrygian heresy.

The Acts of Acacius

79. *The Acts of the Disputation of S. Acacius.*

Behold the Cataphrygians. They were people of an ancient religion which they have abandoned, having been converted to my sacred rites.

Firmilian of Caesarea

80. Epistle 75.7 in The Works of Cyprian.

But you have also responded well to that passage in his epistle where Stephen said that the heretics themselves are also in accord on baptism and that reciprocally they do not baptize those who come to them, but only enter into communion with them, as if we too ought to do this. Although you have already there proved sufficiently that it is ridicules for one to follow the erring, nevertheless we add as a supplement that it is not unusual if the heretics act in this way, for although they disagree in certain minor points, nevertheless in that which is most important they have a unanimity that is one and the same: to blaspheme the Creator, fabricating for themselves certain dreams and fantasies of an unknown God. It thus follows, of course that they agree in the deception of their own baptism as they are in agreement in repudiating the truth of God.

Since it would take too long to respond to their wicked or irrelevant details, this brief summary is sufficient: those who do not possess the true Lord the Father cannot possess the truth of the Son or of the Holy Spirit. In accordance with this, those too who are called Cataphrygians and attempt to employ new prophecies can have neither the Father nor the Son, because they do not have the Holy Spirit. If we ask them what Christ they preach, they will answer that they preach him who sent the Spirit which has spoken through Montanus and Prisca. When we observe that it was not the Spirit of truth in these prophets, but the spirit of error, we recognize that those who lay claim to their false prophecy against the faith of Christ cannot have Christ. And this is also true of the other heretics, whoever they are. If they separate from the Church of God they can have no part in authority or grace, since all authority and grace have been deposited in the Church where the elders preside, who also possess the authority of baptizing, imposition of hands, and ordaining. For as it is not permitted that a heretic ordain or lay on hands, so it is not permitted that he baptize or per-

manum inponere, ita nec baptizare nec quicquam sancte et spiritaliter ge-
rere, quando alienus sit a spiritali et deifica sanctitate.

Quod totum nos iam pridem in Iconio qui Phrygiae locus est collecti in
unum conuenientibus ex Galatia et Cilicia et ceteris proximis regionibus
confirmauimus tenendum contra haereticos firmiter et uindicandum, cum
a quibusdam de ista re dubitaretur.

81. Ibid. 10 (Hartel, pp. 816-18).

Volo autem uobis et de historia quae apud nos facta est exponere ad hoc
ipsum pertinente. Ante uiginti enim et duos fere annos temporibus post A-
lexandrum imperatorem multae istic conflictationes et pressurae accide-
runt uel in commune omnibus hominibus uel priuatim christianis: terrae
etiam motus plurimi et frequentes extiterunt, ut et per Cappadociam et per
Pontum multa subruerent, quaedam etiam ciuitates in profundum recepta
dirupti soli hiatu deuorarentur, ut ex hoc persecutio quoque grauis aduersum nos nominis fieret, quae post longam retro aetatis pacem repente oborta
de inopinato et insueto malo ad turbandum populum nostrum terribilior ef-
fecta est. Serenianus tunc fuit in nostra prouincia praeses, acerbus et dirus
persecutor. In hac autem perturbatione constitutis fidelibus et huc atque il-
luc persecutionis metu fugientibus et patrias suas relinquentibus atque in
alias regionum partes transeuntibus (erat enim transeundi facultas eo quod
persecutio illa non per totum mundum sed localis fuisset), emersit istic
subito quaedam mulier quae in extasin constituta propheten se praeferret
et quasi sancto spiritu plena sic ageret. Ita autem principalium daemoniorum impetu ferebatur ut per longum tempus sollicitaret et deciperet fra-
ternitatem, admirabilia quaedam et portentosa perficiens et facere se terram
moueri polliceretur: non quod daemoni tanta esset potestas ut terram mouere
aut elementum concutere in sua ualeret, sed quod nonnumquam nequam
spiritus praesciens et intellegens terrae motum futurum id se facturum esse
simularet quod futurum uideret. Quibus mendaciis et iactationibus sub-
egerat mentes singulorum ut sibi oboedirent et quocumque praeciperet et
duceret sequerentur, faceret quoque mulierem illam cruda hieme nudis pe-
dibus per asperas niues ire nec uexari in aliquo aut laedi illa discursione,
diceret etiam se in Iudaeam et Hierosolymam festinare, fingens tamquam
inde uenisset. Hic et unum de presbyteris Rusticum, item et alium diaco-
nium fefellit, ut eidem mulieri commiscerentur: quod paulo post detectum

form any function that is holy and spiritual, since he is alienated from that
sanctity which is spiritual and sacred.

We confirmed long ago in Iconium, which is a place in Phrygia, when
we were assembled with those who came together from Galatia and Cilicia
and other neighboring regions, that all this must be firmly held and maintained against the heretics, since some had doubts on that matter.

81. Ibid. 75.10.

But I wish also to relate a story which happened among us pertaining to
this very matter. For approximately twenty-two years ago in the period after
the emperor Alexander there were many conflicts and oppressions here
which affected either all men in common or Christians particularly. There
were also numerous and frequent earthquakes so that many places were
demolished throughout Cappadocia and Pontus, even some cities were
swallowed, seized in the depth of the crack in the broken earth. As a result,
there was also a harsh persecution of the name against us. This arose suddenly, after the long peace of the previous period, and because the evil was
unexpected and we were unaccustomed to it, it was more dreadful in
throwing our people into confusion. Serenianus was governor in our province at that time; he was a bitter and awful persecutor. But when the faithful were set in this confusion and were fleeing here and there out of fear
of persecution, and were leaving their own country and crossing into other
parts (for it was possible to cross over because the persecution was not uni-
versal, but local), a certain woman suddenly appeared here, who having
represented herself to be ecstatic, presented herself as a prophetess and thus
acted as if she were filled with the Holy Spirit. Moreover, she was so driven
by the impetus of the chief demons that for a long time she disturbed and
deceived the brotherhood by performing certain marvelous and porten-
tuous deeds. She also promised to make the earth tremble, not that the demon had power so great that on his own he could move the earth or shake
the elements, but that sometimes an evil spirit, by his foreknowledge and
perception of a future earthquake, pretends that he will cause that which
he has seen will occur. By these lies and boasts he had subjected the minds
of individuals so that they obeyed him and followed wherever he commanded and led. He also made that woman walk barefooted through fro-
zen snow in harsh winter. She was not bothered in any way or injured by
that activity. She also used to say that she was hurrying to Judea and Jerusalem, making out as if she had come from there. The demon also duped
a presbyter named Rusticus here, likewise also another who was a deacon,
so that they had sexual relations with that same woman. This was discovered a little later, for suddenly one of the exorcists appeared to her. He was
a good man and one who always lived well in respect to religious disci-

est. Nam subito apparuit illi unus de exorcistis uir probatus et circa religiosam disciplinam bene semper conuersatus, qui exhortatione quoque fratrum plurimorum qui et ipse fortes ac laudabiles in fide aderant excitatus erexit se contra illum spiritum nequam reuincendum: qui subtili fallacia etiam hoc paulo ante praedixerat uenturum quendam auersum et temptatorem infidelem. Tamen ille exorcista inspiratus dei gratia fortiter restitit et esse illum nequissimum spiritum qui prius sanctus putabatur ostendit. Atqui illa mulier quae prius per praestigias et fallacias daemonis multa ad deceptionem fidelium moliebatur, inter cetera quibus plurimos deceperat etiam hoc frequenter ausa est, ut et inuocatione non contemptibili sanctificare se panem et eucharistiam facere simularet et sacrificium domino sine sacramento solitae praedicationis offerret, baptizaret quoque multos usitata et legitima uerba interrogationis usurpans, ut nihil discrepare ab ecclesiastica regula uideretur.

82. Ibid. 19 (Hartel, pp. 822-23).

Plane quoniam quidam de eorum baptismo dubitabant qui etsi nouos prophetas recipiunt eosdem tamen patrem et filium nosse nobiscum uidentur, plurimi simul conuenientes in Iconio diligentissime tractauimus et confirmauimus repudiandum esse omne omnino baptisma quod sit extra ecclesiam constitutum.

pline. This man, incited by the exhortation also of many brothers, who, themselves also being brave and worthy of praise, supported him in the faith, raised himself up against that evil spirit to conquer it. The spirit, by its subtle intrigue, had predicted a little earlier that some adverse and faithless tempter would come. Nevertheless, that exorcist, inspired by the grace of God, bravely stood his ground and showed that spirit, which was previously thought to be holy, to be most wicked. But nevertheless, that woman, who previously by the deceptions and intrigues of the demon undertook many things to deceive the faithful, among her other activities by which she had deceived many also frequently dared to pretend that by an invocation not to be despised she sanctified the bread and celebrated the eucharist, and so dared to offer the sacrifice of the Lord [not][18] without the sacrament of the usual eucharistic prayer. She also dared to baptize many, employing the customary and lawful words of interrogation so that she appeared to differ in no way from the rule of the Church.

82. Ibid. 75.19.

To be sure, since some had a question about the baptism of those who, although they receive the new prophets, nevertheless appear to recognize the Father and the Son with us, a large number of us convened in Iconium and discussed the matter very carefully. We established that every baptism which has been constituted outside the Church must be totally rejected.

---

[18]I follow Labriolle in supplying a negative here, although there is no manuscript evidence for a negative. Labriolle notes, correctly, that Firmilian's point is that the woman's actions were ritually correct.

Part III

Testimonia
from
the Fourth Century
and Later

Eusebius

83. H.E. 5.14 (GCS, ed. Schwartz, p. 458).

μισόκαλός γε μὴν ἐς τὰ μάλιστα καὶ φιλοπόνηρος ὢν ὁ τῆς ἐκκλησίας
τοῦ θεοῦ πολέμιος μηδένα τε μηδαμῶς τῆς κατὰ τῶν ἀνθρώπων ἀπολιπὼν
ἐπιβουλῆς τρόπον, αἱρέσεις ξένας αὖθις ἐπιφύεσθαι κατὰ τῆς ἐκκλησίας ἐνήργει· ὧν μὲν ἰοβόλων δίκην ἑρπετῶν ἐπὶ τῆς Ἀσίας καὶ Φρυγίας εἷρπον, τὸν μὲν δὴ παράκλητον Μοντανόν, τὰς δ' ἐξ αὐτοῦ γυναῖκας,
Πρίσκιλλαν καὶ Μαξίμιλλαν, ὡς ἂν τοῦ Μοντανοῦ προφήτιδας γεγονυίας
αὐχοῦντες.

84. *Vita Constantini* 3.63-66 (GCS, ed. Heikel, pp. 110-13).

(63) ἐπεὶ δὲ τὰς διαστάσεις ἐκποδὼν ποιησάμενος ὑπὸ σύμφωνον ἁρ-
μονίαν τὴν ἐκκλησίαν τοῦ θεοῦ κατεστήσατο, ἔνθεν μεταβὰς ἄλλο τι
γένος ἀθέων ἀνδρῶν ᾠήθη δεῖν ὥσπερ δηλητήριον τοῦ τῶν ἀνθρώπων ἀφανὲς
καταστῆσαι βίου. . . . καταπεμφθὲν δέ τι τοῖς κατ' ἔθνος ἡγεμόσι [πρόσ-
ταγμα] πᾶν τὸ τῶν τοιούτων δύσφημον φῦλον ἤλαυνεν, πρὸς δὲ τῷ νόμῳ
καὶ ζωοποιὸν διδασκαλίαν εἰς αὐτῶν πρόσωπον διετύπου, σπεύδειν ἐπὶ
μετάνοιαν παρορμῶν τοὺς ἄνδρας· σωτηρίας γὰρ ὅρμον αὐτοῖς ἔσεσθαι
τὴν ἐκκλησίαν τοῦ θεοῦ. ἐπάκουσον δ' ὅπως καὶ τούτοις διὰ τοῦ πρὸς
αὐτοὺς ὡμίλει γράμματος.

(64) Βασιλέως ἐπιστολὴ πρὸς τοὺς ἀθέους αἱρεσιώτας.

"Νικητὴς Κωνσταντῖνος Μέγιστος Σεβαστὸς αἱρετικοῖς.

Ἐπίγνωτε νῦν διὰ τῆς νομοθεσίας ταύτης, ὦ Νοουατιανοί, Οὐα-
λεντῖνοι, Μαρκιωνισταί, Παυλιανοί, οἵ τε κατὰ Φρύγας ἐπικεκλημένοι,
καὶ πάντες ἁπλῶς εἰπεῖν οἱ τὰς αἱρέσεις διὰ τῶν οἰκείων πληροῦντες
συστημάτων, ὅσοις ψεύδεσιν ἡ παρ' ὑμῖν ματαιότης ἐμπέπλεκται, καὶ
ὅπως ἰοβόλοις τισὶ φαρμάκοις ἡ ὑμετέρα συνέχεται διδασκαλία, ὡς τοὺς
μὲν ὑγιαίνοντας εἰς ἀσθένειαν τοὺς δὲ ζῶντας εἰς διηνεκῆ θάνατον
ἀπάγεσθαι δι' ὑμῶν. ὦ τῆς μὲν ἀληθείας ἐχθροί, τῆς δὲ ζωῆς πολέμιοι
καὶ ἀπωλείας σύμβουλοι· πάντα παρ' ὑμῖν τῆς ἀληθείας ἐστὶν ἐναντία,
αἰσχροῖς πονηρεύμασι συνάδοντα. . . .

(65) Τοιγάρτοι ἐπειδὴ τὸν ὄλεθρον τοῦτον τῆς ὑμετέρας ἐξωλείας
ἐπὶ πλεῖον φέρειν οὐκ ἔστιν οἷόν τε, διὰ τοῦ νόμου τούτου προαγορεύ-
ομεν, μή τις ὑμῶν συνάγειν ἐκ τοῦ λοιποῦ τολμήσῃ. διὸ καὶ πάντας
ὑμῶν τοὺς οἴκους, ἐν οἷς τὰ συνέδρια ταῦτα πληροῦτε, ἀφαιρεθῆναι
προστετάχαμεν, μέχρι τοσούτου τῆς φροντίδος ταύτης προχωρούσης,
ὡς μὴ ἐν τῷ δημοσίῳ μόνον, ἀλλὰ μηδ' ἐν οἰκίᾳ ἰδιωτικῇ ἢ τόποις τισὶν
ἰδιάζουσι τὰ τῆς δεισιδαίμονος ὑμῶν ἀνοίας συστήματα συντρέχειν.
πλὴν ὅπερ ἔστι κάλλιον, ὅσοι τῆς ἀληθινῆς καὶ καθαρᾶς ἐπιμέλεσθε θρη-

Eusebius[1]

83. *Church History* 5.14.

Being a hater of good in the highest degree and a lover of evil, the enemy of God's Church, having neglected no kind of scheme at all, again contrived to produce strange heresies against the Church, some of which crept upon Asia and Phrygia like poisonous snakes, boasting that Montanus was the Paraclete, and that his female disciples, Priscilla and Maximilla, had become the prophetesses of Montanus.

84. *Life of Constantine* 3.63-66.

(63) But when he had put disagreements aside and brought the Church of God under harmonious agreement, he turned from there to another task. He thought it necessary to render a certain kind of godless men extinct, as if they were noxious for human life. . . . And when a certain edict had been dispatched to the governors in the provinces, he drove out every blasphemous tribe of such people. But in addition to the law, he also prescribed a life-producing instruction to themselves, urging the men to hasten to repentance, for the Church of God will be a haven of salvation for them. But listen to how he also addressed these men through his letter to them.

(64) The letter of the emperor to the impious heretics.

"Constantine the Great, Conqueror, Augustus, to the heretics.

Recognize now through this legislation, O Novatians, Valentinians, Marcionites, Paulians, and you who are called Cataphrygians, and, in general, all you who set out heresies in full form through your private assemblies, with how many lies your vanity has been interwoven, how your teaching is held together with certain poisonous drugs, so that through you the healthy are made sick and the living are reduced to perpetual death. O enemies of the truth, and adversaries of the life, and counsellors of destruction, for with you all things are contrary to the truth, and in harmony with shamefully wicked things. . . .

(65) Since, therefore, we cannot further bear this destructiveness of your abomination, we make public proclamation by this law that no one of you should henceforth dare to assemble. On this account we have ordered that you be deprived of all your houses in which you hold these assemblies. This attention extends not only to the assemblies of your foolish superstition gathering in a public place, but in a private house or any private places. But the better way is for as many of you as care about true and pure religion

---

[1]For sources pertaining to Montanism in Eusebius, see above, numbers 21, 22, 23, 24, 25, 28, and 29.

σκείας, εἰς τὴν καθολικὴν ἐκκλησίαν ἔλθετε καὶ τῇ ταύτης ἁγιότητι κοινωνεῖτε, δι' ἧς καὶ τῆς ἀληθείας ἐφικέσθαι δυνήσεσθε, κεχωρίσθω δὲ παντελῶς τῆς τῶν ἡμετέρων καιρῶν εὐκληρίας ἡ τῆς διεστραμμένης διδασκαλίας ὑμῶν ἀπάτη, λέγω δὲ ἡ τῶν αἱρετικῶν καὶ σχισματικῶν ἐναγής τε καὶ ἐξώλης διχόνοια. . . . ὑπὲρ δὲ τοῦ τῆς θεραπείας ταύτης καὶ ἀναγκαίαν γενέσθαι τὴν ἰσχὺν προσετάξαμεν, καθὼς προείρηται, ἅπαντα τὰ τῆς δεισιδαιμονίας ὑμῶν συνέδρια, πάντων φημὶ τῶν αἱρετικῶν τοὺς εὐκτηρίους, εἴ γε εὐκτηρίους ὀνομάζειν οἴκους προσήκει, ἀφαιρεθέντας ἀναντιρρήτως τῇ καθολικῇ ἐκκλησίᾳ χωρίς τινος ὑπερθέσεως παραδοθῆναι, τοὺς δὲ λοιποὺς τόπους τοῖς δημοσίοις προσκριθῆναι, καὶ μηδεμίαν ὑμῖν εἰς τὸ ἑξῆς τοῦ συνάγειν εὐμάρειαν περιλειφθῆναι, ὅπως ἐκ τῆς ἐνεστώσης ἡμέρας ἐν μηδενὶ τόπῳ μήτε δημοσίῳ μήτ' ἰδιωτικῷ τὰ ἀθέμιτα ὑμῶν συστήματα ἀθροισθῆναι τολμήσῃ. προτεθήτω."

(66) Οὕτω μὲν τὰ τῶν ἑτεροδόξων ἐγκρύμματα βασιλικῷ προστάγματι διελύοντο, ἠλαύνοντό τε οἱ θῆρες οἱ [τε] τῆς τούτων δυσσεβείας ἔξαρχοι. τῶν δ' ὑπὸ τούτων ἠπατημένων οἱ μὲν νόθῳ φρονήματι βασιλικῆς ἀπειλῆς φόβῳ τὴν ἐκκλησίαν ὑπεδύοντο, τὸν καιρὸν κατειρωνευόμενοι· ἐπεὶ καὶ διερευνᾶσθαι τῶν ἀνδρῶν τὰς βίβλους διηγόρευεν ὁ νόμος, ἡλίσκοντό τ' ἀκπειρημένας κακοτεχνίας μετιόντες, οὗ δὴ χάριν πάντα ἔπραττον εἰρωνείᾳ τὴν σωτηρίαν ποριζόμενοι, οἱ δὲ καὶ σὺν ἀληθεῖ τάχα που λογισμῷ ηὐτομόλουν ἐπὶ τὴν τοῦ κρείττονος ἐλπίδα.

Theodore of Heraclea

85. *In Iohannis* 14.15 (Combefis, *Bibliotheca Patrum Concionatoria* 4 [1662] p. 466).

Nam si illis non diligentibus solum, sed et ultro mortem pro ipso appetentibus, pro eo ac pollicitus erat, Paracletum non misit, ut haereticorum e Phrygia impietas sentit, in sacris mentitus Euangeliis comperietur. Sin autem, veritas cum sit, sanctum iis Spiritum misit, temere errantes comminiscuntur, ac per Montanum et Priscillam, qui ducentis triginta circiter annis apostolica sequiores gratia emerserunt, missum Paracletum dicunt.

Cyril of Jerusalem

86. *Catechesis* 16, *de spiritu sancto* 1.8 (PG 33.928-29).

Μισείσθωσαν οἱ Κατάφρυγας, καὶ Μοντανός, ὁ τῶν κακῶν ἔξαρχος, καὶ αἱ δύο δῆθεν αὐτοῦ προφήτιδες, Μαξιμίλλα καὶ Πρισκίλλα. ὁ γὰρ Μοντανὸς οὗτος, ὁ παρεξεστηκὼς καὶ μανιώδης ἀληθῶς (οὐ γὰρ ἂν εἴτε τοιαῦτα, εἰ μὴ ἐμαίνετο), ἐτόλμησεν εἰπεῖν ἑαυτὸν εἶναι τὸ ἅγιον

to enter the Catholic Church and share in its holiness, through which you can attain the truth. But let the deceit of your distorted teaching be totally removed from the good fortune of our times; what I mean is the accursed and pernicious discord of heretics and schismatics. . . . And that there might be the power necessary to effect this cure, we have ordered, as has already been said, that all the assemblies of your superstition, I mean the houses of prayer of all the heretics, if indeed it is fitting to call them houses of prayer, having been taken from you incontrovertibly, be delivered to the Catholic Church without any delay, and that all the remaining places be held to be state property, and that no provision for assembling be left you for the future, that from this day your lawless assemblies may not dare gather in any place public or private. Let it be published.''

(66) In this way the secret gatherings of the heterodox were destroyed by royal decree, and the beasts, the leaders of their impiety, were driven out. Some who had been deceived by them, because they feared the emperor's threat, slipped into the Church with a spurious intention, concealing their thoughts at the time. Since the law also commanded that the books of the men be searched out, those pursuing the forbidden evil arts were caught. For this reason these did everything in pretence to procure their own safety. But there were also others who came over to the better hope with an attitude that was apparently sincere.

Theodore of Heraclea

85. *On the Gospel of John* 14.15.

For if, as the impiety of the heretics from Phrygia supposes, (the Lord) did not send the Paraclete, as he had indeed promised, to those (apostles) who not only loved him, but furthermore were eager to die on his behalf, he will be discovered to have lied in the Sacred Gospels. But if, since he is the truth, he sent the Holy Spirit to them, (the Phrygians) contrive rashly in error when they say the Paraclete was sent by means of Montanus and Priscilla who emerged as leaders about two hundred and thirty years following the period of the Apostolic grace.

Cyril of Jerusalem

86. *Catechetical Lectures* 16.8

Let the Cataphrygians be hated, and Montanus, the leader of their evils, and his two supposed prophetesses, Maximilla and Priscilla. For this Montanus, who was truly mad and crazy (for he would not have said such things had he not been mad), had the audacity to say that he himself was the Holy

Πνεῦμα· ὁ ἀθλιώτατος, καὶ πάσης ἀκαθαρσίας καὶ ἀσελγείας πεπληρωμέ-
νος· αὔταρκες γὰρ τοῦτο διὰ συσσήμων εἰπεῖν, τῶν παρουσῶν γυναικῶν
σεμνότητος ἕνεκεν. Καὶ Πέπουζαν μικρότατον κωμύδριον ἐν τῇ Φρυγίᾳ
καταλαβὼν, ψευδῶς Ἱερουσαλὴμ ὀνομάσας τοῦτο· καὶ ἀθλιώτατα παιδία
γυναικῶν μικρὰ σφάττων, καὶ κατακόπτων εἰς ἀθέμιτον βρῶσιν, προφάσει
τῶν καλουμένων παρ' αὐτοῖς μυστηρίων (διὸ μέχρις πρώην ἐν τῷ διωγμῷ,
τοῦτο ποιεῖν ἡμεῖς ὑποπτευόμεθα, διὰ τὸ κἀκείνους τοὺς Μοντανοὺς,
ψευδῶς μὲν ὁμωνύμος δὲ, καλεῖσθαι Χριστιανοὺς), ἐτόλμησεν ἑαυτὸν
εἰπεῖν ἅγιον Πνεῦμα, ὁ πάσης ἀσεβείας καὶ ἀπανθρωπίας πεπληρωμένος,
ὁ ἀναπολόγητον ἔχων τὴν καταδίκην.

Council of Laodicia

87. Canon 8 (Hefele, *Histoire des conciles* [1907] 1,2, p. 1000).

Περὶ τοῦ, τοὺς ἀπὸ τῆς αἱρέσεως τῶν λεγομένων Φρυγῶν ἐπιστρέφον-
τας, εἰ καὶ ἐν κλήρῳ νομιζομένῳ παρ' αὐτοῖς τυγχάνοιεν, εἰ καὶ μέ-
γιστοι λέγοιντο, τοὺς τοιούτους μετὰ πάσης ἐπιμελείας κατηχεῖσθαί
τε καὶ βαπτίζεσθαι ὑπὸ τῶν τῆς Ἐκκλησίας ἐπισκόπων τε καὶ πρεσβυτέρων.

Pseudo-Athanasius

88. *Athanasii contra omnes haereses* 10 (PG 28.520).

Εἴπωμεν καὶ πρὸς τὸν δείλαιον Φρύγα τὸν λέγοντα μετὰ τὴν ἐπιδημίαν
τοῦ Σωτῆρος ἐπιδεδημηκέναι Μοντανὸν καὶ Πρίσκιλλαν. ταῦτα γρεῶν
πτύσματα ἴσως ὡς κεκεπφωμένων. πῶς δύναται μετὰ τὴν ἐπιδημίαν τοῦ
Σωτῆρος πάλιν προφήτης ἐπιδεδημηκέναι; οὐκ ἤκουσας, ὅτι "Ὁ νόμος καὶ
οἱ προφῆται ἕως Ἰωάννου"; ἄκουσον σύ, λαὲ τοῦ Κυρίου. ὥσπερ βασιλεὺς
μέλλει κατανταν ἔν τινι πόλει, καὶ ἀποστέλλει σημάντορας λέγων· Ἰδοὺ
ποίῳ σχήματι μέλλω ἔρχεσθαι. ἐὰν δὲ ἐπιδημήσῃ, καὶ ἐπιγνῶσι τὴν ἐνση-
μανθεῖσαν ἐπιδημίαν, προσκυνοῦντες αὐτὸν, οὐκ ἔτι χρεία τοῦ σημαί-
νοντος· αὐτοψὶ γὰρ ἑώρακαν αὐτὸν τὸν σημανθέντα. ἐὰν δέ τις εἰπῇ ἐν
αὐτῇ τῇ πόλει, ὅτι μέλλει ἔσεσθαι ὁ βασιλεὺς οὐκ ἂν καταπτύσωσιν
αὐτοῦ οἱ ἐν τῇ πόλει λέγοντες, ὅτι· Ὃν ἑωράκαμεν καὶ ἔχομεν μεθ'
ἑαυτῶν, πῶς σὺ λέγεις, ὅτι σημαίνω ὑπάρχειν ἄλλον; καὶ οὗτοι τοίνυν
σὺν ταῖς ἄλλαις αἱρέσεσιν ἀπώλοντο.

Debate of a Montanist and an Orthodox Christian

89. Text from G. Ficker, ZKG (1905) 445-63.

Μοντανιστὴς εἶπεν· Ἡμεῖς τῷ ἁγίῳ Παύλῳ πειθόμενοι Μοντανὸν
ἐδεξάμεθα, ὡς ἔχοντα τὸ τέλειον τοῦ ἁγίου πνεύματος, τουτέστι(ν) τὸν

Spirit, this wretched man, filled with all impurity and disregard for moral restraints, for it is sufficient to hint at this on account of the dignity of the women present. And after he had laid hold of Pepuza, a most insignificant little village in Phrygia, and falsely named it Jerusalem, and had slaughtered the wretched little children of the women and cut them up for unlawful food on the falsely alleged motive of their so-called mysteries (wherefore until recently, in the persecution, we were suspected of doing this because those Montanists shared the name Christian with us, though falsely), he who was filled with impiety and inhumanity, who had an irrevocable sentence, had the audacity to say that he himself was the Holy Spirit.

Council of Laodicia

87. Canon 8.

Concerning the fact that those who are converted from the heresy of those called Phrygians, even if they should belong to their supposed clergy, or be said to be great, such people should be instructed with all care, and should be baptized by the bishops and presbyters of the Church.

Pseudo-Athanasius

88. Sermon Against All Heresies 10.

Let us also address the wretched Phrygian who says that Montanus and Priscilla have appeared after the appearance of the Savior. These words are the slobberings of old women, as they have been equally duped. How can a prophet have appeared again after the appearance of the Savior? Have you not heard that "the law and the prophets were until John" (cf. Luke 16:16)? Listen, O people of the Lord. As a king about to arrive at some city sends men to signal his coming, saying: "Behold, I am about to come in such dress," once he makes his appearance, and they recognize the appearance which was signalled, and bow down to him, there is no further need of one to signal him, for they have seen him who was signalled with their own eyes. But if someone in that very city should say, "The king will soon be here," would not those in the city spit at him and say: "We have seen him and have him with us. How can you say, 'I declare that there is another?' " These, therefore, have perished with the other heresies.

Debate of a Montanist and an Orthodox Christian

89. Text from G. Ficker, *Zeitschrift für Kirchengeschichte* (1905) 446-63.

The Montanist said: We, persuaded by Saint Paul, have accepted Montanus as possessing the perfection of the Holy Spirit, that is the Paraclete.

114 THE MONTANIST ORACLES AND TESTIMONIA

παράκλητον. αὐτὸς γὰρ εἶπε(ν) Παῦλος· Ὅταν δὲ ἔλθῃ τὸ τέλειον, τὸ ἐκ μέρους καταργηθήσεται· καὶ· ἐκ μέρους γινώσκομεν καὶ ἐκ μέρους προφητεύομεν.
Ὀρθόδοξος· Ἀληθεύων εἶπεν ὁ ἅγιος Παῦλος ἢ ψευδόμενος;
—Μ: Ἀληθεύων.
—Ο: Κατήργηται οὖν τὰ τοῦ ἀποστόλου;
—Μ: Μὴ γένοιτο.
—Ο: Πῶς οὖν εἶπεν· ὅταν δὲ ἔλθῃ τὸ τέλειον, τὸ ἐκ μέρους καταργηθήσεται, ὡς ἀληθεύων ἢ ὡς ψευδόμενος;
—Μ: Αὐτὸς εἶπεν· ἐκ μέρους γινώσκομεν καὶ ἐκ μέρους προφητεύομεν.
—Ο: Ἀληθῶς λέγεις, ἀλλ᾽ οὐκ ἐνόησας, ὅτι πᾶς λόγος ἐν τῷ αἰῶνι τούτῳ μέρος ἐστὶ τοῦ ἐν τῷ μέλλοντι αἰῶνι φανησομένου μυστηρίου. νῦν γὰρ πιστεύομεν εἰς πατέρα καὶ υἱὸν καὶ ἅγιον πνεῦμα καὶ ἐν τοῖς λόγοις ἔχομεν· τότε δὲ ἡ γνῶσις, ὅτε πρόσωπον πρὸς πρόσωπον ὀψώμεθα. ἄρτι πιστεύομεν, ὅτι αὐτὸς κύριος ἐν κελεύσματι, ἐν φωνῇ ἀρχαγγέλου καὶ ἐν σάλπιγγι θεοῦ καταβήσεται ἀπ᾽ οὐρανοῦ· τότε δὲ πρόσωπον πρὸς πρόσωπον. τῶν οὖν πραγμάτων κατὰ πρόσωπον ὀφθέντων τὸ ἐκ μέρους καταργηθήσεται. οὐκέτι γὰρ ἀπὸ λόγων ἔχομεν τὴν πίστιν, ἀλλὰ ἀπ᾽ αὐτῆς τῆς θέας, καὶ τοῦτό ἐστι(ν) τὸ ἐκ μέρους [καταρ]γηθήσεται.
—Μ: Καταργηθήσεται οὖν καὶ πίστις;
—Ο: Καταργηθήσεται. ἀντὶ τοῦ παύεται. ἀμέλει αὐτῆς ὅλης τῆς περικοπῆς μνησθῶμεν τῇ συνέσει τοῦ πνεύματος. λέγει δὲ οὕτως· Ἀγάπη οὐδέποτε πίπτει· εἴτε δὲ προφητεία, καταργηθήσεται. ἐκ μέρους γὰρ γινώσκομεν καὶ ἐκ μέρους προφητεύομεν· ὅταν δὲ ἔλθῃ τὸ τέλειον, τὸ ἐκ μέρους καταργηθήσεται. ὅτε ἤμην νήπιος, ὡς νήπιος ἐλάλουν, ἐλογιζόμην ὡς νήπιος· ὅτε γέγονα ἀνήρ, κατήργηκα τὰ τοῦ νηπίου. βλέπομεν γὰρ ἄρτι δι᾽ ἐσόπτρου ἐν αἰνίγματι, τότε δὲ πρόσωπον πρὸς πρόσωπον· ἄρτι γιγνώσκω(μεν) ἐκ μέρους, τότε δὲ ἐπιγνώσομαι καθὼς καὶ ἐπεγνώσθην. ὁρᾷς, ὅτι καταργηθήσεται ἐπὶ τὸ βέλτιον· ὅ ἐστι τί; παρόντων τῶν πιστευομένων παύσεται ἡ πίστις. οὐκέτι γὰρ πιστεύομεν, ἀλλ᾽ ὁρῶμεν. πίστις δὲ βλεπομένη οὐκ ἔστι πίστις. ὃ γὰρ βλέπει τις, τί καὶ πιστεύει; καὶ τοῦτό ἐστι· βλέπομεν γὰρ ἄρτι δι᾽ ἐσόπτρου ἐν αἰνίγματι, τότε δὲ πρόσωπον πρὸς πρόσωπον. τότε, πότε; δῆλον, ὅτε τὸ τέλος.
—Μ: Ἰδοὺ οὖν ἦλθε(ν) Μοντανὸς ὁ παράκλητος καὶ ἔδωκεν ἡμῖν τὸ τέλειον.
—Ο: Τὸ τέλειον ὅταν ἔλθῃ, τὸ ἐκ μέρους καταργηθήσεται ἢ οὔ;

For Paul himself said: "When perfection has come, that which is incomplete will be abolished" (1 Cor 13:10), and: "We know in part and we prophesy in part" (1 Cor 13:9).

The Orthodox replied: Did Saint Paul speak the truth or did he lie?

—M: He spoke the truth.

—O: Then have the words of the apostle been abolished?

—M: By no means.

—O: How, then, did he say: "When perfection has come, that which is incomplete will be abolished" (1 Cor 13:10), as the truth, or as a lie?

—M: He himself said: "We know in part, and we prophesy in part" (1 Cor 13:9).

—O: You speak the truth, but you have not considered that every word in this age is part of the mystery which will be revealed in the age to come. For now we believe in the Father and the Son and the Holy Spirit, and we posses them in words; but then we shall know, when we shall see face to face (cf. 1 Cor 13:12). Now we believe that "the Lord himself will descend from heaven with a word of command, with the call of the archangel and the trumpet of God" (1 Thess 4:16); and then we will see him face to face. Therefore, when the realities have been seen face to face, that which is incomplete will be abolished. For we will no longer have faith based on words, but on sight itself; and this is what it means that that which is incomplete will be abolished.

—M: Then faith too will be abolished?

—O: That is correct. What will take its place when it ceases? By all means let us recall the whole passage itself to understand the Spirit. Now he speaks as follows: "Love never fails, but as for prophecy, it will be abolished. For we know in part, and we prohesy in part, but when perfection has come, that which is incomplete will be abolished. When I was a child, I spoke as a child, I reasoned as a child; when I became a man, I put aside childish ways. For now we see in a mirror enigmatically, but then face to face; now I know in part, but then I shall know fully, just as I also have been fully known" (cf. 1 Cor 13:8-12). You see that it will be abolished for what is better. And what is this? Faith will cease when the things which are believed are present. For we shall no longer believe, but we shall see. And faith which is seen is not faith. For why does one also believe something which he sees? And this is the meaning of: "For now we see in a mirror enigmatically, but then face to face" (1 Cor 13:12). When is the "then"? Obviously when the end has come.

—M: Behold, then, Montanus, the Paraclete, has come and has given us perfection.

—O: When perfection has come, will that which is incomplete be abol-

—M: Οὕτως γέγραπται.

—O: Ὁρῶμεν δέ, ὅτι Μοντανὸς καταργεῖται ἕως σήμερον· τὰ δὲ τοῦ ἁγίου Παύλου αὔξουσιν.

—M: Καί τοι γε ὑμεῖς τὰ Παύλου καταργεῖτε λέγοντες μετὰ Χριστὸν μὴ εἶναι προφήτας.

—O: Πλανᾶστε, μὴ εἰδότες τὰς γραφὰς μηδὲ ἃ διδάσκει ἡ ἐκκλησία. ἡμεῖς γὰρ ἴσμεν, ὅτι καὶ μετὰ Χριστὸν προφῆται. αὐτὸς γὰρ Ἰησοῦς εἶπεν, ὅτι· Ἰδοὺ ἐγὼ ἀποστελῶ πρὸς ὑμᾶς προφή[τας] καὶ σοφοὺς καὶ γραμματεῖς καὶ ἐξ αὐτῶν ἀποκτενεῖτε καὶ σταυρώσετε καὶ ἐξ αὐτῶν μαστιγώσετε ἐν ταῖς συναγωγαῖς ὑμῶν. καὶ Παῦλος λέγει· Ζηλοῦτε τὰ χαρίσματα τὰ μείζονα, μᾶλλον δέ, ἵνα προφητεύητε. καὶ πάλιν λέγει· Ἐὰν οὖν συνέλθῃ ἡ ἐκκλησία ὅλη ἐπὶ τὸ αὐτὸ καὶ πάντες γλώσσαις λαλῶσιν, εἰσέλθωσι[ν] δὲ ἰδιῶται [ἢ] ἄπιστοι, οὐκ ἐροῦσιν, ὅτι μαίνεσθε; ἐὰν δὲ πάντες προφητεύσωσι[ν], εἰσέλθῃ δέ τις ἄπιστος ἢ ἰδιώτης, ἐλέγχεται ὑπὸ πάντων, ἀνακρίνεται ὑπὸ πάντων, τὰ κρυπτὰ τῆς καρδίας αὐτοῦ καὶ φανερὰ γίνεται ὑπὸ πάντων, καὶ οὕτως πεσὼν ἐπὶ πρόσωπον προσκυνήσει τῷ θεῷ ἀπαγγέλλων, ὅτι ὄντως θεὸς ἐστὶν ἐν ἡμῖν.

—M: Πῶς οὖν ὑμεῖς λέγετε, ὅτι μετὰ Χριστὸν οὐκ ἐγένετό τις προφήτης;

—O: Ἡμεῖς καὶ μετὰ Χριστὸν ὁμολογοῦμεν γεγενῆσθαι προφήτας καὶ αὐτοὺς τοὺς ἀποστόλους ἔχειν καὶ τῆς προφητείας τὸ χάρισμα. πῶς γὰρ Πέτρος τὸν Ἀνανίαν καὶ τὴν Σαπφείραν ἤλεγξε νοσφισαμένους ἐκ τῆς τιμῆς τοῦ χωρίου, εἰ μὴ χάρισμα προφητείας εἶχε; πῶς δὲ καὶ ὁ ἅγιος Παῦλος ἔλεγε τὰ μέλλοντα ἐπ᾽ ἐσχάτου τῶν ἡμερῶν ἔσεσθαι, εἰ μὴ καὶ αὐτὸς εἶχε[ν] χάρισμα προφητείας;

—M: Πῶς οὖν οὐ δέχεσθε Μοντανὸν τὸν ἅγιον;

—O: Ὅτι ψευδοπροφήτης ἦν οὐδὲν ἀληθὲς λέγων.

—M: Μὴ βλασφήμει, ἄνθρωπε, τὸν παράκλητον.

—O: Ἐγὼ αἰνῶ καὶ δοξάζω τὸν παράκλητον, τὸ πνεῦμα τῆς ἀληθείας, Μοντανὸν δὲ βδελύσσομαι ὡς τὸ βδέλυγμα τῆς ἐρημώσεως.

—M: Πῶς;

—O: Πρῶτον, ὅτι λέγει· Ἐγώ εἰμι ὁ πατὴρ καὶ ἐγώ εἰμι ὁ υἱὸς καὶ ἐγὼ ὁ παράκλητος.

—M: Ὑμεῖς δὲ λέγετε, ὅτι· Ἄλλος ἐστὶν ὁ πατὴρ καὶ ἄλλος ὁ υἱὸς καὶ ἄλλο τὸ πνεῦμα τὸ ἅγιον.

—O: Ἐὰν ἡμεῖς λέγωμεν, οὐδὲν ἀξιόπιστον· ἐὰν δὲ υἱὸς διδάσκῃ, ἄλλον

ished or not?

—M: It has been so written.

—O: But we see that Montanus is being done away with to this very day, but the teachings of Saint Paul are growing in power.

—M: And yet you abolish the teachings of Paul when you say there are no prophets after Christ.[2]

—O: You err, because you know neither the Scriptures nor what the Church teaches. For we know that there are prophets also after Christ. For Jesus himself said: "Behold I am sending you prophets and wise men and scribes. Some of them you will kill and crucify, and some of them you will beat in your synagogues" (Matt 23:34). And Paul says: "Be zealous for the greater gifts" (1 Cor 12:31), "and especially that you may prophesy" (1 Cor 14:1). And again he says: "If, then, the whole Church should gather at the same place and all speak in tongues, and the uninitiated or unbelievers should enter, will they not say that you are mad? But if all prophesy, and an unbeliever or uninitiated person should enter, he is reproved by all, he is judged by all, the secrets of his heart are also made manifest by all, and thus he will fall on his face and worship God and declare that God is really among us" (cf. 1 Cor 14:23-25).

—M: How then do you say that there was no prophet after Christ?

—O: We also admit that there have been prophets after Christ, and that the apostles themselves also had the gift of prophecy. For how did Peter rebuke Ananias and Sapphira who appropriated something for themselves from the price of the field (cf. Acts 5:3), if he did not have the gift of prophecy? And how too did Saint Paul speak about the things that will be at the end of days (cf. 1 Cor 15), if he too did not himself have the gift of prophecy?

—M: On what basis, then, do you not accept Montanus, the saint?

—O: Because he was a false prophet, and said nothing true.

—M: Man, do not blaspheme the Paraclete!

—O: I praise and glorify the Paraclete, the Spirit of truth, but I loathe Montanus as the abomination of desolation (cf. Matt 24:15).

—M: Why?

—O: First, because he says: "I am the Father, and I am the Son, and I am the Paraclete."

— M: But you yourselves say: The Father is one, and the Son is another, and the Holy Spirit another.

—O: If we should say it, it is nothing worthy of faith, but if the Son teaches

---

[2]Cf. the use of Luke 16:16 by the orthodox in number 88.

εἶναι τὸν πατέρα καὶ ἄλλον τὸν παράκλητον, τὸ πνεῦμα τὸ ἅγιον, ἀνάγκη πείθεσθαι.

—Μ: Δεῖξον, ποῦ διδάσκει.

—Ο: Ὅταν λέγῃ· Ἐγὼ ἐρωτήσω τὸν πατέρα, καὶ ἄλλον παράκλητον δώσει ὑμῖν, τὸ πνεῦμα τῆς ἀληθείας, ἵνα ᾖ μεθ᾽ ὑμῶν εἰς τὸν αἰῶνα, ὃ ὁ κόσμος οὐ δύναται λαβεῖν, ὅτι οὐ θεωρεῖ αὐτό· ὑμεῖς δὲ γιγνώσκετε, ὅτι παρ᾽ ὑμῖν μένει καὶ ἐν ὑμῖν ἔσται. πῶς οὐχὶ φανερῶς ἄλλον παράκλητον ἀκούων ἄλλον παρ᾽ αὐτὸν τὸν λέγοντα νοεῖς;

—Μ: Εἰ ἄλλος καὶ ἄλλος καὶ ἄλλος, τρεῖς θεοί.

—Ο: Μὴ γένοιτο.

—Μ: Πῶς· μὴ γένοιτο;

—Ο: Ὅτι ἡ θεία γραφὴ τὰ τὴν αὐτὴν ἔχοντα φύσιν καὶ βουλὴν ἑνοῖ.

—Μ: Μὴ γένοιτο.

—Ο: Ἀκούεις Παύλου τοῦ ἀποστόλου λέγοντος, ὅτι· Ἐν Χριστῷ Ἰησοῦ οὐκ ἔνι δοῦλος οὐδὲ ἐλεύθερος· οὐκ ἔνι ἄρσεν καὶ θῆλυ· οὐκ ἔνι Ἕλλην καὶ Ἰουδαῖος, ἀλλὰ πάντες ἐν Χριστῷ Ἰησοῦ εἷς ἐστε. καὶ αὐτοῦ τοῦ Χριστοῦ ἀκούομεν λέγοντος περὶ τοῦ ἀνδρὸς καὶ τῆς γυναικός, ὅτι οὐχέτι εἰσὶ δύο, ἀλλὰ σὰρξ μία. εἰ δὲ τὰ ἐν διαστάσει ὄντα οὐκέτι εἰσὶ δύο διὰ τὸ ταὐτὸν τῆς βουλῆς καὶ τῆς φύσεως, πῶς δυνατὸν τὰ ἀσώματα ὑπὸ ἀριθμὸν καὶ θέσιν γενέσθαι.

—Μ: Οὐκ ἔστιν οὖν εἷς θεός;

—Ο: Εἷς θεὸς τῷ λόγῳ τῆς φύσεως, τῇ δὲ ὑποστάσει ἄλλος ἐστὶν ὁ πατὴρ καὶ ἄλλος ὁ υἱὸς καὶ ἄλλος τὸ πνεῦμα τὸ ἅγιον.

—Μ: Πῶς οὖν ὁ υἱὸς λέγει· Ἐν ἐκείνῃ τῇ ἡμέρᾳ γνώσονται, ὅτι ἐγὼ ἐν τῷ πατρὶ καὶ ὁ πατὴρ ἐν ἐμοί; καὶ πάλιν λέγει· Ἄν τις ἀγαπᾷ με, τὸν λόγον μου τηρήσει, καὶ ὁ πατήρ μου τηρήσει αὐτόν, καὶ πρὸς αὐτὸν ἐλευσόμεθα καὶ μονὴν παρ᾽ αὐτῷ ποιησόμεθα. ὁ μὴ ἀγαπῶν με τοὺς λόγους μου οὐ τηρεῖ· καὶ ὁ λόγος ὁ ἐμὸς οὐκ ἔστιν ἐμός, ἀλλὰ τοῦ πέμψαντός με. ταῦτα λελάληκα ὑμῖν παρ᾽ ὑμῖν μένων· ὁ δὲ παράκλητος, τὸ πνεῦμα τὸ ἅγιον, ὃ πέμψει ὁ πατὴρ ἐν τῷ ὀνόματί μου, ἐκεῖνο ὑμᾶς διδάξει πάντα καὶ ὑπομνήσει πάντα, ἃ εἶπον ἐγώ.

—Ο: Ἄκων συναινεῖς τῷ λόγῳ τῆς ἀληθείας. εἰ γὰρ πείθῃ τοῖς εἰρημένοις, ὀρθοποδήσεις πρὸς τὴν ἀλήθειαν. ἤκουσας, ὅτι λέγει· Ἐν ἐκείνῃ τῇ ἡμέρᾳ γνώσεσθε, ὅτι ἐγὼ ἐν τῷ πατρὶ καὶ ὁ πατὴρ ἐν ἐμοί, καὶ οὐκ εἶπεν· Ἐν ἐκείνῃ τῇ ἡμέρᾳ γνώσεσθε πάντες, ὅτι ἐγὼ πατὴρ καὶ υἱός εἰμι. ἀκούεις δὲ, ὅτι λέγει· Καὶ πρὸς αὐτὸν ἐλευσόμεθα ἐγὼ καὶ ὁ πατήρ· οὐκ εἶπε πρὸς αὐτόν· Ἐλεύσομαι ἐγὼ καὶ ὁ πατὴρ καὶ ὁ υἱὸς καὶ μονὴν ποιήσω· ἀλλὰ καὶ τὸ· Ὁ λόγος ὁ ἐμὸς οὐκ ἔστιν ἐμός, ἀλλὰ τοῦ

that the Father is one, and the Paraclete, the Holy Spirit, another, it must be believed.

—M: Show where he teaches it.

—O: When he says: "I will ask the Father, and he will give you another Paraclete, the Spirit of truth, that he may be with you forever. The world cannot receive him, because it does not see him; but you know him, because he abides with you, and will be in you" (cf. John 14:16-17). How is it that when you hear him mention clearly another Paraclete, you do not think of another besides him who is speaking?

—M: If there is one, and another, and another, there are three Gods.

—O: By no means.

—M: How do you say, "By no means"?

—O: Because the divine Scripture unites those which have the same nature and will.

—M: By no means.

—O: You hear Paul the apostle saying: "In Christ Jesus there is neither slave nor free; there is no male and female; there is no Greek and Jew, but you are all one in Christ Jesus" (cf. Gal 3:28). And we hear Christ himself say of husband and wife, that they are no longer two, but one flesh (cf. Matt 19:6). Now if things which exist separately are no longer two because of an identity of will and nature, how can incorporeal things be subject to number and position?

—M: Is there not, then, one God?

—O: God is one by reason of his nature, but in hypostasis the Father is one, the Son another, and the Holy Spirit another.

—M: How, then, does the Son say: "In that day they will know that I am in the Father and the Father is in me" (cf. John 14;10)? And again he says: "If anyone love me, he will keep my word, and my Father will keep him, and we will come to him and make our home with him. He who does not love me does not keep my words, and my word is not mine, but his who sent me. I have spoken these words to you while I am with you; but the Paraclete, the Holy Spirit, whom the Father will send in my name, will teach you all things, and will remind you of all the words which I have spoken" (cf. John 14:23-26).

—O: You are involuntarily in agreement with the true doctrine. For if you believe in what you have said, you will walk in the truth. You have heard that he says: "In that day you will know that I am in the Father and the Father in me." He did not say: "In that day you will all know that I am the Father and the Son." And you hear that he says: "I and the Father will come to him." He did not say: "I and the Father and the son will come to him and make our home." But also, the saying: "My word is not mine,

πέμψαντός με, οὐδὲν ἕτερον δηλοῖ ἢ τῶν ὑποστάσεων τὴν ἰδιότητα· καὶ ὅταν δέ· ταῦτα λελάληκα ὑμῖν παρ' ὑμῖν μένων, ἀκούσῃς, ὁ δὲ παράκλητος τὸ πνεῦμα τὸ ἅγιον, ὃ πέμψει ὁ πατὴρ ἐν τῷ ἐμῷ ὀνόματι, ἐκεῖνος διδάξει ὑμᾶς πάντα, ἃ εἶπον ὑμῖν, πῶς οὐ σαυτὸν ἐρυθριάσας ὁμολογήσεις τῶν τριῶν ὑποστάσεων τὴν εὐκρίνειαν;

—Μ: Ἐν ἡμέρᾳ . . . κρίσεως αἱ τρεῖς ὑποστάσεις καθέζονται κρῖναι ζῶντας καὶ νεκρούς.

—Ο: Τὸ καθέζονται σωματικῶς ἀκούων πνευματικῶς νόει, ἵνα μὴ τόπους καὶ χωρισμοὺς σωμάτων ὑπολάβῃς, ἀλλὰ τὸ πάγιον τῆς φύσεως. πανταχοῦ γὰρ ὁ πατήρ, πανταχοῦ ὁ υἱός, πανταχοῦ τὸ πνεῦμα τὸ ἅγιον, καὶ ὥσπερ οὐδὲν μέσον ἐστὶ(ν) νοῦ καὶ λόγου καὶ πνοῆς, οὕτως οὐδὲν μέσον πατρὸς καὶ υἱοῦ καὶ ἁγίου πνεύματος. νοῆσαι δὲ δεῖ τὸν πατέρα τέλειον ἐν τελείᾳ ὑποστάσει, καὶ τὸν υἱὸν τέλειον ἐν τελείᾳ ὑποστάσει, καὶ τὸ πνεῦμα τὸ ἅγιον τέλειον ἐν τελείᾳ ὑποστάσει, παρὰ τοῦ πατρὸς ἐκπορευόμενον.

—Μ: Πῶς ἐγχωρεῖ; αὐτὸς λέγει· Ἐγὼ καὶ ὁ πατὴρ ἕν ἐσμεν.

—Ο: οὐκ εἶπεν· Ἕν εἰμι, ἀλλ' ἕν ἐσμεν, ἵνα τῶν ὑποστάσεων τὸ ἐνυπόστατον γνῶμεν. ἐκεῖνο δὲ θαυμάζω, ὅτι μέμνησαι τῶν εὐαγγελίων καὶ οὐκ ὀρθοποδεῖς πρὸς τὴν ἀλήθειαν αὐτῶν.

—Μ: Ἐγὼ τοῖς εὐαγγελίοις πείθομαι.

—Ο: Δεῖξον οὖν, ποῦ γέγραπται ἐν τοῖς εὐαγγελίοις, ὅτι· Ἐγώ εἰμι καὶ ὁ πατὴρ καὶ ὁ υἱὸς καὶ τὸ πνεῦμα.

—Μ: Ὁ ἑωρακὼς ἐμὲ ἑώρακεν τὸν πατέρα.

—Ο: Ἀλλὰ τὸν πατέρα· οὐχ ἑαυτὸν φήσας εἶναι πατέρα, ἀλλὰ τοιοῦτον οἷον τὸν πατέρα.

—Μ: θέλεις γνῶναι, ὅτι ὀρφανοί εἰσιν οἱ μὴ δεχόμενοι τὸν παράκλητον; ἄκουε τοῦ Κυρίου λέγοντος· Συμφέρει ὑμῖν, ἵνα ἐγὼ ἀπέλθω· ἐὰν μὴ ἀπέλθω, ὁ παράκλητος οὐκ ἐλεύσεται πρὸς ὑμᾶς· ἐὰν δὲ πορευθῶ, πέμψω αὐτὸν πρὸς ὑμᾶς· καὶ ἐλθὼν ἐκεῖνος ἐλέγξει τὸν κόσμον περὶ ἁμαρτίας καὶ περὶ δικαιοσύνης καὶ περὶ κρίσεως. καὶ μετ' ὀλίγα λέγει· Οὐκ ἀφήσω ὑμᾶς ὀρφανούς· ἔρχομαι πρὸς ὑμᾶς. οἱ τοίνυν μὴ δεξάμενοι τὸν παράκλητον ὀρφανοί εἰσιν.

—Ο: Ἀληθῶς οὐ μόνον ὀρφανοί εἰσιν, ἀλλὰ καὶ ἄθεοι οἱ μὴ δεξάμενοι τὸν παράκλητον.

—Μ: Διὰ τί οὖν οὐ δέχεσθε αὐτόν;

—Ο: Ἡμεῖς καὶ ἐδεξάμεθα καὶ δεχόμεθα, ὑμεῖς δὲ οὔτε ἔγνωτε οὔτε ἐδέξασθε, ἀλλ' ἠπατήθητε παρὰ Μοντανοῦ, καὶ τοιαύτην ἀπάτην, ἣν οὐκ ἂν ἠπατήθησαν ἄνθρωποι μὴ γενόμενοι σκεύη τοῦ διαβόλου. πρῶτον γὰρ

but his who sent me,'' shows nothing else than the distinctive character of the hypostases. And also when you hear, "I have spoken these words to you while I am with you, but the Paraclete, the Holy Spirit, whom the Father will send in my name, will teach you all the things which I have said,'' how, in embarrassment, do you not admit the clear distinction of the three hypostases?

—M: On the day of judgment the three hypostases sit to judge the living and the dead (cf. 1 Pet 4:5).

—O: When you hear the physical expression, "they sit,'' understand it spiritually, so that you do not take it to mean physical places and separations, but stability of nature. For the Father is everywhere, and the Son is everywhere, and the Holy Spirit is everywhere; and just as there is nothing between mind and speech and breath, so there is nothing between the Father, Son, and Holy Spirit. And you must understand that the Father is perfect, and the Holy Spirit, which proceeds from the Father, is perfect, with a perfect hypostasis.

—M: How is this possible? He himself says: "I and the Father are one" (John 10:30).

—O: He did not say: "I am one,'' but: "We are one,'' that we may know the independent existence of the hypostases. But I am amazed at the fact that you have remembered the Gospels, but you do not walk in their truth.

—M: I believe in the Gospels.

—O: Show me, then, where it is written in the Gospels: "I am the Father, and the Son, and the Spirit.''

—M: "He who has seen me has seen the Father" (John 14:9).

—O: But "the Father.'' He did not say that he himself was the Father, but that it was as though [one saw] the Father.

—M: Are you willing to recognize that those who do not receive the Paraclete are orphans? Listen to the Lord as he says: "It is to your benefit that I go away; If I do not go away, the Paraclete will not come to you. But if I go, I will send him to you, and when he has come he will reprove the world of sin, and of justice, and of judgment" (John 16:7-8). And after a few words, he says: "I will not leave you orphans; I will come to you" (John 14:18). Those, therefore, who have not received the Paraclete are orphans.

—O: As a matter of fact, those who have not received the Paraclete are not only orphans, but also atheists.

—M: Then why do you not receive him?

—O: We both have received him and continue to do so. It is you who have neither known him nor received him, but have been deceived by Montanus, and your deception is of the kind that men would not experience un-

πείθει ὑμᾶς εἰπεῖν τοὺς ἀποστόλους ὀρφανοὺς καὶ τὸν Κύριον Ἰησοῦν ψεύστην τὸν εἰρηκότα αὐτοῖς· Οὐκ ἀφήσω ὑμᾶς ὀρφανούς· ἔρχομαι πρὸς ὑμᾶς.

—Μ: Ἡμεῖς γὰρ λέγομεν, ὅτι οὐκ ἦν ὁ Χριστὸς ἐν τοῖς ἀποστόλοις;
—Ο: Ὁ λέγων, ὅτι οὐκ ἦν ἐν τοῖς ἀποστόλοις ὁ παράκλητος, ἀλλ' ἐν Μοντανῷ πάντως οὐδὲ τὸν Χριστὸν δώσει ἐν αὐτοῖς. οὐδεὶς γὰρ δύναται εἰπεῖν Κύριον Ἰησοῦν, εἰ μὴ ἐν πνεύματι ἁγίῳ. καὶ εὑρέθησαν καθ' ὑμᾶς ὀρφανοὶ καὶ ὁ Κύριος Ἰησοῦς Χριστὸς ψεύστης, καὶ Μοντανὸς ὁ τοῦ Ἀπόλλωνος ἱερεὺς ἀληθής. τί δὲ ταύτης τῆς ἀπάτης ἐστὶν ἀθλιώτερον;
—Μ: Λέγομεν καὶ ἡμεῖς, ὅτι οἱ ἀπόστολοι ἔσχον ἐκ τοῦ πνεύματος, ἀλλ' οὐ τὸ πλήρωμα τοῦ παρακλήτου εἶχον.
—Ο: Καὶ ὁ λέγων· Ἡμεῖς δὲ πάντες ἀνακεκαλυμμένῳ προσώπῳ τὴν δόξαν Κυρίου κατοπτριζόμεθα, οὐκ εἶχε τὸ πνεῦμα, ἀλλὰ Μοντανὸς ὁ ἱερεὺς τοῦ εἰδώλου;
—Μ: Παῦλος γὰρ οὐκ ἦν διώκτης;
—Ο: Ἀλλὰ σκεῦος ἐκλογῆς γέγονε.
—Μ: Καὶ Μοντανός.
—Ο: Ἀλλ' ἐκ τούτου γινώσκεται ὁ ἀληθὴς προφήτης ἐκ τοῦ τὰ τοῦ θεοῦ αὐτὸν λέγειν, καὶ ὁ ψευδοπροφήτης ἐν ᾧ τὰ ἐναντία αὐτὸν τῷ θεῷ λέγειν.
—Μ: Καὶ πότε Μοντανὸς ἐναντία τῷ θεῷ εἶπεν;
—Ο: Ὅταν μὲν ὁ θεὸς καὶ σωτὴρ ἡμῶν λέγῃ τὸν παράκλητον ἄλλον εἶναι παρ' ἑαυτὸν καὶ τοῖς ἀποστόλοις ἀποστέλλειν αὐτὸν ἐπαγγέλλεται, Μοντανὸς δὲ λέγει· Ἐγώ εἰμι ὁ πατὴρ καὶ ὁ υἱὸς καὶ τὸ ἅγιον πνεῦμα, δῆλον, ὅτι ἐναντία τῷ υἱῷ λέγει καὶ ἔστι ψευδοπροφήτης.
—Μ: Καὶ ἡμεῖς λέγομεν, ὅτι εἶχον οἱ ἀπόστολοι τὸν ἀρραβῶνα τοῦ πνεύματος, ἀλλ' οὐ τὸ πλήρωμα.
—Ο: Ὅτι οἱ ἀπόστολοι ναοὶ τοῦ πνεύματος ἦσαν καὶ πάντες οἱ ἅγιοι, ἄκουε Παύλου λέγοντος· Οὐκ οἴδατε, ὅτι τὰ σώματα ὑμῶν ναὸς τοῦ ἐν ὑμῖν ἁγίου πνεύματός ἐστι(ν) καὶ ἐν ἄλλοις· ὑμεῖς δὲ οὐκ ἐστὲ ἐν σαρκί, ἀλλ' ἐν πνεύματι, εἴπερ πνεῦμα θεοῦ οἰκεῖ ἐν ὑμῖν. τοσούτων οὖν μαρτυριῶν οὐσῶν τῶν λεγουσῶν, ὅτι τὸ πνεῦμα ἦν καὶ ἔστιν ἐπὶ τοὺς πιστεύοντας, πῶς σὺ λέγεις μὴ εἶναι ἐπὶ τοὺς ἀποστόλους;
—Μ: Εἶπον, ὅτι ἀρραβὼν ἦν τοῦ πνεύματος ἐν αὐτοῖς.
—Ο: Αὐτὸ τὸ πνεῦμα ἀρραβών ἐστι τῶν ἐπηγγελμένων ἀγαθῶν, οἷον ἐπαγγελίαν ἔχομεν ἀφθαρσίας. πόθεν ἡ ἀπόδειξις, ὅτι ἐσόμεθα ἄφθαρτοι ἐκ τοῦ πνεύματος, οὗ ἔδωκεν ἡμῖν, καὶ οὕτως πᾶσαν ἐπαγγελίαν ἐλπίζομεν πληροῦσθαι ἐκ τῆς τοῦ πνεύματος τοῦ ἁγίου παρουσίας ὡς εἶναι αὐτὸ ἀρραβῶνα τῶν ἐπηγγελμένων ἀγαθῶν; λέγει δὲ οὕτως ὁ Παῦλος· Ὁ δὲ

less they had become the instruments of the devil. For in the first place, he persuades you to say that the apostles were orphans, and that the Lord Jesus was a liar, who said to them: "I will not leave you orphans; I will come to you" (John 14:18).

—M: Do we say that the Christ was not in the apostles?

—O: He who says that the Paraclete was not in the apostles, but in Montanus, will in no way grant that Christ was in them. "For no one can say Jesus is Lord, except in the Holy Spirit" (cf. 1 Cor 12:3). And, according to you, they were found to be orphans, and the Lord Jesus Christ to be a liar, and Montanus, the priest of Apollo, to be true. Now what is more wretched than this fraud?

—M: We also say that the apostles possessed some of the Spirit, but they did not possess the fulness of the Paraclete.

—O: And did he who said: "But we all with unveiled face behold the glory of the Lord" (cf. 2 Cor 3:18), not possess the Spirit, but Montanus, the priest of the idol, did?

—M: Was Paul not a persecutor?

—O: But he became a "chosen vessel" (Acts 9:15).

—M: So did Montanus.

—O: But the true prophet is known by the fact that he speaks the words of God, and the false prophet in that he says things that are contrary to God.

—M: When did Montanus say things contrary to God?

—O: When God, even our Savior, says that the Paraclete is other than himself and promises to send him to the apostles (cf. John 14:16), but Montanus says: "I am the Father, and the Son, and the Holy Spirit." It is obvious that he is saying things contrary to the son, and is a false prophet.

—M: We also say that the apostles possessed the pledge of the Spirit, but not the fulness (cf. 2 Cor 1:22; 5:5).

—O: That the apostles and all the saints were temples of the Spirit, hear Paul when he says: "Do you not know that your bodies are a temple of the Holy Spirit in you" (1 Cor 6:19) and elsewhere: "But you are not in flesh, but in spirit, if the Spirit of God dwells in you" (Rom 8:9). Therefore, since there are so many testimonies which say that the Spirit was and is on the believers, how do you say he is not on the apostles?

—M: I said that the pledge of the Spirit was in them.

—O: The Spirit himself is the pledge of the good things which have been promised. For example, we have the promise of incorruption. Whence is the proof that we shall be incorruptible? It is from the Spirit which he has given us. In this way we have hope that every promise will be fulfilled, on the basis of the presence of the Holy Spirit, as the Spirit himself is the pledge of the good things which have been promised. And Paul speaks as follows:

βεβαιῶν ἡμᾶς σὺν ὑμῖν εἰς Χριστὸν καὶ χρίσας ἡμᾶς θεός, ὁ καὶ σφρα-
γισάμενος ἡμᾶς καὶ δοὺς τὸν ἀρραβῶνα τοῦ πνεύματος ἐν ταῖς καρδίαις
ἡμῶν, ὅ ἐστιν ὅτι ἐβεβαιώθη σὺν ὑμῖν εἰς Χριστόν. πόθεν τοῦτο ἐκ τοῦ
πνεύματος, οὗ δέδωκεν ἡμῖν; ἡ γὰρ ἀπόδειξις, ὧν ἐπηγγείλατο Χριστός,
ἐκ τῆς τοῦ πνεύματος παρουσίας ἐστίν· ἐπηγγείλατο βασιλείαν οὐρα-
νῶν, ἐπηγγείλατο ἀφθαρσίαν, ἀθανασίαν, σοφίαν, ἁγιασμόν, ἀπολύ-
τρωσιν. τίς ταύτης τῆς δωρεᾶς ἀπόδειξις καὶ πόθεν ἡμῖν τὸ ἀσφαλές;
ἐκ τοῦ πνεύματος, οὗ ἔδωκεν ἡμῖν. ὁ γὰρ τὸ αἴτιον τῶν χαρισμάτων δεδωκὼς
δώσει καὶ τὰ ἑπόμενα καὶ διὰ τοῦτο ἀρραβὼν εἴρηται τὸ πνεῦμα τῆς
μελλούσης ἀποκαλύπτεσθαι δόξης.
—Μ: Διὰ τί δὲ καὶ τὰς ἁγίας Μαξίμιλλαν καὶ Πρίσκιλλαν ἀποστρέφεσθε
καὶ λέγετε μὴ ἐξὸν εἶναι προφητεύειν γυναιξίν; οὐκ ἦσαν καὶ τῷ
Φιλίππῳ θυγατέρες τέσσαρες προφητεύουσαι καὶ Δεββῶρα οὐκ ἦν
προφῆτις; καὶ ὁ ἀπόστολος οὐ λέγει· Πᾶσα γυνὴ προσευχομένη [ἢ] προφητεύουσα ἀκατακαλύπτῳ τῇ κεφαλῇ εἰ οὐκ ἔστιν γυναιξὶν προφητεύειν
οὐδὲ προσεύχεσθαι; εἰ δὲ προσεύχονται, καὶ προφητευέτωσαν.
—Ο: Ἡμεῖς τὰς προφητείας τῶν γυναικῶν οὐκ ἀποστρεφόμεθα, καὶ ἡ ἁγία
Μαρία προεφήτευσε λέγουσα· Ἀπὸ τοῦ νῦν μακαριοῦσί με πᾶσαι αἱ γενεαί. καὶ ὡς καὶ αὐτὸς εἶπας ἦσαν τῷ ἁγίῳ Φιλίππῳ θυγατέρες προφητεύουσαι καὶ Μαρία ἡ ἀδελφὴ Ἀαρὼν προεφήτευσεν. Ἀλλ᾽ οὐκ ἐπιτρέπομεν
αὐταῖς λαλεῖν ἐν ἐκκλησίαις οὐδὲ αὐθεντεῖν ἀνδρῶν, ὥστε καὶ βίβλους
ἐξ ὀνόματος αὐτῶν γράφεσθαι. τοῦτο γάρ ἐστιν ἀκατακαλύπτως αὐτὰς
προσεύχεσθαι καὶ προφητεύειν, καὶ οὖν κατήσχυνε τὴν κεφαλὴν του-
τέστι(ν) τὸν ἄνδρα. Μὴ γὰρ οὐκ ἠδύνατο ἡ ἁγία θεοτόκος Μαρία ἐξ ὀνόματος ἑαυτῆς βιβλία γράψαι; Ἀλλ᾽ οὐκ ἐποίησεν, ἵνα μὴ καταισχύνῃ τὴν
κεφαλὴν αὐθεντοῦσα τῶν ἀνδρῶν.
—Μ: Τὸ γὰρ ἀκατακαλύπτῳ τῇ κεφαλῇ προσεύχεσθαι ἢ προφητεύειν ἐστὶ
τὸ μὴ γράφειν βιβλία;
—Ο: Καὶ πάνυ.
—Μ: Ἐὰν οὖν λέγῃ ἡ ἁγία Μαρία· Ἀπὸ τοῦ νῦν μακαριοῦσί(ν) με πᾶσαι
αἱ γενεαί, μετὰ παρρησίας λέγει καὶ ἀνακεκαλυμμένως, ἢ οὔ;
—Ο: Ἔχει κάλυμμα τὸν εὐαγγελιστήν. οὐ γὰρ ἐξ ὀνόματος αὐτῆς τὸ
εὐαγγέλιον ἀναγέγαπται.
—Μ: Μή μοι τὰς ἀλληγορίας ὡς δόγματα λάμβανε.
—Ο: Μάλιστα μὲν οὖν ὁ ἅγιος Παῦλος καὶ τὰς ἀλληγορίας εἰς τὰς τῶν
δογμάτων βεβαιώσεις ἔλαβε λέγων, ὅτι· Ἀβραὰμ δύο γυναῖκας ἔσχεν,
ἅτινά εἰσιν ἀλληγορούμενα. αὗται γάρ εἰσιν αἱ δύο διαθῆκαι. δῶμεν

"But he who confirms us with you in Christ, and who has anointed us, is God, who has also sealed us and given us the pledge of the Spirit in our hearts" (2 Cor 1:21-22). That is to say that he was confirmed with you in Christ. Whence is it that this depends on the Spirit which he has given us? The proof of Christ's promises depends on the presence of the Spirit. He promised the kingdom of heaven; he promised incorruptibility, immortality, wisdom, sanctification, redemption. What is the proof of this gift, and whence is our assurance? From the Spirit which he has given us. For he who has given the cause of the gifts will also give their consequences, and for this reason the Spirit has been said to be the pledge of the glory which will be revealed (cf. Rom 8:18).

—M: And why do you also repudiate the saints Maximilla and Priscilla, and say that it is not permissible for a woman to prophesy? Did not Philip have four daughters who prophesied, and was not Deborah a prophetess (cf. Acts 21:9; Judg 4:4)? And does not the apostle say: "Every woman who prays or prophesies with uncovered head . . . " (1 Cor 11:5)? If it is not possible for a woman to prophesy, neither can she pray. But if they can pray, let them also prophesy.

—O: We do not repudiate the prophecies of women. Even the holy Mary prophesied and said: "Henceforth all generations will call me blessed" (Luke 1:48). And as even you yourself said, the holy Philip had four daughters who prophesied, and Mary the sister of Aaron prophesied (cf. Exod 15:20f). But we do not permit them to speak in Churches nor to have authority over men (cf. 1 Tim 2:12), with the result that books too are written under their names. For this is what it means for women to pray and prophesy without a veil, and this, then, has brought shame on her head (cf. 1 Cor 11:5), that is her husband, For could not the holy Mary, mother of God, have written books under her own name? But she did not, so that she might not bring shame on her head by exercising authority over men.

—M: Is not writing books the meaning of the statement about praying or prophesying with uncovered head?

—O: It certainly is.

—M: Then if the holy Mary says, "Henceforth all generations will call me blessed" (Luke 1:48), is she being outspoken and speaking in an unveiled manner or not?

—O: She has the evangelist as her veil. For the Gospel has not been written under her name.

—M: Don't take allegories as though they were doctrines with me.

—O: Saint Paul especially, then, also took allegories for the confirmation of dogmas when he said: "Abraham had two wives" (cf. Gal 4:22), "which things are allegories. For they are two covenants" (Gal 4:24). But let us

δέ, ὅτι οὐ διὰ ἀλληγορίαν τὸ τῆς κεφαλῆς κάλυμμα. στῆσόν μοι ἐπὶ πάντων τὴν ἀλληγορίαν, ἐὰν ᾖ πενιχρὰ γυνὴ καὶ μὴ ἔχῃ, τί κατακαλύπτεται, οὐ δεῖ αὐτὴν προσεύχεσθαι οὐδὲ προφητεύειν; —Μ: Καὶ δύναται εἰς τοσοῦτον εἶναι πενιχρά, ὡς μὴ ἔχειν τί σκεπάσεται; —Ο: Πολλάκις μὲν εἴδομεν οὕτως πενιχρὰς γυναῖκας ὥστε μὴ ἔχειν, τί σκεπάσονται. ἐπειδὴ δὲ αὐτὸς οὐ θέλεις εἶναι πενιχρὰς γυναῖκας ὥστε μὴ ἔχειν τί σκεπάσονται, τί ποιεῖς ἐπὶ τῶν βαπτιζομένων; Ἄρα οὐ δεῖ αὐτὰς βαπτιζομένας προσεύχεσθαι; τί δὲ λέγεις καὶ ἐπὶ τῶν ἀνδρῶν τῶν πολλάκις διὰ κάκωσιν σκεπαζομένων τὴν κεφαλήν; Ἄρα καὶ τούτους κωλύεις προσεύχεσθαι ἢ προφητεύειν; —Μ: Ἐν ἐκείνῃ τῇ ὥρα, ᾖ προσεύχεται ἢ προφητεύει, ἀνακαλύπτεται. —Ο: Οὐ δεῖ αὐτὸν ἀδιαλείπτως προσεύχεσθαι, ἀλλὰ παρακούειν τοῦ ἀποστόλου διδάσκοντος αὐτόν, τοῦ λέγοντος· Ἀδιαλείπτως προσεύχεσθε. καὶ τὴν γυναῖκα δὲ συμβουλεύεις βαπτιζομένην μὴ προσεύχεσθαι. —Μ: Διὰ τοῦτο οὖν οὐ δέχεσθε Πρίσκιλλαν καὶ Μαξίμιλλαν, ἐπειδὴ βιβλία συνέταξαν; —Ο: Οὐ διὰ τοῦτο μόνον, ἀλλ᾽ ὅτι καὶ ψευδοπροφήτιδες γεγόνασι μετὰ τοῦ ἐξάρχου αὐτῶν Μοντανοῦ. —Μ: Πόθεν, ὅτι ψευδοπροφήτιδες γεγόνασιν; —Ο: Τὰ αὐτὰ Μοντανῷ εἰρήσασιν; —Μ: Ναί. —Ο: Ἠλέγχθη δὲ Μοντανὸς ἐναντία ταῖς θείαις γραφαῖς εἰρηκώς, καὶ αὐταὶ ἄρα αὐτῷ συνεκβληθήσονται.

Ambrosiaster

90. *Ad Timotheum prima* 3.11 (CSEL 81, ed. Vogels, p. 268).

Catafrygae occasionem erroris captantes, propter quod post diaconos mulieres adloquitur, etiam ipsas diaconissas (diaconas) debere ordinari vana praesumptione defendunt, cum sciant apostolos septem diaconos eligisse. numquid nulla mulier tunc idonea inventa est, cum inter undecim apostolos sanctas mulieres fuisse legamus? sed cum (ut) heretici animum suum verbis, non sensu legis adstruere videantur, apostoli verbis contra sensum

grant that the covering of the head does not have reference to an allegory. Put a stop to the allegorical meaning for me in the presence of everyone: Suppose there is a poor woman and she does not have the means to veil herself. Must she neither pray nor prophesy?

—M: Is it possible for a woman to be so poor that she does not have the means to cover herself?

—O: We have frequently seen women so poor that they did not have the means to cover themselves. But since you yourself are not willing to admit that there are women so poor that they do not have the means to cover themselves, what do you do in the case of those who are baptized? Is it not necessary that the women themselves pray when they are baptized? And what do you say also in the case of men who often cover their head on account of distress? Do you also prevent them from praying or prophesying?

—M: He uncovers himself at the time he prays or prophesies.

—O: It is not necessary, then, for him to pray without ceasing, but he must disregard the teaching of the apostle who says: ''Pray without ceasing'' (1 Thess 5:17). And you also counsel a woman not to pray when she is baptized.

—M: Is it because Priscilla and Maximilla composed books that you do not receive them?

—O: It is not only for this, but also because they were false prophetesses with their leader Montanus.

—M: Why do you say they were false prophetesses?

—O: Did they not say the same things as Montanus?

—M: Yes.

—O: Montanus has been refuted as having said things contrary to the divine Scriptures. Therefore, these women too will be cast out along with him.

Ambrosiaster

90. *Commentary on the First Epistle to Timothy* 3.11

The Cataphrygians, who strive after an opportunity for error, argue with vain presumption that they themselves too ought to be ordained as deaconesses because he addresses women after the deacons (cf. 1 Tim 3:8-11), although they know that the apostles chose seven deacons (cf. Acts 6:3ff). Was no woman found to be fit then, when we read that there were holy women among the eleven apostles? But as the heretics appear to add their own meaning to the words, not understanding the sense of law, they rely on the words of the apostle against the meaning of the apostle, so that although he teaches that a woman ought to be silent in the Church (cf. 1

nituntur apostoli, ut, cum ille mulierem in ecclesia in silentio esse debere praecipiat, illi e contra etiam auctoritatem in ecclesia vindicent ministerii.

91. *Ad Thesalonicenses prima* 5 (CSEL 81, ed. Vogels, pp. 232-33).

hinc est unde in alia (unde et Iohannis apostoli) epistola: nolite, inquit, omni spiritui credere, sed probate spiritus, si ex deo sunt. quia, si multa bona dicat, in aliquo autem quod fidei adversum est promat, sciatur non esse spiritus sanctus. nihil enim erroris poterit in sancto spiritu reperiri. . . . quemadmodum in Montano et Priscilla et Maximilla profetis Catafrygarum spiritus mundi imitatione quadam boni simulavit, ut per multa verisimilia necnon et vera mentiretur se esse spiritum sanctum.

Basil of Caesarea

92. Epist. 188.1 (*Saint Basile Lettres* II [1961], ed. Courtonne, pp. 121-22).

Τὸ μὲν οὖν περὶ τοὺς Καθαροὺς ζήτημα καὶ εἴρηται πρότερον, καὶ καλῶς ἀπεμνημόνευσας, ὅτι δεῖ τῷ ἔθει τῶν καθ' ἑκάστην χώραν ἕπεσθαι, διὰ τὸ διαφόρως ἐνεχθῆναι περὶ τοῦ βαπτίσματος αὐτῶν τοὺς τότε περὶ τούτων διαλαβόντας˙ τὸ δὲ τῶν Πεπουζηνῶν οὐδένα μοι λόγον ἔχειν δοκεῖ˙ καὶ ἐθαύμασα πῶς κανονικὸν ὄντα τὸν Διονύσιον παρῆλθεν. ἐκεῖνο γὰρ ἔκρινον οἱ παλαιοὶ δέχεσθαι βάπτισμα, τὸ μηδὲν τῆς πίστεως παρεκβαῖνον˙ ὅθεν τὰς μὲν αἱρέσεις ὠνόμασαν, τὰ δὲ σχίσματα, τὰς δὲ παρασυναγωγάς. αἱρέσεις μὲν τοὺς παντελῶς ἀπερρηγμένους, καὶ κατ' αὐτὴν τὴν πίστιν ἀπηλλοτριωμένους, σχίσματα δὲ τοὺς δι' αἰτίας τινὰς ἐκκλησιαστικὰς καὶ ζητήματα ἰάσιμα πρὸς ἀλλήλους διενεχθέντας˙ παρασυναγωγὰς δὲ τὰς συνάξεις τὰς παρὰ τῶν ἀνυποτάκτων πρεσβυτέρων ἢ ἐπισκόπων καὶ παρὰ τῶν ἀπαιδεύτων λαῶν γινομένας. . . .

Αἱρέσεις δὲ, οἷον ἡ τῶν Μανιχαίων, καὶ Οὐαλεντίνων, καὶ Μαρκιονιστῶν, καὶ αὐτῶν τούτων τῶν Πεπουζηνῶν˙ εὐθὺς γὰρ περὶ αὐτῆς τῆς εἰς θεὸν πίστεως ἡ διαφορά. ἔδοξε τοίνυν τοῖς ἐξ ἀρχῆς, τὸ μὲν τῶν αἱρετικῶν παντελῶς ἀθετῆσαι, τὸ δὲ τῶν ἀποσχισάντων, ὡς ἔτι ἐκ τῆς ἐκκλησίας ὄντων, παραδέξασθαι˙ τοὺς δὲ ἐν ταῖς παρασυναγωγαῖς, μετανοίᾳ ἀξιολόγῳ καὶ ἐπιστροφῇ βελτιωθέντας, συνάπτεσθαι πάλιν τῇ ἐκκλησίᾳ, ὥστε πολλάκις καὶ τοὺς ἐν βαθμῷ, συναπελθόντας τοῖς ἀνυποτάκτοις, ἐπειδὰν μεταμεληθῶσιν, εἰς τὴν αὐτὴν παραδέχεσθαι τάξιν.

Οἱ τοίνυν Πεπουζηνοὶ προδήλως εἰσὶν αἱρετικοί˙ εἰς γὰρ τὸ πνεῦμα τὸ ἅγιον ἐβλασφήμησαν, Μοντανῷ καὶ Πρισκίλλῃ τὴν τοῦ παρακλήτου

Tim 2:11-12), they, on the contrary, even demand the authority of ministry in the Church.

91. *On the Second Epistle to the Thessalonians* 5.

Hence there is also in another epistle (of the apostle John): "Do not believe every spirit," he says, "but test the spirits, whether they are of God" (1 John 4:1). Even if he should say many good things, but in some one thing express something which is contrary to the faith, it would be known that he is not the Holy Spirit. For one will find no error in the Holy Spirit.

For example, in Montanus and Priscilla and Maximilla, the prophets of the Cataphrygians, the spirit of the world simulated the Spirit in a kind of imitation of the good, so that by means of many things which seemed true, and also by some that were, he falsely declared himself to be the Holy Spirit.

Basil of Caesarea

92. Epistle 188.1.

Your inquiry concerning the Cathari has been discussed previously, and you have recalled correctly that we must follow the custom of those in each region because those who then made decisions about these matters held different views concerning their baptism. But the baptism of the Pepuzans seems to me to have no status, and I am amazed how it escaped the notice of Dionysius who was versed in ecclesiastical regulations. For the ancients decided to accept that baptism which deviates from the faith in no way. For this reason they specified heresies, schisms, and rival assemblies. Heresies are those who are broken off completely, and alienated in relation to the faith itself; schisms are those who are at odds with one another because of some ecclesiastical matters and subjects of dispute which are curable; and rival assemblies are assemblies which have come into existence from insubordinate presbyters or bishops and from uninstructed laymen. . . .

Now so far as heresies are concerned, there is, for example, that of the Manichaeans, and that of the Valentinians, and that of the Marcionites, and that of these very Pepuzans, for there is an immediate difference concerning the faith in God itself. It seemed good, therefore, to those of old to reject completely the baptism of the heretics, but to admit that of the schismatics, since they still belonged to the Church, and to join those in the rival assemblies to the Church again after they had been improved by repentance worthy of mention and conversion. Consequently they often received into the same rank even those in orders who branched off together with the insubordinate, when they repented.

The Pepuzans, then, are obviously heretical. For they have blasphemed against the Holy Spirit by unlawfully and shamelessly attributing the name

προσηγορίαν ἀθεμίτως καὶ ἀναισχύντως ἐπιφημίσαντες. εἴτε οὖν ὡς ἀνθρώπους θεοποιοῦντες, κατάκριτοι· εἴτε ὡς τὸ πνεῦμα τὸ ἅγιον τῇ πρὸς
ἀνθρώπους συγκρίσει καθυβρίζοντες, καὶ οὕτω τῇ αἰωνίῳ καταδίκῃ ὑπ-
εύθυνοι, διὰ τὸ ἀσυγχώρητον εἶναι τὴν εἰς τὸ πνεῦμα τὸ ἅγιον
βλασφημίαν. τίνα οὖν λόγον ἔχει τὸ τούτων βάπτισμα ἐγκριθῆναι τῶν
βαπτιζόντων εἰς πατέρα καὶ υἱὸν καὶ Μοντανὸν ἢ Πρίσκιλλαν; οὐ γὰρ
ἐβαπτίσθησαν οἱ εἰς τὰ μὴ παραδεδομένα ἡμῖν βαπτισθέντες. ὥστε, εἰ
καὶ τὸν μέγαν Διονύσιον τοῦτο παρέλαθεν, ἀλλ᾿ ἡμῖν οὐ φυλακτέον τὴν
μίμησιν τοῦ σφάλματος.

Epiphanius

93. *Panarion* 48.14-15 (GCS, ed. Holl, pp. 238-41).

(14) Τιμῶσι δὲ οἱ τοιοῦτοι καὶ τόπον τινὰ ἔρημον ἐν τῇ Φρυγίᾳ,
Πέπουζάν ποτε καλουμένην πόλιν, νῦν δὲ ἠδαφισμένην, καὶ φασιν ἐκεῖσε
κατιέναι τὴν ἄνωθεν Ἱερουσαλήμ. ὅθεν ἐκεῖ ἀπερχόμενοι μυστήριά τινα
ἐπιτελοῦσιν ἐν τῷ τόπῳ καὶ ἁγιάζουσιν [ἑαυτούς], ὡς ὑπολαμβάνουσιν.
ἔστι γὰρ καὶ τὸ γένος ἐν τῇ Καππαδοκίᾳ καὶ Γαλατίᾳ καὶ ἐν τῇ
προειρημένῃ Φρυγίᾳ, ὅθεν κατὰ Φρύγας ἡ αἵρεσις καλεῖται· ἀλλὰ καὶ
ἐν Κιλικίᾳ καὶ ἐν Κωνσταντινουπόλει τὸ πλεῖστον.

Ἵνα δὲ μηδὲν καταλείψωμεν τῶν πρὸς ὄνομα ἑκάστης αἱρέσεως ὑφ᾿ ἡμῶν
προδεδηλωμένης, καὶ περὶ τοῦ Τασκοδρουγιτῶν ὀνόματος αὖθις ἐροῦμεν·
ἔστι γὰρ τὸ ὄνομα τοῦτο ἢ ἐν αὐτῇ ταύτῃ ἢ ἐν τῇ μετ᾿ αὐτὴν τῶν
Κυϊντιλλιανῶν καλουμένη· ἀπ᾿ αὐτῶν γὰρ τούτων ὁρμᾶται καὶ τοῦτο τὸ
ὄνομα. καλοῦνται δὲ διὰ τοιαύτην αἰτίαν Τασκοδρουγῖται· τασκὸς παρ᾿
αὐτοῖς πάσσαλος καλεῖται, δρουγγος δὲ μυκτὴρ εἴτ᾿ οὖν ῥύγχος καλεῖται, καὶ ἀπὸ τοῦ τιθέναι ἑαυτῶν τὸν δάκτυλον τὸν λεγόμενον λιχανὸν
ἐπὶ τὸν μυκτῆρα ἐν τῷ εὔχεσθαι, δῆθεν κατηφείας χάριν καὶ ἐθελοδι-
καιοσύνης, ἐκλήθησαν ὑπό τινων Τασκοδρουγῖται τουτέστιν πασσαλο-
ρυγχῖται. ἐν ταύτῃ δὲ τῇ αἱρέσει ἢ ἐν τῇ συζύγῳ αὐτῆς τῇ τῶν
Κυϊντιλλιανῶν· εἴτ᾿ οὖν Πρισκιλλιανῶν καὶ Πεπουζιανῶν καλουμένη,
δεινόν τι καὶ ἀθέμιτον ἔργον φασὶ γίνεσθαι. παῖδα γὰρ κομιδῇ νήπιον
ὄντα κατὰ ἑορτήν τινα δι᾿ ὅλου τοῦ σώματος κατακεντῶντες χαλκαῖς ῥα-
φίσι τὸ αἷμα αὐτοῦ προσπορίζονται ἑαυτοῖς, εἰς ἐπιτήδευσιν δῆθεν
θυσίας.

(15) Ἀρκεῖ δὲ ἡμῖν ἃ καὶ περὶ ταύτης εἰρήκαμεν, ὦ ἐπιπόθητοι.
ἐπηγγειλάμεθα γὰρ ἀπὸ ἑκάστης ἧς ἴσμεν αἱρέσεως μὴ φθονῆσαι, ἀλλὰ
ὑποφῆναι ἅ τε δι᾿ ἀκοῆς ἅ τε διὰ συγγραμμάτων, ἅ τε δι᾿ ἐγγράφων καὶ ἃ

Paraclete to Montanus and Priscilla. They are condemned, therefore, either because they make men divine, or because they insult the Holy Spirit by comparing him to men, and are thus liable to eternal condemnation because blasphemy against the Holy Spirit is unforgivable (cf. Matt 12:31). What basis to be accepted, then does the baptism have of these who baptize into the Father and the Son and Montanus or Priscilla? For they have not been baptized who have been baptized into names which have not been handed down to us. So, although this escaped the notice of the great Dionysius, we, however, must not preserve the imitation of the error.

Epiphanius[3]

93. *Panarion* 48.14-15.

(14) And such people also honor a certain deserted place in Phrygia, a city once called Pepuza, but which has now been razed, and they say the Jerusalem from above will descend there. This is why they go and celebrate certain mysteries at the place and consecrate it, as they think. For the sect exists also in Cappadocia and Galatia, and in Phrygia which I mentioned previously, whence the sect is called Cataphrygians. It is found also in Cilicia, and, above all, in Constantinople.

But to omit nothing of those matters pertaining to the name of each heresy previously exposed by us, we will again comment on the name of the Tascodrougites. For this name is either in this very heresy, or in that one which followed it named from the Quintillians, for this name too originates from these very people. Now they are called Tascodrougites for the following reason. They call a peg "tascos," and a nostril, also a nose, "drouggos." And from the fact that they place their finger, which is called the forefinger, on their nostril when they pray, to be sure because of sorrow or affected righteousness, some called them Tascodrougites, that is, "Nose Pegs."

Now in this heresy, or in that called its yoke-fellow, that of the Quintillians, also of the Priscillians and Pepuzians, they say some terrible wicked deed is done. For at a certain feast, they pierce a child, just an infant, throughout its whole body with bronze needles and procure its blood for themselves, in their devotion to sacrifice, of course.

(15) But what we have said about this heresy, my friends, is sufficient. For we have promised to hold nothing back from each heresy, but to bring to light the things which we have grasped, some through hearing, some by

---

[3]For Epiphanius, *Panarion* 48.1-13, see number 26 above.

τε ὑπό τινων ἀληθῶς πιστωσαμένων τὴν ἡμῶν ἔννοιαν κατειλήφαμεν, ἵνα μηδέν τι περιττὸν ὧν γε ἔγνωμεν ποιησάμενοι [μὴ] ὑπὸ συνείδησιν δόξωμεν εἶναι μὴ ὀρθὰ καὶ αὐτοὶ ἐφευρίσκοντες κατὰ ἀνθρώπων λέγειν.

. . . ὡς δὲ καὶ τὴν ἐνταῦθα ἱκανῶς ἔχειν ἡγηφσάμενοι περὶ ταύτης τῆς αἱρέσεως ἐργασίαν σὺν δυνάμει Χριστοῦ ἐπὶ τὰς ἑξῆς προβῆναι ἑαυτοὺς ἐπιδῶμεν, τὸν μὲν ἰὸν καὶ τὰ ἀγκιστροειδῆ τῶν ὀδόντων αὐτῆς φάρμακα ἐν τῷ τῆς ἀληθείας τοῦ σταυροῦ ξύλῳ καταθλάσαντες, τῇ αἱμορροίᾳ ἐχίδνῃ ἐοικυίας, ἧς ἡ λύμη τῶν δεδηγμένων τὸ αἷμα παντὸς τοῦ σώματος ἐκκρίνει καὶ οὕτως τὸν θάναντον ἐμβάλλει. αὕτη γὰρ καὶ ἡ τῶν Κυϊντιλλιανῶν αἵρεσις τοῦτο ἐπιτελεῖ. ἀφθόρου γὰρ παιδὸς κατακεντᾷ τὸ σῶμα καὶ τὸ αἷμα πρὸς μετάληψιν ἀποφέρεται, * δῆθεν τοῦτο εἰς μυσταγωγίαν ὀνόματος Χριστοῦ, τοὺς ἠπατημένους πλανήσασα.

94. *Panarion* 49.1-3 (GCS, ed. Holl, pp. 241-44).

(1) Κυϊντιλλιανοὶ δὲ πάλιν, οἱ καὶ Πεπουζιανοὶ καλούμενοι, Ἀρτοτυρῖταί τε καὶ Πρισκιλλιανοὶ λεγόμενοι, οἱ αὐτοὶ μὲν ὄντες [τοῖς] κατὰ Φρύγας καὶ ἐξ αὐτῶν ὁρμώμενοι, διῄρηνται δὲ κατά τινα τρόπον. φασὶ γὰρ οὗτοι οἱ Κυϊντιλλιανοὶ εἴτ' οὖν Πρισκιλλιανοὶ ἐν τῇ Πεπούζῃ ἢ Κυϊντιλλαν ἢ Πρίσκιλλαν (οὐκ ἔχω [γὰρ] ἀκριβῶς λέγειν), μίαν δὲ ἐξ αὐτῶν ὡς προεῖπον ἐν τῇ Πεπούζῃ κεκαθευδηκέναι καὶ τὸν Χριστὸν πρὸς αὐτὴν ἐληλυθέναι συνυπνωκέναι τε αὐτῇ τούτῳ τῷ τρόπῳ, ὡς ἐκείνη ἀπατωμένη ἔλεγεν· "ἐν ἰδέᾳ, φησί, γυναικός, ἐσχηματισμένος ἐν στολῇ λαμπρᾷ ἦλθε πρός με Χριστὸς καὶ ἐνέβαλεν ἐν ἐμοὶ τὴν σοφίαν καὶ ἀπεκάλυψέ μοι τουτονὶ τὸν τόπον εἶναι ἅγιον καὶ ὧδε τὴν Ἰερουσαλὴμ ἐκ τοῦ οὐρανοῦ κατιέναι." διό φασι καὶ ἄχρι τῆς δεῦρο μυεῖσθαί τινας οὕτω γυναῖκας ἐκεῖσε ἐν τῷ τόπῳ καὶ ἄνδρας, πρὸς τὸ ἐπιμεινάσας αὐτὰς ἢ αὐτοὺς τὸν Χριστὸν θεωρῆσαι. γυναῖκες γοῦν παρ' αὐτοῖς καλοῦνται προφήτιδες. οὐ πάνυ δὲ σαφῶς οἶδα εἰ παρ' αὐτοῖς ἢ παρὰ τοῖς κατὰ Φρύγας· ὁμοῦ γάρ εἰσι καὶ τὸ αὐτὸ φρόνημα κέκτηνται.

(2) Κέχρηνται δὲ οὗτοι παλαιᾷ καὶ καινῇ διαθήκῃ καὶ ἀνάστασιν νεκρῶν ὁμοίως φάσκουσι. Κυϊντιλλαν δὲ ἔχουσιν ἀρχηγὸν ἅμα Πρισκίλλῃ, τῇ καὶ παρὰ τοῖς κατὰ Φρύγας. φέρουσι δὲ μαρτυρίας πολλὰς ματαίας, χάριν διδόντες τῇ Εὔᾳ ὅτι πρώτη βέβρωκεν ἀπὸ τοῦ ξύλου τῆς φρονήσεως· καὶ τὴν ἀδελφὴν τοῦ Μωυσέως προφήτιδα λέγουσιν, εἰς μαρτυρίαν τῶν παρ' αὐτοῖς καθισταμένων γυναικῶν ἐν κλήρῳ· ἀλλὰ καί, φησί, τέσσαρες θυγατέρες ἦσαν τῷ Φιλίππῳ προφητεύουσαι. πολλάκις δὲ ἐν τῇ αὐτῶν ἐκκλησίᾳ εἰσέρχονται λαμπαδηφοροῦσαι ἑπτά τινες παρθένοι, λευχείμονες δῆθεν ἐρχόμεναι, ἵνα προφητεύσωσι τῷ λαῷ. αἱ δὲ τρόπον τινὰ ἐνδεικνύμεναι ἐνθουσιασμοῦ τοῖς παροῦσι λαοῖς ἀπάτην ἐργάζονται κλαίειν τε ποιοῦσιν πάντας ὡς εἰς οἶκτον μετανοίας ἄγουσαι,

written documents, and some by those truly proven in our faith, so that we not appear to be composing something consciously which exceeds what we have come to know and to speak incorrectly, inventing things ourselves against the men. . . .

But since we have herein sufficiently related the activity concerning this heresy, let us devote ourselves to advance to those which follow, having crushed its venom and the barbed poisons of its teeth by the wood of the cross of truth. It is like the Haimorroia viper whose bite removes the blood from the whole body of those who have been bitten, and in this way inflicts death. For this heresy of the Quintillians brings this about. For it pricks the body of an uncorrupted child, and, having misled those who have been deceived, the blood is taken away for consumption, to be sure, in the initiation into the mysteries of the name of Christ.

94. *Panarion* 49.1-3.

(1) Now the Quintillians again, who are also called Pepuzians, and those called Artotyrians and Priscillians are the same as the Cataphrygians, and have their origin from them, but differ in a certain way. For these Quintillians, or Priscillians say that in Pepuza either Quintilla or Priscilla, I cannot say precisely, but one of them, as I said before, had been asleep in Pepuza and the Christ came to her and slept with her in the following manner, as that deluded woman described it. "Having assumed the form of a woman," she says, "Christ came to me in a bright robe and put wisdom in me, and revealed to me that this place is holy, and that it is here that Jerusalem will descend from heaven." For this reason, they say, even to the present some women and men are thus initiated there, at that place, that, if they wait, they may behold the Christ.

Women are called prophetesses among them, but I do not know very clearly whether it is among them or the Cataphrygians. For they are together and hold the same doctrine.

(2) They use the Old and New Testament, and likewise say that there is a resurrection of the dead. And they have Quintilla as their leader, together with Priscilla who was also with the Cataphrygians. And they bear many vain testimonies, granting grace to Eve because she first ate of the tree of knowledge (cf. Gen 3:6). And they consider Moses' sister as a prophetess (cf. Exod 15:20), in support of the women appointed to the clergy among them. "But," she says, "Philip had four daughters who prophesied" (cf. Acts 21:9). And frequently in their assembly seven virgins dressed in white and carrying torches enter, coming, of course, to prophesy to the people. And these, by manifesting a certain kind of frenzy, produce deception in the people present, and make them weep; they pour forth tears as if they

δάκρυα χεόμεναι καὶ σχήματί τινι ἐποδυρόμεναι τὸν τῶν ἀνθρώπων βίον. ἐπίσκοποί τε παρ' αὐτοῖς γυναῖκες καὶ πρεσβύτεροι γυναῖκες καὶ τὰ ἄλλα· ὧν μηδὲν διαφέρειν φασίν "ἐν γὰρ Χριστῷ Ἰησοῦ οὔτε ἄρσεν οὔτε θῆλυ." ταῦτά ἐστιν ἃ κατειλήφαμεν. Ἀρτοτυρίτας δὲ αὐτοὺς καλοῦσιν ἀπὸ τοῦ ἐν τοῖς αὐτῶν μυστηρίοις ἐπιτιθέντας ἄρτον καὶ τυρὸν [καὶ] οὕτως ποιεῖν τὰ αὐτῶν μυστήρια.

(3) Πᾶσα δὲ ἀνθρώπων χλεύη ἐν τῷ ἀποστῆναι [καθέστηκεν] ἀπὸ τῆς ὀρθῆς πίστεως καὶ εἰς ἀμηχανίαν τρέπεσθαι καὶ εἰς διαφορὰς ἐνθουσιασμῶν τε καὶ ὀργίων. ἐκβακχευόμεναι γὰρ αἱ διάνοιαι ἀεὶ τοὺς μὴ κατέχοντας τὴν ἄγκυραν τῆς ἀληθείας, ἀλλ' ἐπιδιδόντας ἑαυτοὺς τῷ * φέρουσι κατὰ πᾶσαν ὁτιοῦν αἰτίαν. κἄν τε γὰρ γυναῖκες παρ' αὐτοῖς εἰς ἐπισκοπὴν καὶ πρεσβυτέριον καθίστανται διὰ τὴν Εὔαν, ἀκούσωσι τοῦ κυρίου λέγοντος "πρὸς τὸν ἄνδρα σου ἡ ἀποστροφή σου καὶ αὐτός σου κυριεύσει." λέληθε δὲ αὐτοὺς καὶ ὁ ἀποστολικὸς λόγος ὅτι "γυναικὶ οὐκ ἐπιτρέπω λαλεῖν οὔτε αὐθεντεῖν ἀνδρός" καὶ πάλιν "οὐ γάρ ἐστιν ἀνὴρ ἐκ γυναικός, ἀλλὰ γυνὴ ἐξ ἀνδρός," καὶ ὁ Ἀδὰμ οὐκ ἠπάτηται, ἀλλ' ἡ Εὔα πρώτη ἀπατηθεῖσα ἐν παραβάσει γέγονεν."

95. *Panarion* 51.33 (GCS, ed. Holl, pp. 306-308).

(33) Εἶτά τινες ἐξ αὐτῶν πάλιν ἐπιλαμβάνονται τούτου τοῦ ῥητοῦ ἐν τῇ αὐτῇ Ἀποκαλύψει καὶ φάσκουσιν ἀντιλέγοντες ὅτι "εἶπεν πάλιν· γράψον τῷ ἀγγέλῳ τῆς ἐκκλησίας τῆς ἐν Θυατείροις, καὶ οὐκ ἔνι ἐκεῖ ἐκκλησία Χριστιανῶν ἐν Θυατείροις. πῶς οὖν ἔγραφε τῇ μὴ οὔσῃ;" καὶ εὑρίσκονται οἱ τοιοῦτοι ἑαυτοὺς ἀναγκάζοντες ἐξ αὐτῶν ὧν κηρύττουσι ὑπὲρ τῆς ἀληθείας ὁμολογεῖν. ἐὰν γὰρ εἴπωσιν "οὐκ ἔνι νῦν ἐκκλησία εἰς Θυάτειρα" δεικνύουσι προπεφητευκέναι τὸν Ἰωάννην. ἐνοικησάντων γὰρ τούτων ἐκεῖσε [καὶ] τῶν κατὰ Φρύγας καὶ δίκην λύκων ἀρπαξάντων τὰς διανοίας τῶν ἀκεραίων πιστῶν, μετήνεγκαν τὴν πᾶσαν πόλιν εἰς τὴν αὐτῶν αἵρεσιν, οἵ τε ἀρνούμενοι τὴν Ἀποκάλυψιν κατὰ τοῦ λόγου τούτου εἰς ἀνατροπὴν κατ' ἐκεῖνο καιροῦ ἐστρατεύοντο. νῦν δὲ διὰ τὸν Χριστὸν ἐν τῷ χρόνῳ τούτῳ, μετὰ χρόνον ϟιβ' ἐτῶν, ἔστιν [ἐκεῖ] ἡ ἐκκλησία καὶ αὔξει, [εἰ] καὶ ἄλλοι τινὲς ἐκεῖσε τυγχάνουσι· τότε δὲ ἡ πᾶσα ἐκκλησία ἐκενώθη εἰς τὴν κατὰ Φρύγας. διὸ καὶ ἐσπούδασε τὸ ἅγιον πνεῦμα ἀποκαλύψαι ἡμῖν πῶς ἤμελλε πλανᾶσθαι ἡ ἐκκλησία μετὰ τὸν χρόνον τῶν ἀποστόλων, τοῦ τε Ἰωάννου καὶ τῶν καθεξῆς, ὃς ἦν χρόνος μετὰ τὴν τοῦ σωτῆρος ἀνάληψιν * , ἐπὶ ἐνενήκοντα τρισὶν ἔτεσιν, ὡς μελλούσης τῆς ἐκεῖσε ἐκκλησίας πλανᾶσθαι καὶ χωνεύεσθαι ἐν τῇ κατὰ Φρύγας αἱρέσει. οὕτω γὰρ εὐθὺς διελέγχει [αὐτοὺς] ὁ κύριος ἐν τῇ Ἀποκαλύψει λέγων "γράψον τῷ ἀγγέλῳ τῆς ἐν Θυατείροις ἐκκλησίας·

were sustaining the sorrow of repentance, and with a certain bearing they lament the life of men.

And women are bishops among them, and presbyters, and the other offices, as there is no difference, they say, for "in Christ Jesus there is neither male nor female" (cf. Gal 3:28).

These are the things which we have grasped. But they call them Artotyrians from the fact that they set forth bread and cheese in their mysteries, and in this way celebrate their mysteries.

(3) Men are totally absurd when they separate from the orthodox faith and turn to illogicality and the disagreements which stem from enthusiastic inspiration and secret rites. For the thought of those who do not retain the anchor of the truth, but deliver themselves to one who carries them about for any cause whatever, is subject to Bacchic frenzy. For even if women among them are appointed to the office of bishop and presbyter because of Eve, they hear the Lord saying: "Your resort shall be to your husband, and he shall rule over you" (Gen 3:16). And the apostolic word has also escaped their notice: "I do not permit a women to speak, nor to have authority over a man" (cf. 1 Tim 2:12). And again: "For man is not from woman, but woman from man" (1 Cor 11:8), and: "Adam was not deceived, but Eve was first deceived and transgressed" (cf. 1 Tim 2:14).

95. *Panarion* 51.33.

(33) Then, again, some of them attack this statement in the same Apocalypse and, disputing it, say that he said again: "Write to the angel of the Church in Thyatira" (cf. Rev 2:18), and there is no Church of Christians there in Thyatira. How, then, did he write to a Church which did not exist?

Such people find that they compel themselves to make assertions against the truth by the things which they proclaim. For if they say: "There is no Church in Thyatira now," they show that John has prophesied. For because these people dwell there, and the Cataphrygians who, like wolves, have overpowered the thoughts of the innocent faithful, they have transferred the whole city to their heresy. Those who reject the Apocalypse fight to refute this word during that time.

But now in this time, because of the Christ, after one-hundred-twelve years, there is a Church, and it is flourishing, and there are others there too, but at that time the whole Church was deserted to the Cataphrygians. For this reason also the Holy Spirit hastened to reveal to us how the Church was to go astray after the time of the apostles, that is John and those who followed. It was in the ninety-third year after the Savior's ascension when the Church there was to go astray and be melted down in the Cataphrygian heresy. For immediately the Lord rebuked them as follows in the Apocalypse: "Write to the angel of the Church in Thyatira: Thus says the one

τάδε λέγει ὁ ἔχων τοὺς ὀφθαλμοὺς αὐτοῦ ὡς φλόγα πυρὸς καὶ οἱ πόδες αὐτοῦ ὅμοιοι χαλκολιβάνῳ· οἶδά σου τὰ ἔργα καὶ τὴν πίστιν καὶ ἀγάπην καὶ τὴν διακονίαν, καὶ ὅτι τὰ ἔσχατά σου πλείονα τῶν πρώτων. ἔχω δὲ κατὰ σοῦ, ὅτι ἀφεῖς τὴν γυναῖκα Ἰεζάβελ ἀπατᾶν τοὺς δούλους μου, λέγουσαν ἑαυτὴν προφῆτιν, διδάσκουσαν φαγεῖν εἰδωλόθυτα καὶ πορνεύειν. καὶ ἔδωκα αὐτῇ χρόνον μετανοῆσαι καὶ οὐ θέλει μετανοῆσαι ἐκ τῆς πορνείας αὐτῆς." οὐχ ὁρᾶτε, ὦ οὗτοι, ὅτι περὶ τῶν γυναικῶν λέγει τῶν ἐν οἰήσει προφητείας ἀπατωμένων καὶ ἀπατωσῶν πολλούς; φημὶ δὲ περὶ Πρισκίλλας καὶ Μαξιμίλλας καὶ Κυϊντίλλας, ὧν ἡ ἀπάτη οὐ λέληθε τὸ πνεῦμα τὸ ἅγιον, ἀλλὰ προεθέσπισε προφητικῶς ἐν τῷ στόματι τοῦ ἁγίου Ἰωάννου, πρὸ κοιμήσεως αὐτοῦ προφητεύσαντος ἐν χρόνοις Κλαυδίου Καίσαρος και ἀνωτάτω, ὅτε εἰς τὴν Πάτμον νῆσον ὑπῆρχεν· ὁμολογοῦσι γὰρ καὶ οὗτοι ἐν θυατείροις ταῦτα πεπληρῶσθαι. ἄρα γοῦν κατὰ προφητείαν ἔγραφε τοῖς ἐκεῖ ἐν Χριστῷ κατ᾽ ἐκεῖνο καιροῦ πεπολιτευμένοις ὅτι ἤμελλεν ἑαυτὴν γυνὴ προφῆτιν καλεῖν. καὶ διέπεσεν ὁ κατὰ τῆς ἀληθείας ἐπεγειρόμενος πανταχόθεν ἐπινενοημένος λόγος, δεικνυμένου τοῦ κατὰ τὴν Ἀποκάλυψιν λόγου προφητικοῦ ὄντος ἐκ πνεύματος ἁγίου κατὰ ἀλήθειαν.

96. *Panarion* 79 1 (GCS 37, ed. Holl, p. 476).

(1) . . . Καὶ αὐτό[θι] γὰρ ἔδοξεν ἀπὸ γυναικῶν ὁ διάβολος ἐξεμεῖν, ὡς καὶ ἄνω παρὰ Κυϊντίλλῃ καὶ Μαξιμίλλῃ καὶ Πρισκίλλῃ περιγέλαστα [τὰ] διδάγματα, οὕτω καὶ ἐνταῦθα.

Pacian of Barcelona

97. Epistola I ad Sympronianum novatianum (PL 13.1053).

(1) Tantae enim a capite christiano haereses exstiterunt, ut nominum ipsorum sit uolumen immensum. Nam ut Judaeorum haereticos praetermittam, Dositheum samaritanum, Sadducaeos et Pharisaeos, quanti apostolorum temporibus emerserint, dinumerare perlongum est: Simon magus, et Menander, et Nicolaus, et caeteri quos fama recondit obscura. Quid? posterioribus temporibus Ebion et Apelles et Marcion et Valentinus et Cerdon, nec longe post eos Cataphryges et Novatiani, ut examina nouella praetercam. quis ergo mihi primum per litteras refutandus est? ipsa, si uoles, nomina omnium charta non capiet, nisi quod scriptis tuis, paenitentiam usquequaque damnantibus, secundum Phrygas te assensisse, pronuntias. uerum his ipsis, domine charissime, tam multiplex et diuersus est error, ut

who has eyes like a flame of fire and whose feet are like burnished bronze. I know your works and your faith, and love, and service, and that your last works are greater than the first. But I have this against you, that you permit the woman Jezebel, who calls herself a prophetess and teaches to eat meat offered to idols and to commit sexual immorality, to deceive my servants. I have given her time to repent, and she does not wish to repent of her sexual immorality'' (cf. Rev 2:18-21).

Do you not see that he is speaking of women who deceive themselves with the concept of prophecy, and deceive many others? Now I mean Priscilla, Maximilla, and Quintilla, whose fraud has not escaped the notice of the Holy Spirit. The Spirit spoke prophetically by the mouth of Saint John before his death, when he prophesied a very long time ago in the times of Claudius Caesar, when he was on the island of Patmos, for these too agree that these words have been fulfilled in Thyatira. John wrote, therefore indeed, in a prophetic manner to those living in Christ there at that time, that a woman was to call herself a prophetess.

And the contrived argument raised up on every side against the truth has collapsed, since the word in the Apocalypse proves to be a prophetic word from the Holy Spirit, and a word in conformity with truth.

96. *Panarion* 79.1.

(1) . . . For indeed the devil seemed to vomit forth such teaching from women; as in the case of the ridiculous teachings of Quintilla, Maximilla, and Priscilla discussed above, so also here. . . .

Pacian of Barcelona

97. Epistle 1, To Sympronianus 1-2.

(1) . . . It would take a large volume to list the names of all the heresies which have existed since the rise of Christianity. For, to pass over the heretics of the Jews, the Samaritan Dositheus, the Sadducees and Pharisees, it would be very tedious to enumerate how many have emerged since the times of the apostles: Simon Magus, Menander, Nicolas, and others whom obscurity has concealed. What? Later there was Ebion, Apelles, Marcion, Valentinus, and Cerdo, nor long after them, the Cataphrygians and Novatians, to pass by recent multitudes. Whom, then, should I first refute in my letter? If you wish such a refutation, this paper will not contain even the names of all of them. However, in your writings in which you everywhere condemn penitence, you announce that you hold a view that accords with the Phrygians. But, my dear Sir, the error among these very people is so manifold and diverse that it is not a matter of one thing among them,

non hoc unum in illis quod contra paenitentiam sapiunt, sed quasi quaedam capita Lernaea caedenda sint.

(2) Et primum hi plurimis nituntur auctoribus: nam puto, et Graecus Blastus ipsorum est. Theodotus quoque et Praxeas uestros aliquando docuere: ipsi illi Phryges nobiliores qui se animatos mentiuntur a Leucio, institutos a Proculo gloriantur. Montanum et Maximillam et Priscillam secuti, quam multiplices controuersias excitarunt de paschali die, de Paraclito, de apostolis, de prophetis, multaque alia, sicut et hoc de catholico nomine, de uenia paenitentiae. quare si omnia ista discutere uelimus, docili praesentia opus est.

Filastrius of Brescia

98. *Diuersarum Haereseon Liber* 49 (CSEL 38, ed. Marx, p. 26).

Alii autem post istos surrexerunt cata Frigas, in Frigia prouincia habitantes. isti prophetas et legem accipiunt, patrem, et filium, et spiritum confitentur, carnis surrectionem expectant, quae et catholica ecclesia praedicat: quosdam autem suos prophetas, id est, Montanum nomine, et Priscillam et Maximillam adnuntiant, quos neque prophetae neque Christus nuntiauit. Addunt etiam plenitudinem sancti spiritus non per apostolos beatos Christo dante fuisse concessam, sed per illos suos pseudoprophetas aestimant inpertitam, et separant se a catholica ecclesia per illos suos pseudoprophetas, et falsos doctores.

Hi mortuos baptizant, publice mysteria celebrant, Pepuzam uillam suam, quae sic dicitur in Frigia, Hierusalem appellant, ubi Maximilla et Priscilla et ipse Montanus uitae tempus uanum et infructuosum habuisse dinoscuntur. Ubi et mysterium cynicon et infantis execranda celebratur impietas. Dicunt enim eos de infantis sanguine in pashca miscere in suum sacrificium, suisque ita ubique emittere perniciosis et falsis satellitibus.

Didymus of Alexandria

99. *De trinitate* 2.15 (PG 39.720).

Μετερχόμενοι τοίνυν εἰς τὴν ὀρθοδοξίαν, κἂν τυχὸν ὦσιν βεβαπτισμένοι, βαπτίζονται μὲν (οὐ γὰρ λέγομεν ἀναβαπτίζονται, ἐπειδὴ μὴ ἔχουσι τὸ ἀληθὲς βάπτισμα)· οἱ δὲ Εὐνομιανοὶ μὲν, διὰ τὸ μίαν κατά-

namely that they are opposed to penitence, but the heads of the Lernaean hydra must be cut off, as it were.

(2) And first of all these rely on numerous authorities, for I think the Greek Blastus also belongs to them. Theodotus and Praxeas too have sometimes instructed your people; those more famous Phrygians themselves who declare falsely that they have descended from Leucius, boast that they have been instructed by Proclus. Take Montanus and his disciples Maximilla and Priscilla. How many controversies have they stirred up about the day of the Passover, about the Paraclete, about apostles, about prophets, and many other things, such as this too about the name Catholic, about the pardon of penitence! For this reason, if we wish to discuss all these subjects, we must have your docile presence.

Filastrius of Brescia

98. *Book of Heresies* 49.

But after those the Cataphrygians arose, dwelling in the province of Phrygia. They accept the prophets and the law; they confess the Father, the Son, and the Spirit; they expect the resurrection of the flesh, things which the Catholic Church also preaches. But they proclaim certain prophets of their own, that is, one named Montanus, and Priscilla, and Maximilla, whom neither the prophets nor Christ proclaimed. They add too that the fulness of the Holy Spirit was not granted when Christ gave it through the blessed apostles, but they think it was imparted through those pseudo prophets of theirs. And they separate themselves from the Catholic Church by their pseudo prophets and false teachers.

They baptize the dead; they celebrate their mysteries in public; they apply the name Jerusalem to their village Pepuza, which is thus said to be in Phrygia, where Maximilla and Priscilla, and Montanus himself are recognized to have spent their useless and fruitless lives. This is also where both the Cynic mystery and the accursed impiety of an infant is celebrated. For they say that on the Passover they mix some blood of an infant in their sacrifice, and so they send it forth everywhere to their pernicious and deceptive accomplices.

Didymus of Alexandria

99. *On the Trinity* 2.15.

When, therefore, they pass over into orthodoxy, they are baptized, even if they have perhaps been baptized (for we do not say they are rebaptized, since they do not possess the true baptism). This is the case with the Eu-

δυσιν ποιεῖσθαι, λέγοντες μόνον εἰς τὸν θάνατον τοῦ Κυρίου βαπτί-
ζεσθαι· Φρύγες δέ, διὰ τὸ μὴ εἰς τὰς τρεῖς ἁγίας ὑποστάσεις βαπτίζειν,
ἀλλὰ πιστεύειν τὸν αὐτὸν εἶναι πατέρα, καὶ υἱόν, καὶ ἅγιον πνεῦμα.

100. Ibid. 3.18 (PG 39.881).

Εἰ ταῦτα οὕτως ἔχει, ἀμάχως τὸ "πορεύομαι" καὶ "ὁ πέμψας," ὡς μορφὴν
δούλου λαβών, εἶπε, καὶ διὰ τὸ Ἰουδαίους ἀπιστεῖν τῇ οἰκονομίᾳ καὶ
ὅτι τῇ συμφωνίᾳ τοῦ θεοῦ καὶ πατρὸς ἐπεφάνη· καὶ οὐ διὰ τοῦτο μόνον,
ἀλλ᾽ ὥστε καὶ τοὺς παχεῖς τὸν νοῦν καὶ χερσώδεις Μοντανιστὰς ἐντρέ-
πεσθαι, τὸν αὐτὸν υἱοπατέρα ὁμοῦ καὶ παράκλητον νοοῦντας· σὺν αὐτοῖς
δὲ καὶ Μανιχαῖον, κ.τ.λ.

101. Ibid. 3.23 (PG 39.924).

Αλλ᾽ οὕτως εἴρηνται, τοῦτο μὲν διὰ τὸ μὴ σύγχυσιν νοῆσαι τῶν θείων
ὑποστάσεων, ἑκάστην δὲ διευκρινηθῆναι· τοῦτο δὲ διὰ τὸ ἐκβάλλεσθαι
Ἑλλήνων μὲν τὴν πολυθείαν διὰ τοῦ, "Εἷς θεὸς ὁ πατήρ," Ἰουδαίων δὲ
τὴν περὶ τὸν Χριστὸν ἀθέτησιν διὰ τοῦ, "Εἷς κύριος Ἰησοῦς Χριστός,"
Μοντανιστῶν δὲ τὴν ἄνοιαν, μελλόντων τὰς τρεῖς πανυμνήτους ὑποστάσεις ὡς ἓν πρόσωπον θρησκεύειν, διὰ τοῦ, "Εἷς" καὶ "Εἷς" καὶ "Εἷς."

102. Ibid. 3.38 (PG 39.977)

Τὸ δέ, "Οὐκ ἀφήσω ὑμᾶς ὀρφανούς· ἔρχομαι πρὸς ὑμᾶς," ἐδίδαξεν, ὡς
ὃν τρόπον τὸ πνεῦμα τοῦ θεοῦ ἦν καὶ πρὸ τῆς γνωστῆς αὐτοῦ ἐπιδημίας
ἐν πᾶσιν, οὕτω καὶ μετὰ τὴν ἀνάληψιν ὁ υἱός, ἐν ἀπεριγράφῳ μίᾳ θεότητι
καὶ θελήσει τῶν ὑποστάσεων οὐσῶν, οὐκ αὐτὸς ὢν ἄμφω καὶ πνεῦμα τοῦ
θεοῦ (ὡς ἐνόησεν Μοντανός, καὶ τούτῳ μάλιστα ἐπερείδεται τῷ μέρει
τῆς γραφῆς, μὴ βλέπων μηδ᾽ ἀκούων ὡς ἄλλος περὶ ἄλλου καὶ ἄλλου προσώπου
λέγει· "Ἐρωτήσω τὸν πατέρα καὶ πέμψει ἄλλον παράκλητον")· ἀλλ᾽ ὡς σὺν
τῷ πνεύματι παρὼν ἰδιοσύστατος, καθά ἐστιν ἀεὶ πανταχοῦ καὶ ὁ πατήρ.

103. Ibid. 3.41 (PG 39.984-89).

Καὶ Μοντανιστῶν ἡ πλάνη ἐν τούτοις·
(1) Πρῶτον, ὅτι ἀπομαντεύονται ἓν πρόσωπον εἶναι τῶν τριῶν θείων
ὑποστάσεων· Μοντανὸς γάρ, φησίν, εἶπεν· Ἐγώ εἰμι ὁ πατὴρ καὶ ὁ υἱὸς
καὶ ὁ παράκλητος." καὶ πρὸς σύστασιν δῆθεν τούτου προφέρουσιν, πάσης
ἰδιωτείας ἐπέκεινα νοοῦντες, ὅπερ θαυμασίως εἶπεν ὁ υἱός· "Ἐγὼ ἐν
τῷ πατρί, καὶ ὁ πατὴρ ἐν ἐμοί"· καὶ "Ἐλευσόμεθα ἐγὼ καὶ ὁ πατήρ μου,

nomians because they perform a single immersion and say that they are baptized only into the death of the Lord; it is the case with the Phrygians because they do not baptize into the three holy hypostases, but believe the same one is Father, Son, and Holy Spirit.

100. Ibid. 3.18.

If these things are so it is without doubt that the Savior said, "I go" (cf. John 14:28), and "he who sent me" (cf. John 14:24), as "having received the form of a slave" (Phil 2:7), and because the Jews do not believe in the divine economy and that he appeared in harmony with God and the Father; and not for this reason alone, but also so that the thick-witted and barren Montanists might be ashamed because they think the Son-Father together with the Paraclete are the same person, and with them also the Manichean, etc.

101. Ibid. 3.23.

But these things have been said in this way, first for the sake of avoiding confusion of the divine hypostases, and to clearly distinguish each one, and then to exclude the polytheism of the Greeks by the phrase, "One God the Father" (1 Cor 8:6), and the Jew's rejection of Christ by the phrase, "One Lord Jesus Christ" (1 Cor 8:6), and the foolishness of the Montanists who would worship the three hypostases which are praised by all as one person, by the words "one," and "one," and "one" (cf. 1 Cor 8:6).

102. Ibid. 3.38.

Now Jesus taught, "I will not leave you orphans; I will come to you" (John 14:18), to show that as the Spirit of God was in all before his known coming, so also would the Son be after his ascension, in one unlimited divinity and will of the hypostases, not that he himself is both, and in addition the Spirit of God (as Montanus thought, and he relies especially on this passage of Scripture, though he neither perceives nor understands that one person is speaking of another and of still another person: "I will ask the Father, and he will send another Paraclete" [cf. John 14:16]), but as a distinct entity being present with the Spirit, just as the Father too is always everywhere.

103. Ibid. 3.41.

The error of the Montanists consists in the following.

(1) First, that they rave irrationally that there is one person of the three divine hypostases. For Montanus says, he said: "I am the Father, and the Son, and the Paraclete." And in support of this then, their thoughts surpassing the bounds of all stupidity, they cite that which the Son spoke in a marvelous manner: "I am in the Father, and the Father is in me" (John

142   THE MONTANIST ORACLES AND TESTIMONIA

καὶ μονὴν παρ' αὐτῷ ποιήσομεν'" καὶ, "Ἐγὼ καὶ ὁ πατὴρ ἕν ἐσμεν'" καὶ, "Ὁ ἑωρακὼς ἐμὲ ἑώρακεν τὸν πατέρα'" καὶ, "Ὁ παράκλητος, ὃν πέμψει ὁ πατὴρ ἐν τῷ ἐμῷ ὀνόματι." ταῦτα δὲ πάντα, ὡς καὶ ἀνωτέρω εἴρηται, ἓν καὶ ἓν καὶ ἓν πρόσωπον ἰδιοσυστάτως δηλοῖ ἐν μιᾷ θεότητι καὶ συμφωνίᾳ. οὐ γὰρ εἶπεν· "Ἐγὼ καὶ ὁ πατὴρ ἕν εἰμι," ἀλλά, "ἕν ἐσμεν." καὶ κατηγορεῖ ταῦτα τῆς ἀνοίας αὐτῶν καὶ κακοδοξίας.

(2) Δεύτερον, ὅτι τοῦ Ἀποστόλου γράψαντος Κορινθίοις ἐν τῇ πρώτῃ ἐπιστολῇ· "Εἴτε προφητεῖαι καταργηθήσονται, εἴτε γλῶσσαι παύσονται, εἴτε γνῶσις καταργηθήσεται· ἐκ μέρους γὰρ γινώσκομεν, καὶ ἐκ μέρους προφητεύομεν· ὅταν δὲ ἔλθῃ τὸ τέλειον, τότε τὸ ἐκ μέρους καταργηθήσεται'" ἐκεῖνοι λέγουσιν τὸν Μοντανὸν ἐληλυθέναι, καὶ ἐσχηκέναι τὸ τέλειον τὸ τοῦ παρακλήτου, τοῦτ' ἔστιν τὸ τοῦ ἁγίου πνεύματος· οὐ προσέχοντες τοῖς προσκειμένοις. Ἔχει γὰρ εὐθύς· '"οτε ἤμην νήπιος, ἐλάλουν ὡς νήπιος, ἐλογιζόμην ὡς νήπιος· ὅτε γέγονα ἀνήρ, κατήργηκα τὰ τοῦ νηπίου. Βλέπομεν γὰρ ἄρτι δι' ἐσόπτρου ἐν αἰνίγματι· τότε δὲ πρόσωπον πρὸς πρόσωπον. ἄρτι γινώσκομεν ἐκ μέρους· τότε δὲ ἐπιγνωσόμεθα, καθὼς καὶ ἐπεγνώσθημεν." τοῦτ' ἔστιν· ἅπερ νῦν ἀκούοντες ὑπὸ τῶν γραφῶν πιστεύομεν εἶναι, μετὰ τὴν ἀνάστασιν τῇ ὄψει θεασόμεθα, καὶ τῷ πράγματι γνωσόμεθα, τῆς μερικῆς γνώσεως παυσαμένης· ἡ γὰρ γνῶσις, ἡ ἐξ ἀκοῆς, τῆς αὐτόπτου γνώσεως καὶ τῆς πείρας μέρος ἐστίν. οἷον νῦν ἀκούοντες πιστεύομεν περὶ τῆς δευτέρας παρουσίας τοῦ δεσπότου, καὶ περὶ τοῦ βήματος αὐτοῦ, καὶ τῆς τρισμακαρίας φωνῆς· "Δεῦτε, οἱ εὐλογημένοι τοῦ πατρός μου, κληρονομήσατε τὴν ἡτοιμασμένην ὑμῖν βασιλείαν'" τότε τῇ θέᾳ καὶ τῇ πείρᾳ μαθησόμεθα. νῦν ἀκούοντες πιστεύομεν περὶ τῶν ἁγίων ἀγγέλων· τότε κατὰ πρόσωπον λειτουργοῦντας αὐτοὺς ὀψόμεθα. νῦν ἀκούοντες πιστεύομεν, '"Ἃ ὀφθαλμὸς οὐκ ἴδεν, καὶ οὖς οὐκ ἤκουσεν, καὶ ἐπὶ καρδίαν ἀνθρώπου οὐκ ἀνέβη, ὅσα ἡτοίμασεν ὁ θεὸς τοῖς ἀγαπῶσιν αὐτόν'" τότε οὐκ ὄψονται μόνον, ἀλλὰ καὶ ἐν ἀπολαύσει αὐτῶν οἱ ἄξιοι γένωνται. τὰ γὰρ νῦν κάτω τῆς ψυχῆς ἡμῶν ὄμματι τῶν ἐπουρανίων ἀφανῆ καθεστῶτα, ὁ μέλλων βίος φανερὰ ποιήσει.

Ἀλλ' εἶπεν, φησὶν, ὁ Χριστός· "Ἔτι πολλὰ ἔχω λέγειν ὑμῖν, ἀλλ' οὐ δύνασθε βαστάζειν ἄρτι· ὅταν δὲ ἔλθῃ ἐκεῖνος, τὸ πνεῦμα τῆς ἀληθείας, ὁδηγήσει ὑμᾶς εἰς πᾶσαν τὴν ἀλήθειαν'" καὶ, '"Ἀφ' ἑαυτοῦ οὐ λαλήσει, ἀλλ' ἐκ τοῦ ἐμοῦ λήψεται, καὶ ἀναγγελεῖ ὑμῖν'" καὶ, "Ἐκεῖνος ἐμὲ δοξάσει'" καὶ πάλιν· "Οὐκ ἀφήσω ὑμᾶς ὀρφανούς· ἔρχομαι πρὸς ὑμᾶς."

14:11), and: "I will come, and my Father, and we will make our abode in him" (cf. John 14:23), and: "I and the Father are one" (John 10:30), and "He who has seen me has seen the Father" (John 14:9), and: "The Paraclete, whom the Father will send in my name" (cf. John 14:26). But all these statements, as has also been said above, reveal one, and another, and another person as existing personally in a single divinity and harmony. For he did not say: "I and the Father, I am one," but "we are one." These words refute their foolishness and false opinion.

(2) Second, that when the apostle wrote to the Corinthians in the first epistle: "Whether prophecies, they shall be made void, or tongues, they shall cease, or knowledge, it shall be made void, for we know in part and we prophesy in part, but when perfection comes, then that which is in part shall be made void" (1 Cor 13:8-10), they say that Montanus has come and that he possessed the perfection of the Paraclete, that is, that of the Holy Spirit, for they do not pay attention to the words that are added. For there follows immediately the words: "When I was a child, I spoke as a child, I thought as a child; when I became a man, I put aside the ways of a child. For now we see indistinctly in a mirror, but then face to face. Now we know in part, but then we shall know fully just as also we were fully known" (1 Cor 13:11-12). This means: The things which we now hear on the authority of the Scriptures we believe to be; after the resurrection we shall see them with our eyes and know them in reality, when partial knowledge has ceased, for the knowledge which depends on hearing is a part of the knowledge of an eye-witness and of experience. For example, now because we hear, we believe concerning the second coming of the Master, and his judgment, and the thrice-blessed word: "Come, blessed of my Father; inherit the kingdom which has been prepared for you" (Matt 25:34); then we shall learn by sight and experience. Now when we hear, we believe concerning the holy angels; then we shall see them directly performing their service. Now when we hear, we believe, "Eye has not seen nor has ear heard nor has it entered the heart of man what God has prepared for those who love him" (1 Cor 2:9); but then those who are worthy will not only see them, but will also enjoy them. For the life to come will make manifest the invisible things of the heavenly realm which have now been ordained here below for the eye of our soul.

But, he says, Christ said: "I still have many things to say to you, but you are not able to bear them now; but when the Spirit of truth comes, he will lead you into all truth" (John 16:12-13), and: "He will not speak from himself, but he will receive from me and will announce to you" (cf. John 16:13), and: "He will glorify me" (John 16:14), and again: "I will not leave you orphans; I will come to you" (John 14:18). He came, then I sup-

ἦλθεν οὖν δῆθεν, ὅταν Μοντανός. οὐχ οὕτως δέ· μὴ γένοιτο! ἐπεὶ πρὸς
τοῦτον τὸν ἀδιανόητον αὐτῶν λόγον εὑρίσκονται πρὸ Μοντανοῦ οἵ τε
τὸν Χριστὸν ἐσχηκότες, οἵ τε ἀπόστολοι οἱ τὴν τάξιν δεξάμενοι παρὰ
τοῦ θεοῦ, καὶ ἐν ἑαυτοῖς ἐσχηκότες λαλοῦντα τὸν Χριστόν, καὶ οἰκοῦν
τὸ πνεῦμα τοῦ θεοῦ, καὶ διὰ τῆς ἐπιθέσεως τῶν χειρῶν καὶ ἄλλοις παρέχοντες αὐτὸ κατὰ τὴν αὐτοῦ βούλησιν, καὶ μετὰ παρρησίας διδάσκον-
τες, καὶ παρὰ πᾶσιν πιστευόμενοι καὶ μὴ ὡς Μοντανὸς ἀπιστούμενος.
. . . τί δὲ σημαίνει τὸ, "Ἔρχομαι πρὸς ὑμᾶς," εἴρηται ἀνωτέρω· εἴχομεν
γὰρ (εἰ καὶ ἔχουσιν οἱ ἄξιοι τελείως) τόν τε Χριστὸν τὸν εἰπόντα·
"Ἔρχομαι πρὸς ὑμᾶς"· τό τε ἅγιον πνεῦμα, περὶ οὗ εἶπεν· "Ὅταν ἔλθῃ
ἐκεῖνος." οὐδὲ γὰρ ἀτελές τι ἐποίει ὁ δεσπότης, ἐμφυσῶν μετὰ τὴν ἀνάστασιν εἰς πρόσωπα τῶν ἀποστόλων, καὶ λέγων· "Λάβετε πνεῦμα ἅγιον"
οὐδ᾽ ἐψεύδετο, ἢ αὐτὸς λέγων· "Ὅτι παρ᾽ ὑμῖν μένει, καὶ ἐν ὑμῖν ἐστιν,"
ἢ ἀπόστολος γράφων· "Οὐκ οἴδατε, ὅτι ναὸς θεοῦ ἐστε, καὶ τὸ πνεῦμα τοῦ
θεοῦ οἰκεῖ ἐν ὑμῖν;" οὔτε ἡ σοφία λέγουσα· "Πνεῦμα κυρίου πεπλήρωκεν
τὴν οἰκουμένην· καὶ τὸ συνέχον τὰ πάντα, γνῶσιν ἔχει φωνῆς." οὔτε μὴν
ἀτελέστεροι Μοντανοῦ οἱ ἀπόστολοι καὶ οἱ πρὸ αὐτῶν ἅγιοι ἐτύγχανον
ὄντες. ἐπεφάνη δὲ τῇ Πεντηκοστῇ, ἔνθα καὶ ἤδη ἦν τὸ πάντα συνέχον
ἅγιον πνεῦμα, καὶ ἐδέχθη, ὡς ἔχουσιν αἱ Πράξεις οὕτως. . . .

(3) Τρίτον ὅτι κατασκευάζουνται, δεῖξαι, τόν τε Μοντανὸν ἐσχηκέναι
τὸ τέλειον τοῦ παρακλήτου, τήν τε Πρισκίλλαν καὶ Μαξιμίλλαν προφήτιδας. . . . ἔγραψαν Μοντανῷ. λέγουσιν, ὅτι ὑμεῖς οὐ πιστεύετε μετὰ
τὴν πρώτην ἐπιφάνειαν τοῦ δεσπότου εἶναι προφήτας· εἶπεν δὲ, φησὶν,
ὁ σωτήρ· "Ἰδοὺ ἐγὼ ἀποστέλλω πρὸς ὑμᾶς προφήτας, καὶ σοφοὺς, καὶ γραμ-
ματεῖς· καὶ ἐξ αὐτῶν ἀποκτενεῖτε, καὶ σταυρώσετε, καὶ ἐξ αὐτῶν μαστιγώσετε ἐν ταῖς συναγωγαῖς ὑμῶν." λέγει δὲ, οὐχ ὡς ἐκεῖνοι νομίζουσιν,
ἀλλὰ τοὺς ἀποστόλους προειπόντας πολλὰ τῶν μελλόντων καὶ τῶν ἐσχάτων
καιρῶν, καὶ τῆς ἐν οὐρανοῖς βασιλεία· ἐξ ὧν καὶ ἀπεκτάνθησαν, ὡς Στέ-
φανος καὶ Ἰάκωβος· καὶ ἐσταυρώθησαν, ὡς Πέτρος· καὶ ἐμαστιγώθησαν, ὡς
Παῦλος. ἔσθ᾽ ὅτε δὲ εἶπεν καὶ τοὺς μάρτυρας καὶ τοὺς σοφοὺς ἐπισκο-
πομάρτυρας. προφήτιδας δὲ οἶδεν ἡ γραφὴ τὰς Φιλίππου τέσσαρας θυγατέρας, τὴν Δεβόρραν, Μαριὰμ τὴν ἀδελφὴν Ἀαρὼν, καὶ τὴν θεοτόκον
Μαριάμ, εἰποῦσαν, ὡς τὸ Εὐαγγέλιον εἶπεν· "Ἀπὸ τοῦ νῦν μακαριοῦσίν
με πᾶσαι αἱ γυναῖκες καὶ αἱ γενεαί"· βίβλους δὲ συνταγείσας ἐξ ὀ-
νόματος αὐτῶν οὐκ οἶδεν· ἀλλὰ καὶ ἐκώλυσεν ὁ ἀπόστολος, Τιμοθέῳ τὸ
πρῶτον γράψας· "Γυναιξὶν διδάσκειν οὐκ ἐπιτρέπω"· καὶ πάλιν ἐν τῇ

pose, when Montanus came. In no way! Since, in relation to this stupid assertion of theirs, both those who have possessed Christ before Montanus are found, and the apostles who received their position from God and who have had Christ speaking in themselves, and in whom the Spirit of God dwells, and who also grant the Spirit to others through the laying on of hands according to his will, and who teach boldly, and are believed by all, and not disbelieved as Montanus. . . . But what "I will come to you" means has been explained above. For we have (although those who are worthy possess him perfectly) both Christ who said, "I will come to you," and the Holy Spirit of whom he said: "When he comes." For the Master was not doing something without a purpose when he breathed into the face of the apostles after the resurrection and said: "Receive the Holy Spirit" (John 20:22). Nor did he lie when he himself said: "Because he remains with you, and is in you" (John 14:17), or the apostle, when he wrote: "Do you not know that you are the temple of God, and the Spirit of God dwells in you?" (1 Cor 3:16), or Wisdom, when she said: "The Spirit of the Lord has filled the world, and that which contains all things has knowledge of sound" (Wis 1:7). Neither the apostles nor the saints who preceded them were less perfect than Montanus. But the Holy Spirit who contains all things appeared at Pentecost; he was present at that place and at that time, and he was received, as it is recorded in the Acts. . . .

(3) Third, that they contend to prove that Montanus had possessed the perfection of the Paraclete, and that the prophetesses Priscilla and Maximilla . . . wrote for Montanus. They say that you do not believe that there are prophets after the first appearance of the Master. But, he says, the Savior said: "Behold I am sending prophets to you, and wise men, and scribes; you will kill some of them, and crucify them, and some of them you will beat in your synagogues" (Matt 23:34). But he is speaking not [of later prophets] as those think, but of the apostles who predicted many of the things to come, and many things of the last times, and of the kingdom in heaven; some of them also were killed, as Stephen and James, and they were crucified, as Peter, and they were beaten, as Paul. And there are times when he meant the bishop-martyrs by the "martyrs" and "wise men." But Scripture knows as prophetesses the four daughters of Philip (cf. Acts 21:9), Deborah (cf. Judg 4:4), Mariam the sister of Aaron (cf. Exod 15:20), and Mary the mother of God, who said, as the Gospel has it: "From now all women and generations will call me blessed" (cf. Luke 1:48). But Scripture knows no books composed under the name of any women. On the contrary, the apostle even forbid it when he wrote to Timothy the first time: "I do not permit a woman to teach" (1 Tim 2:12), and again in the first epistle to the Corinthians: "Every woman who prays and prophesies with

πρὸς Κορινθίους πρώτη ἐπιστολῇ· "Πᾶσα γυνὴ προσευχομένη καὶ προφητεύουσα ἀκατακαλύπτῳ τῇ κεφαλῇ, καταισχύνει τὴν κεφαλήν"· ὅ ἐστιν, μὴ ἐξεῖναι γυναικὶ ἀναίδην ἐξ οἰκείας προστάξεως βίβλους συγγράφειν καῖ ἐ. . . . δάσκειν καὶ τούτῳ ὑβρίζειν τὴν κεφαλὴν, τοῦτ' ἔστιν τὸν ἄνδρα· "κεφαλὴ" γάρ "γυναικὸς ὁ ἀνὴρ· κεφαλὴ δὲ ἀνδρὸς, Χριστός." καὶ ἡ κατασιγάζουσα τὰς γυναῖκας αἰτία πρόδηλος· ἐπειδὴ ἡ ἐξ ἀρχῆς τῆς γυναικὸς διδασκαλία οὐ καλῶς τὸ κοινὸν ἔβλαβε γένος. "Ὁ" γὰρ "ἀνὴρ," ὡς γράφει ὁ ἀπόστολος, "οὐκ ἠπατήθη, ἀλλ' ἡ γυνή." ὥστε παρὰ πάντας Μοντανὸς οὐδὲ ἔγνω, οὐδὲ ἔσχεν τὸ ἅγιον πνεῦμα, τοῦτο οἰηθείς· καὶ ταῦτα, μετὰ τὴν ἀνάληψιν τοῦ σωτῆρος, καὶ τὴν ἐπιφοίτησιν τοῦ ἁγίου πνεύματος, πλέον ἢ μετὰ ἑκατὸν ἔτη γενόμενος ἱερεὺς πρῶτον εἰδώλου, καὶ οὕτω τὴν τυφλὴν ταύτην εἰσηγησάμενος αἵρεσιν.

104. *Fragmenta in Actus Apostolorum* 10.10 (PG 39.1677).

"Ἐγένετο δὲ ἐπ' αὐτὸν, φησὶν, ἔκστασις, καὶ θεωρεῖ τὸν οὐρανόν ἀνεῳγμένον." οἱ γυναικῶν παραπαιουσῶν ἑλόμενοι εἶναι μαθηταὶ, οὗτοι δέ εἰσιν οἱ ἀπὸ τῆς Φρυγίας, φασὶ τοὺς προφήτας, κατεχομένους ὑπὸ τοῦ ἁγίου πνεύματος, μὴ παρακολουθεῖν ἑαυτοῖς παραφερομένοις κατὰ τὸν τῆς προφητείας καιρόν. δοκοῦσι δὲ ἀπόδειξιν ἔχειν ταύτης τῆς κικωδοξίας, καὶ δὴ τῆς προκειμένης γραφῆς, λεγούσης ἐξεστακέναι τὸν Πέτρον. Ἀλλ' ἴστωσαν ὁ ἠλίθιοι οἱ ἀληθῶς πυραπαίοντες, ὡς πολλὰ σημαίνει ἡ λέξις αὕτη. δηλοῖ γὰρ καὶ τὴν ἐπὶ θαυμασμῷ ἔκπληξιν, καὶ τὸ ἔξω τῶν αἰσθητῶν γενέσθαι, ποδηγούμενον ἐπὶ τὰ πνευματικὰ, καὶ τὸ παρακόπτειν, ὅπερ οὐ λεκτέον οὔτε ἐπὶ Πέτρου, οὔτε ἐπὶ προφητῶν, ἀλλὰ τὰ ἄλλα ἐκ τῆς λέξεως σημαινόμενα. ἀμέλει γοῦν ὁ ἐκστὰς Πέτρος παρηκολούθει, ὡς ἀπαγγέλλων ἃ εἶδε καὶ ἤκουσε, καὶ τίνος σύμβολα τὰ δειχθέντα ἦν. ταῦτα καὶ περὶ τῶν προφητῶν πάντων ἐρεῖς παρακολουθούντων, οἷς ἔλεγον τὰ θεωρούμενα. σοφοὶ γὰρ ἦσαν νοοῦντες ἀπὸ τοῦ ἰδίου στόματος ἃ προέφερον, τοῦ κυρίου μετὰ τὴν ἀνάστασιν φανερῶς ἐντειλαμένου μαθητεῦσαι παντὰ τὰ ἔθνη. ἢ πῶς οἱ ἐν Ἱεροσολύμοις ἀπόστολοι ἀκούσαντες τὰ κατὰ τὸν Κορνήλιον, διεκρίνοντο πρὸς τὸν Πέτρον; πάνυ μὲν οὖν ἐδεῖτο τῆς περὶ τῶν ἐθνῶν θείας ἀποκαλύψεως ὁ τῶν ἀποστόλων ἔξαρχος, Πέτρος, ὁ πανάγιος.

105. *Fragmenta in epistolam ad Corinthios secundam* 5.12 (PG 39.1704-1705).

Κἂν τε γὰρ ἔξω τῶν ἀνθρωπίνων γενόμενοι τῷ θεῷ ἐκστῶμεν, ἀλλ' οὖν σωφρονοῦμεν ὑμῖν, τῆς θείας ἐκστάσεως οὐ μανίαν, ἀλλὰ νηφαλιότητα ἐχούσης. οὐ προσεκτέον γὰρ τοῖς ἀπὸ τῶν Φρυγῶν λέγουσι τοὺς ἀπο-

her head uncovered dishonors her head'' (1 Cor 11:5), which means it is not permitted a woman shamelessly to compose books on her own authority and . . . to teach, and in this to insult her head, that is her husband. For "the head of the woman is her husband, and the head of the man is Christ" (cf. 1 Cor 11:3). And the reason which imposes silence on the women is obvious. It is because the teaching of the woman in the beginning mislead the common race in no happy manner. For "the man," as the apostle writes, "was not deceived, but the woman" (1 Tim 2:14). Consequently, since he has thought this, Montanus has neither known nor possessed the Holy Spirit over and above all other men. And this is why, more than a hundred years after the resurrection of the Savior and the appearance of the Holy Spirit he has come forward for the first time as the priest of an idol, and thus introduced this blind heresy.

104. *Fragments from the Exposition of Didymus on the Acts of the Apostles* 10.10.

"And ecstasy came upon him," it says, "and he saw heaven opened" (Acts 10:10-11). Those who have chosen to be disciples of delirious women, that is those from Phrygia, say that when prophets are possessed by the Holy Spirit they do not understand themselves as they are carried along at the moment of the prophecy. And they appear to have proof of this heretical opinion also from the Scripture text before us which says that Peter fell into ecstasy. But let those senseless people who are truly delirious know how many meanings this word has. For it signifies both the trance caused by wonder, and that state of being outside the senses being led to spiritual things, and to be deranged. We must not apply the last meaning in the case either of Peter or the prophets, but the other meanings of the word. Peter, at any rate, kept his understanding when he experienced ecstasy, since he reported what he saw and heard, and of what the things portrayed were symbols (cf. Acts 10:34ff). You will say the same things also of all the prophets since they maintained their understanding in the words in which they relate what they have seen. For they were wise men who understood the words they brought forth from their own mouth, since the Lord manifestly commanded them after the resurrection to make disciples of all the nations (cf. Matt 28:19). Or how did the apostles in Jerusalem contend with Peter when they heard the matters concerning Cornelius (cf. Acts 11:2)? The all-holy Peter, then, chief of the apostles, had great need of this divine revelation concerning the Gentiles.

105. *Commentary on the second epistle of the apostle Paul to the Corinthians* 5.12.

Even if, being outside of human matters, we should fall into ecstasy with God, at any rate we are of sound mind with you, for the divine ecstasy does not involve madness, but sobriety. For we must not agree with those from

στόλους καὶ προφήτας ἐξίστασθαι, ὥστε παραπαίειν (παρηκολούθουν γὰρ οἷς ἔλεγον καὶ ἔπραττον, εἰ καί τινες ἄλλοι)· ἠπατήθησαν δὲ οἱ ἠλίθιοι ἐκ τῆς ὁμωνυμίας. οὐ γὰρ μόνον τὸ παραπαίειν καὶ παρακόπτειν σημαίνει ἡ "ἐξέστη" φωνή, ἀλλὰ καὶ τὸ ἐκπλαγῆναι ἐπὶ θαυμασμῷ οὕτω γὰρ ἐξέστη Ἰσαὰκ ἔκστασιν μεγάλην. καὶ ἐκστήσονταί τινες ἐπὶ τῷ κυρίῳ καὶ ἐπὶ τοῖς ἀγαθοῖς αὐτοῦ, κατὰ τὸν προφήτην. εἰ δὲ καὶ ἄλλα τινὰ δηλοῦται ὑπὸ τῆς φωνῆς, ἐπιστήτω ὁ ἐντυγχάνων ταῖς γραφαῖς.

Jerome

106. Ep. 41, ad Marcellam (CSEL 54, ed. Hilberg, pp. 311-14).

(1) Testimonia, quae de Ioannis Euangelio congregata tibi quidam Montani sectator ingessit, in quibus saluator noster se ad patrem iturum missurumque paraclitum pollicetur, in quod promissa sint tempus et quo completa sint tempore, *Apostolorum Acta* testantur: decima die post ascensum Domini, hoc est quinquagesima post resurrectionem, spiritum sanctum descendisse linguasque credentium esse diuisas, ita ut unusquisque omnium gentium sermone loqueretur, quando quidam adhuc parum credentium eos musto ebrios adserebant et Petrus stans in medio apostolorum omnisque conuentus ait: "viri Iudaei, et omnes qui habitatis in Hierusalem, hoc uobis notum sit, et percipite auribus uerba mea. non enim sicut uos aestimatis, hi ebrii sunt—nam est hora diei tertia—, sed hoc est, quod dictum est per Iohel prophetam: 'in nouissimis diebus,' dicit dominus, 'effundam de spiritu meo in omnem carnem, et prophetabunt filii et filiae eorum; et iuuenes uisiones uidebunt et seniores somnia somniabunt; et quidem in seruos meos et ancellas effundam de spiritu meo.' "

(2) Si igitur apostolus Petrus, super quem dominus fundauit ecclesiam, et prophetiam et promissionem domini illo tempore completam memorauit, quomodo possumus nobis tempus aliud uindicare?

quodsi uoluerint respondere et Philippi deinceps quattuor filias prophetasse et prophetam Agabum repperiri et in diuisionibus spiritus inter apostolos, et doctores, prophetas quoque apostolo scribente formatos ipsumque Paulum multa de futuris heresibus et de fine saeculi prophetasse, sciant a nobis non tam prophetiam repelli, quae domini signata est passione, quam eos non recipi, qui cum scripturae ueteris et nouae auctoritate non congruant.

Phrygia who say the apostles and prophets fell into ecstasy so that they lost their wits (for they did not understand what they said and did, although certain others did). But the fools were deceived by the equivocal sense of the word. For the word "ecstasy" means not only to lose one's wits and to be deranged, but also to be amazed because of wonder. For in this sense Isaac fell into great ecstasy (cf. Gen 27:33). And some, according to the prophet, will be struck with ecstasy because of the Lord and his good things. And if there are also some other meanings of the word, let the reader give attention to the Scriptures.

Jerome

106. Epistle 41, To Marcella.

(1) Regarding the proofs some follower of Montanus presented to you, proofs gathered from the Gospel of John, in which our Savior promises that he will go to the Father and will send the Paraclete (cf. John 16:5-7), the Acts of the Apostles shows for what time the promises were made and at what time they were fulfilled. On the tenth day after the Lord's ascension, that is on the fiftieth day after the resurrection, the Holy Spirit descended and the tongues of the believers were divided so that each one spoke in the language of all the nations. When some of those who still had too little faith declared that they were drunk on new wine, Peter, standing in the midst of the apostles and the whole assembly, said: "Men of Judea, and all you who dwell in Jerusalem, let this be known to you, and listen to my words. For these men are not drunk, as you suppose, for it is the third hour of the day, but this is that which was said by the prophet Joel: 'In the last days,' says the Lord, 'I will pour out of my Spirit on all flesh, and their sons and daughters will prophesy, and the young men will see visions, and the old men will dream dreams. And I will indeed pour out of my Spirit on my servants and on my handmaids' " (Acts 2:14-18).

(2) If, then, the apostle Peter, on whom the Lord has founded the Church, has related that both the prophecy and the promise of the Lord were fulfilled at that time, how can we claim another time for ourselves?

But if they wish to reply that the four daughters of Philip prophesied after this (cf. Acts 21:9), and that a prophet named Agabus is encountered (cf. Acts 11:28; 21:10-11), and that prophets have also been inserted between apostles and teachers when the apostle writes about the distributions of the Spirit (cf. 1 Cor 12:28), and that Paul himself prophesied many things about future heresies and the end of the world, let them know that it is not so much that prophecy, which has been confirmed by the Lord's passion, is rejected by us as that those prophets are not received who do not agree with the authority of the Old and New Testament.

(3) Primum in fidei regula discrepamus. nos patrem et filium et spiritum sanctum in sua unumquemque persona ponimus, licet substantia copulemus; illi Sabelli dogma sectantes trinitatem in unius personae angustias cogunt. nos secundas nuptias non tam adpetimus, quam concedimus Paulo iubente, ut uiduae adulescentulae nubant; illi in tantum scelerata putant iterata coniugia, ut, quicumque hoc fecerit, adulter habeatur. nos unam quadragesimam secundum traditionem apostolorum toto nobis orbe congruo, ieiunamus; illi tres in anno faciunt quadragesimas, quasi tres passi sint saluatores, non quo et per totum annum excepto pentecosten ieiunare non liceat, sed quod aliud sit necessitate, aliud uoluntate munus offerri. apud nos apostolorum locum episcopi tenent; apud eos episcopus tertius est. habent enim primos de Pepusa Phrygiae patriarchas, secundos, quos appelant κοινωνούς, atque ita in tertium, id est paene ultimum, gradum episcopi deuoluuntur, quasi exinde ambitiosior religio fiat, si quod apud nos primum est, apud illos nouissimum sit. illi ad omne paene delictum ecclesiae obserant fores; nos cotidie legimus: "malo paenitentiam peccatoris quam mortem," et: "numquid, qui cadit, non resurgit? dicit dominus," et: "convertimini ad me filii conuertentes, et ego curabo contritiones uestras." rigidi autem sunt. non quo et ipsi peiora non peccent, sed quod hoc inter nos et illos sit, quod illi erubescunt confiteri peccata quasi iusti, nos, dum paenitentiam agimus, facilius ueniam promeremur.

(4) Praetermitto scelerata mysteria, quae dicuntur de lactente puero et deuictuor martyre confarrata. malo iniqua non credere; sit falsum omne, quod sanguinis est. aperta est conuincenda blasphemia dicentium deum primum uoluisse in ueteri testamento per Moysen et prophetas saluare mundum: quod quia non potuerit explere, corpus sumpsisse de virgine, et in Christo sub specie filii praedicantem mortem obisse pro nobis et, quia per duos gradus mundum saluare nequiuerit, ad extremum per spiritum sanctum in Montanum, Priscam et Maximillam, insanas feminas, descendisse et plenitudinem, quam Paulus non habuerit dicens: "ex parte cognoscimus et ex parte prophetamus," et: "nunc uidemus per speculum in aenigmate," abscisum et semiuirum habuisse Montanum. haec coargutione non indigent; perfidiam eorum exposuisse superasse est. nec necesse

(3) In the first place, we disagree on the rule of faith. We consider the Father, the Son, and the Holy Spirit each in his own person, although we unite them in substance. They, following the doctrine of Sabellius compress the Trinity into the restrictedness of one person.

We do not so much recommend second marriages as allow them, since Paul orders that young widows marry (cf. 1 Tim 5:14). They consider second marriages to be so wicked that they hold whoever has contracted one to be an adulterer. We have one forty day fast at Lent in accordance with the apostolic tradition, the whole world being in agreement with us. They have three forty day fasts a year, as if three Saviors suffered; not that it is not permissible to fast throughout the whole year, with the exception of Pentecost, but that it is one thing for a gift to be offered of necessity, and another voluntarily.

With us the bishops hold the place of the apostles; with them the bishop is third. For they have first the patriarchs from Pepuza in Phrygia; second, those they call *koinonoi,* and thus bishops are relegated to the third, that is nearly the last, rank, as if accordingly, their religion would be more admired if that which is first with us should be last with them.

They bar the doors of the Church to almost every offense; we read daily: "I prefer the repentance of a sinner to his death" (cf. Ezek 18:23), and: "Shall he who falls not rise?" says the Lord (Jer 8:4), and: "Return to me you sons who are turning back, and I will heal your griefs" (cf. Jer 3:22). But their rigidity does not mean that they themselves do not also commit more serious sins; the difference between us and them is that they are embarrassed to confess their sins, as if they were just, while we do penance and acquire pardon more easily.

(4) I pass over their polluted mysteries which are said to be celebrated with reference to a suckling child and a victorious martyr. I prefer not to believe these infamous things; let everything which involves blood be false. It is clear that the blasphemies must be refuted of those who say God first wished to save the world through Moses and the prophets in the Old Testament; but because he had not been able to fulfill his wish, he assumed the body of a virgin and, speaking in Christ under the form of the Son, he experienced death for us. And because he was unable to save the world by these two steps, finally he has descended through the Holy Spirit in Montanus and those insane women, Priscilla and Maximilla, and that Montanus, a castrated half-man, possessed a fulness which Paul did not possess, for Paul says: "We know in part, and we prophesy in part" (1 Cor 13:9), and: "Now we see in a mirror indistinctly" (1 Cor 13:12).

These things need no refutation. To have exposed their faithlessness is to have overcome them. Nor is it necessary that the rather brief discussion

est, ut singula deliramenta, quae proferunt, brevior epistulae sermon sub-uertat, cum et tu ipsas Scripturas adprime tenes non tam ad eorum mota sis quaestiones, quam, quid sentirem, a me uolueris sciscitari.

107. *Commentariorum in epistolam ad Galatas* 2.3 (PL 26.382).

Longum est si uelim de apostolo, et de Scripturis omnibus singularum gentium, uel virtutes obseruare, uel uitia; cum ad haec ipsa quae diximus, inde deuoluti simus quod Galatae stulti et uecordes pronuntiati sint. scit mecum qui uidit Ancyram metropolim Galatiae ciuitatem, quot nunc us-que schismatibus dilacerata sit, quot dogmatum uarietatibus constuprata. omitto Cataphrygas, Ophitas, Borboritas et Manichaeos; nota enim iam haec humanae calamitatis uocabula sunt. quis unquam Passaloryncitas, et Ascodrobos, et Artotyritas, et caetera magis portenta quam nomina in ali-qua parte Romani orbis audiuit? antiquae stultitiae usque hodie manent uestigia.

108. *Commentariorum in epistolam ad Ephesios* 2.3 (PL 26.510).

Aut igitur iuxta Montanum, patriarchas et prophetas in ecstasi locutos accipiendum, et nescisse quae dixerint; aut si hoc impius est (''spiritus'' quippe ''prophetarum prophetis subiectus est'') intellexerunt utique quae locuti sunt.

109. *Liber de viris inlustribus* 24 (*Texte und Untersuchungen* 14 [1896], ed. Richard-son, p. 22).

Melito Asianus, Sardensis episcopus. . . . huius elegans et declama-torium ingenium Tertullianus, in septem libris quos scripsit aduersus ec-clesiam pro Montano, cauillatur, dicens eum a plerisque nostrorum prophetam putari.

110. Ibid. 26 (Richardson, pp. 22-23).

Apollinaris, Asiae Hieropolitanus episcopus, sub imperatore Marco Antonino Vero floruit, cui et insigne uolumen Pro fide Christianorum de-dit. extant eius et alii quinque Aduersum gentes libri, et De ueritate duo, et Aduersum Cataphrygas, tunc primum cum Prisca et Maximilla, insanis uatibus, incipiente Montano.

111. Ibid. 37 (Richardson, p. 26).

Rhodon, genere Asianus, at Tatiano, de quo supra diximus, Romae in Scripturis eruditus . . . composuit . . . Aduersum Phrygas insigne opus, temporibusque Commodi et Seueri floruit.

of this letter overthrow the individual absurdities which they put forth, since you, being especially a master of the Scriptures themselves, have not been disturbed so much at their questions as you have wished to ask my opinion of them.

107. *Commentary on the Epistle to the Galatians* 2.3.

It would take a long time if I wished, on the basis of the Apostle and all the Scriptures, to note either the virtues or the vices of the nations individually. We have now arrived at those very words which we mentioned where the Galatians have been pronounced to be fools and senseless (cf. Gal 3:1). He who has seen Ancyra, the chief city of Galatia, knows along with me by how many schisms it is ripped to this day, by what a variety of doctrines it is ravished. I pass over the Cataphrygians, the Ophites, the Borborites, the Manicheans, for these designations of human calamity are already known. Who has ever heard of the Passalorynchites, the Ascodrogites, the Artotyrites, and the other monstrosities more than names in any part of the Roman world? Vestiges of ancient stupidity remain to the present day.

108. *Commentary on the Epistle to the Ephesians* 2.3.

Moreover, according to Montanus, it is to be understood that the patriarchs and prophets spoke in ecstasy and did not understand what they said, or if this is impious ("the Spirit of the prophets," to be sure, "has been subjected to the prophets" [1 Cor 14:32]), they have understood, at any rate, what they said.

109. *On Illustrius Men* 24.

Melito the Asian was bishop of Sardis. . . . Tertullian, in the seven books he wrote against the Church for Montanus, satirized his elegant and rhetorical genius, saying that most of us thought him to be a prophet.

110. Ibid. 26.

Apollinaris, bishop of Hierapolis in Asia, flourished in the reign of Marcus Antoninus Verus, to whom he also dedicated a distinguished volume for the faith of the Christians. Five other books of his are also extant: *Against the Nations,* two *On the Truth,* and *Against the Cataphrygians* written at the time when Montanus was first beginning with the insane prophets Prisca and Maximilla.

111. Ibid. 37.

Rhodo, an Asian by race, instructed in the Scriptures at Rome by Tatian, about whom we spoke above, . . . composed . . . a significant work against the Phrygians. He flourished in the times of Commodus and Severus.

112. Ibid. 39 (Richardson, p. 27).

Miltiades, cuius Rhodon in opere suo, quod aduersum Montanum, Priscam Maximillamque composuit, recordatus est, scripsit contra eosdem uolumen praecipuum.

113. Ibid. 40 (Richardson, pp. 27-28).

Apollonius, uir disertissimus, scripsit Aduersus Montanum, Priscam et Maximillam insigne et longum uolumen, in quo adserit Montanum et insanas uates eius periisse suspendio, et multa alia, in quibus de Prisca et Maximilla refert: "Si negant eas accepisse munera, confiteantur non esse prophetas qui accipiunt, et mille hoc testibus approbabo. Sed ex aliis fructibus probantur prophetae. Dic mihi, crinem fucat prophetes? stibio oculos linit prophetes? Vestibus ornatur et gemmis prophetes? Tabula ludit et tesseris propheta? Fenus accipit? Respondeant, utrum haec fieri liceat, an non, meum est probare, quia fecerint." Dicit in eodem libro, quadragesimum esse annum usque ad tempus quo et ipse scribebat librum, ex quo haeresis κατὰ Φρύγας habuerit exordium. Tertullianus sex uolumnibus aduersum ecclesiam editis, quae scripsit De ἐκστάσει, septimum proprie Aduersum Apollonium elaborauit, in quo omnia quae ille arguit, conatur defendere. Floruit autem Apollonius autem Commodo Seueroque principibus.

114. Ibid. 41 (Richardson, p. 28).

Serapion, undecimo Commodi imperatoris anno Antiochiae episcopus ordinatus, scripsit Epistulam ad Caricum et Pontium de haeresin Montani, in qua et hoc addidit: "Ut autem sciatis falsi huius dogmatis, id est, nouae prophetiae ab omni mundo insaniam reprobari, misi uobis Apollinaris beatissimi, qui fuit in Hierapoli Asiae episcopus, litteras."

115. Ibid. 53 (Richardson, pp. 31-32).

Tertullianus presbyter, nunc demum primus post Victorem et Apollonium Latinorum ponitur. . . . Hic usque ad mediam aetatem presbyter ecclesiae, inuidia postea et contumeliis clericorum Romanae ecclesiae ad Montani dogma delapsus, in multis libris nouae prophetiae meminit. Specialiter autem aduersum ecclesiam texuit uolumina, De pudicitia, De persecutione, De ieiuniis, De monogamia, De ecstasi libros sex, et septimum, quem aduersum Apollonium composuit.

112. Ibid. 39.

Miltiades, of whom Rhodo made mention in the work which he composed against Montanus, Prisca, and Maximilla, wrote an excellent volume against the same people.

113. Ibid. 40.

Apollonius, a most eloquent man, wrote a long and distinguished volume against Montanus, Prisca, and Maximilla, in which he asserts that Montanus and his insane prophetesses hung themselves, and many other things, among which he relates of Prisca and Maximilla: "If they deny that they have accepted gifts, let them acknowledge that those who accept gifts are not prophets, and I will prove this by a thousand witnesses. But prophets are tested by other fruits. Tell me, does a prophet dye his hair? Does he daub his eyes with black powder? Is a prophet adorned with clothes and gems? Does a prophet play with a checkerboard and dice? Does he accept interest? Let them respond whether these things ought to be allowed or not; my task is to prove that they have done these things." He says in the same book that he was writing the book in the fortieth year after the Cataphrygian heresy had arisen. Tertullian, after the six volumes which he wrote on ecstasy against the Church were published, elaborated a seventh exclusively against Apollonius, in which he attempts to defend all of Apollonius's accusations. Apollonius flourished in the reigns of Commodus and Severus.

114. Ibid. 41.

Serapion, ordained bishop of Antioch in the eleventh year of the emperor Commodus, wrote a letter to Caricus and Pontius about the heresy of Montanus, in which he also added this: "But that you might know that the madness of this false teaching, that is of the new prophecy, is condemned by the whole world, I have sent you the letter of the blessed Apollinaris who was bishop of Hierapolis in Asia."

115. Ibid. 53.

Tertullian the presbyter is now at last placed first of the Latins after Victor and Apollonius. . . . He was a presbyter of the Church up to the middle of his life; later, when he had lapsed into the doctrine of Montanus because of the envy and reproaches of the clergy of the Roman Church, he mentions the new prophecy in many books. Moreover he composed volumes specifically against the Church: *On Modesty, On Persecution, On Fasts, On Monogamy,* six books *On Ecstasy,* and a seventh which he composed against Apollonius.

116. Ibid. 59 (Richardson, pp. 34-35).

Gaius sub Zephyrino, Romanae urbis episcopo, id est, sub Antonino, Seueri filio, disputationem Aduersus Proclum, Montani sectatorem, ualde insignem habuit, arguens eum temeritatis super noua prophetia defendenda, et in eodem uolumine epistulas quoque Pauli tredecim tantum enumerans, quartam decimam, quae fertur ad Hebraeos, dicit non eius esse, sed apud Romanos usque hodie quasi Pauli apostoli non habetur.

117. *Commentariorum in Naum prophetam*, Prologus (PL 25.1232).

Non enim loquitur (Naum) in ἐκστάσει, ut Montanus et Prisca Maximillaque delirant; sed quod prophetat, liber est uisionis intelligentis uniuersa quae loquitur, et pondus hostium facientis in suo populo uisionem.

118. *Commentariorum in Abacuc prophetam*, Prologus (PL 25.1274).

Necnon et hoc animaduertendum, quod assumptio uel pondus, quae grauia esse iam diximus, prophetiae uisio est, et aduersum Montani dogma peruersum intelligit quod uidet: nec ut amens loquitur, nec in morem insanientium feminarum dat sine mente sonum. Unde et apostolus iubet, ut si prophetantibus aliis, alii fuerit reuelatum, taceant qui prius loquebantur. . . . Ex quo intelligitur, cum quis uoluntate reticet, et alteri locum dat ad loquendum, posse et loqui et tacere cum uelit.

119. *Adversus Jovinianum* 2.3 (PL 23.299).

Verum ne Montanus et Nouatus hic rideant, qui contendunt non posse renouari per poenitentiam eos qui crucifixerunt sibimet filium dei, et ostentui habuerunt, consequenter hunc errorem soluit, et ait: "Confidimus, etc. . . ."

120. *Commentariorum in evangelium Matthaei* 1.9 (PL 26.58).

Nonnulli putant idcirco post dies quadraginta Passionis ieiunia debere committi: licet statim dies Pentecostes et spiritus sanctus adueniens, indicant nobis festiuitatem. Et ex huius occasione testimonii Montanus, Prisca, et Maximilla etiam post Pentecosten faciunt quadragesimam: quod "ablato sponso, filii sponsi debeant ieiunare."

116. Ibid. 59.

Gaius had, under Zephyrinus, bishop of the city of Rome, that is under Antoninus the son of Severus, a very significant argument against Proclus, a follower of Montanus, accusing him of rashness respecting his defence of the new prophecy. In the same volume he enumerates only thirteen epistles of Paul. He says the fourteenth, which is called *To the Hebrews,* is not Paul's. It is not regarded as the apostle Paul's among the Romans to the present day.

117. *Commentary on Nahum,* prologue.

Nahum does not speak in ecstasy, as Montanus, Prisca, and Maximilla rave, but what he prophesies is the book of the vision of a man who understands everything which he says, and in the midst of his own people produces a vision respecting the burden of their enemies.

118. *Commentary on Habakkuk,* prologue.

This too must be noted, that the "assumption" or "burden" which we have already said to be "heavy," is the vision of the prophecy, and contrary to the perverse teaching of Montanus, he understands what he sees. He neither speaks as though he were out of his senses, nor does he utter a sound without his understanding, in the manner of those insane women. On this basis also the Apostle orders that if a revelation is given to one while others are prophesying, those who were speaking first should be silent (cf. 1 Cor 14:30). . . . From this it is understood that when someone keeps silent at will, and gives place to another to speak, he can both speak and be silent when he wishes.

119. *Against Jovinianus* 2.3.

But let not Montanus and Novatus laugh here, men who assert that those who "have crucified to themselves the son of God" and "have made him a mockery" (cf. Heb 6:6) cannot be renewed by penitence. Consequently Paul refuted this error and said: "We are confident" (cf. Heb 6:9ff.), etc.
. . .

120. *Commentary on the Gospel of Matthew* 1 (9,15).

There are some who think, therefore, that fasts ought to be begun after the forty days of the Passion, although the day of Pentecost and the coming of the Holy Spirit indicate to us immediately a time of festivity. And from the pretext of the evidence of this statement Montanus, Prisca, and Maximilla make Lent also after Pentecost because "when the bridegroom has been taken away, the sons of the bridegroom ought to fast" (cf. Matt 9:15).

121. *Commentariorum in Isaiam prophetam*, Prologus (PL 24.19-20).

Neque uero ut Montanus cum insanis feminis somniat, prophetae in ecstasi sunt locuti, ut nescierint quid loquerentur, et cum alios erudirent, ipsi ignorarent quid dicerent. De quibus apostolus ait: "Nescientes quae loquantur, neque de quibus affirment": sed iuxta Salomonem qui loquitur in Prouerbiis: "Sapiens intelligit quae profert de ore suo; et in labiis suis portabit scientiam." . . . Quomodo sapientes prophetae instar brutorum animantium quid dicerent, ignorabant?

122. Epistula 133.4, ad Ctesiphontem (CSEL 56, ed. Hilberg, p. 248).

Montanus, immundi spiritus praedicator, multas ecclesias per Priscam et Maximillam, nobiles et opulentes feminas, primum auro corrupit; dein heresi polluit.

Macarius Magnes

123. *Macarii Magnetis quae supersunt* 4.15 (ed. Blondel [1876], p. 184).

῎Αλλος ἐν Φρυγίᾳ Μοντανὸς οὕτω λεγόμενος ὀνόματι τοῦ Κυρίου ἀσκητικὸν ὑποδὺς καὶ πεπλασμένον σχῆμα, δαίμονος ὀλεθρίου φανεὶς οἰκητήριον, τῇ πλάνῃ τὴν Μυσῶν μέχρι τῆς Ἀσιανῶν ἐπενείματο πᾶσαν· καὶ τοσοῦτον ἴσχυσεν ὁ φωλεύων ἐν αὐτῷ δαίμων καὶ κρυπτόμενος ὡς τὴν οἰκουμένην μικροῦ βάψαι τῷ τῆς πλάνης φαρμάκῳ. . . . Αὐτίκα γοῦν ὡς Ἀντιχρίστοις ἢ ἀντιθέοις οἱ τούτοις πειθόμενοι οὐκέτι χριστιανοὶ χρηματίζειν ἐθέλουσιν, ἀλλ' ἐπ' ὀνόματι τῶν ἐξάρχων φιλοῦσιν ὀνομάζεσθαι Μανιχαῖοι καὶ Μοντανῖται καὶ Μαρκιωνισταὶ καὶ Δροσεριανοὶ καὶ Δοσιθεανοί.

Pseudo-Athanasius

124. *Synopsis Scripturae Sacrae Liber XVI, Canticum Canticorum* 24 (PG 28.352).

Πάλιν τε ὥσπερ δεικνύντος τοῦ Ἰωάννου τὸν Ἀμνὸν, "ἕως Ἰωάννου ὁ νόμος καὶ οἱ προφῆται εἰσίν"· οὕτως τὰ ἐν τῷ ῎Αισματι τῶν ἀσμάτων σημαινόμενα τέλος ἐστὶ πάντων ἐν πάσῃ τῇ θείᾳ γραφῇ σημαινομένων. τί γὰρ ἄλλο μετὰ τὴν τοῦ Χριστοῦ παρουσίαν προσδοκᾶν δεῖ ἢ κρίσιν καὶ ἀνταπόδοσιν; καὶ διὰ τοῦτο οἱ κατὰ Φρύγας παρεισάγοντες προφήτας μετὰ τὸν κύριον σφάλλονται, καὶ ὡς αἱρετικοὶ κατεκρίθησαν.

121. *Commentary on Isaiah,* prologue.

It is not indeed, as Montanus has foolishly said with his insane women, that the prophets spoke in ecstasy, that they did not know what they were saying, and although they instructed others, they themselves were ignorant of what they were saying. The apostle says of such people: "Knowing neither what they say, nor the things of which they make assertions" (1 Tim 1:7). But according to Solomon, who says in Proverbs: "A wise man understands what he brings forth from his mouth, and on his lips he will bear knowledge" (cf. Prov 16:23). . . . . How can wise prophets be ignorant of what they say, like irrational animals?

122. Epistle 133.4, To Ctesiphon.

Montanus, the preacher of an unclean spirit, by means of Prisca and Maximilla, noble and wealthy women, first corrupted many Churches with gold, then polluted them with heresy.

Macarius Magnes

123. *The Remaining Works of Macarius Magnes* 4.15.

In Phrygia there was another heretic called Montanus who, in the name of the Lord, assumed an ascetical and fabricated character, and appeared as the dwelling place of a destructive demon, and consumed all the land of the Mysians with his error even to that of the Asians. And the demon lurking and hidden in him was strong enough to dip nearly the whole world in the poison of his error. . . . . Presently, then, those who believe in these anti-Christs, as it were, or enemies of God no longer want to be called Christians, but desire to be named by the name of their leaders: Manicheans, Montanists, Marcionites, Droserians, and Dositheans.

Pseudo-Athanasius

124. *Synopsis of Sacred Scripture, The Song of Songs* 16.

And again, just as John indicated in respect to the Lamb, "the Law and the prophets were until John" (cf. Luke 16:16), so the things that are signified in the Song of Songs are the culmination of all the things signified in all Holy Scripture. For what else ought we expect after the coming of the Lord, than judgment and retribution? For this reason, the Cataphrygians erred when they introduced prophets after the Lord, and were condemned as heretics.

Pontifical Book

125. *Liber Pontificalis* I (ed. Duchesne [1955] p. 220).

Innocentius, natione Albanense, ex patre Innocentio, sedit ann. XV m. II d. XXI. hic constitutum fecit de omnem ecclesiam et de regulis monasteriorum et de iudaeis et de paganis et multos Catafrigas inuenit, quos exilio monasterii religauit.

Augustine

126. *De agone christiano* 28.30 (CSEL 41, ed.Zycha, pp. 130-31).

Nec eos audiamus, qui dicunt spiritum sanctum, quem in euangelio dominus promisit discipulis, aut in Paulo apostolo uenisse aut in Montano et Priscilla, sicut Cataphryges dicunt, aut in nescio quo Manete uel Manichaeo, sicut Manichaei dicunt. tam enim caeci sunt isti, ut scripturas manifestas non intellegant, aut tam neglegentes salutis suae, ut omnino non legant. quis enim, cum legerit, non intelleget uel in euangelio quod post domini resurrectionem scriptum est dicente domino: "ego mitto promissa patris mei in uos; uos autem sedete hic in ciuitate quousque induamini uirtutem ab alto?" et in *Actibus apostolorum*, posteaquam dominus a discipulorum oculis abscessit in caelum, decem diebus peractis die pentecostes non adtendunt apertissime uenisse spiritum sanctum; et cum essent illi in ciuitate, sicut eos ante monuerat, impleuisse illos, ita ut loquerentur linguis. nam diuersae nationes quae tunc aderant, unusquisque audientium suam linguam intellegebant. sed isti homines decipiunt eos, qui neglegentes catholicam fidem et ipsam fidem suam, quae in scripturis manifesta est, nolunt discere, et quod est grauius et multum dolendum, cum in catholica neglegenter uersentur, haereticis aurem diligenter accommodant.

127. *Contra Faustum* 32.17 (CSEL 25, ed. Zycha, pp. 777-78).

Huc accedit, quia ea dicta sunt in promissione paracleti, ut Manichaeum post tam multos annos uenientem ab ista suspicione prorsus excludant. quia enim post resurrectionem et ascensionem domini continuo uenturus erat spiritus sanctus, apertissime dictum est a Iohanne: "spiritus enim nondum erat datus, quia Iesus nondum fuerat clarificatus." si haec itaque causa erat ut non daretur, quia nondum erat clarificatus Iesus, procul dubio clarifi-

Pontifical Book

125. *Pontifical Book* 1.

Innocent, an Albanian by birth, whose Father was named Innocent, occupied the episcopal see fifteen years two months and twenty-five days. He issued a decree concerning the whole Church, concerning the rules of monasteries, and concerning Jews and pagans, and he discovered many Cataphrygians whom he confined to exile in a monastery.

Augustine

126. *On the Christian Contest* 28.

Let us not listen to those who say the Holy Spirit, whom the Lord promised to his disciples in the Gospel, has come either in the apostle Paul, or in Montanus and Priscilla, as the Cataphrygians say, or in, I know not which, Manes or Manichea, as the Manicheans say. For those people are so blind that they do not understand the clear Scriptures, or they are so negligent of their own salvation that they do not read them at all. For who does not understand when he reads in the Gospel, for example, what has been written after the Lord's resurrection when he says: "I am sending the promise of my Father on you, but stay here in the city until you be endued with power from on high" (Luke 24:49)? And in the Acts of the Apostles, after the Lord withdrew from the disciples' eyes into heaven, these people do not notice that at the end of ten days, on the day of Pentecost, the Holy Spirit came in a very open manner. And while the disciples were in the city as the Lord had instructed them, the Spirit filled them so that they spoke in tongues. For the diverse nations which were present then understood, each one hearing his own language (cf. Acts 2:1-11). But those men deceive those people who, being negligent of the Catholic faith, are not willing to learn about their own faith itself which is manifest in the Scriptures, and what is more serious and to be greatly deplored, while they remain heedlessly in the Catholic Church, they apply their ear diligently to the heretics.

127. *Against Faustus* 32.17.

In addition it happens that the things said in the promise of the Paraclete exclude completely the idea that it is Manichaeus who comes so many years later. For John said very clearly that the Holy Spirit was to come immediately after the resurrection and ascension of the Lord: "For the Spirit was not yet given, because Jesus was not yet glorified" (John 7:39). If this, then, was the reason the Spirit was not given, because Jesus was not yet glorified, without doubt the glorification of Jesus now was the reason the

cato Iesu iam causa erat, ut statim daretur. nam et Cataphrygae se promissum paracletum suscepisse dixerunt, et hinc a fide catholica deuiarunt,
conantes prohibere quod Paulus concessit, et damnare secundas nuptias,
quas ille permisit, sub his verbis insidiantes, quia scriptum est de paracleto: "ipse uos inducet in omnem ueritatem," quod uidelicet non omnem
ueritatem Paulus et ceteri apostili docuisset ac locum Cataphrygarum paracleto reseruassent. ad hoc et illud traxerunt, quod Paulus ait: "ex parte enim
scimus, et ex parte prophetamus; cum autem uenerit quod perfectum est,
quod ex parte est euacuabitur," ut scilicet ex parte sciens et prophetans
apostolus dixerit: "quod uult faciat; non peccat, si nubat," et ideo perfectum paracleti Phrygiae hoc euacuauerit. ad haec cum eis dictum fuerit, quod
sint ecclesiae tanto ante promissae et toto orbe diffusae auctoritate dam-
nati, respondent hinc etiam in se illud esse completum, quod de paracleto
dictum est, quod "mundus eum accipere non potest."

128. *De haeresibus* 26-28 (CC 46, ed. Plaetse et Beukers, pp. 302-303).

(26) Cataphryges sunt quorum auctores fuerunt Montanus tamquam
paracletus, et duae prophetissae ipsius, Prisca et Maximilla. his nomen
prouincia Phrygia dedit, quia ibi exstiterunt ibique uixerunt et etiam nunc
in eisdem partibus populos habent. aduentum spiritus sancti a domino
promissum, in se potius quam in apostolis fuisse asserunt redditum. secundas nuptias pro fornicationibus habent, et ideo dicunt eas permisisse
apostolum Paulum, quia "ex parte sciebat, et ex parte prophetabat, nondum enim uenerat quod perfectum est." hoc autem perfectum in Montanum et in eius prophetissas uenisse delirant. sacramenta perhibentur
habere funesta, nam de infantis anniculi sanguine quem de toto eius cor-
pore minutis punctionum uulneribus extorquent, quasi eucharistiam suam
conficere perhibentur, miscentes eum farinae panemque inde facientes. qui
puer si mortuus fuerit, habetur apud eos pro martyre; si autem uixerit, pro
maximo sacerdote.

(27) Pepuziani a loco quodam nominati sunt qua ciuitatem desertam dicit Epiphanius. hanc autem isti diuinum aliquid esse arbitrantes, Ierusalem
uocant; tantum dantes mulieribus principatum, ut sacerdotio quoque apud
eos honorentur, dicunt enim Quintillae et Priscillae in eadem ciuitate Pepuza Christum specie feminae reuelatum; unde ab hac Quintilliani etiam
nuncupantur. faciunt et ipse de sanquine infantis quod Cataphryges facere

Spirit was given immediately. For the Cataphrygians too have said that they received the promised Paraclete. On this account they have deviated from the Catholic faith, presuming to forbid what Paul has allowed, and to condemn second marriages which he permitted. They use the following words in an insidious way. Because it has been written of the Paraclete, "He will lead you into all truth" (John 16:13), they say that Paul and the other apostles obviously did not teach all the truth, and that they reserved a place for the Paraclete of the Phrygians. In addition to this, they have also dragged in Paul's statement: "For we know in part, and we prophesy in part; but when that which is perfect has come that which is in part will be done away" (1 Cor 13:9-10). Consequently, the Apostle, of course, knew and prophesied in part when he said: "Let him do what he wishes; he does not sin if he marry" (1 Cor 7:36), and, therefore, the perfection of the Phrygian Paraclete has abolished this. When they are told that they are condemned by the authority of the Church which was promised so long ago and which has been spread over the whole world, they respond that here too that which was said of the Paraclete has been fulfilled in themselves: "The world cannot receive him" (John 14:17).

128. *On Heresies* 26-28.

(26) There are the Cataphrygians whose instigators were Montanus as Paraclete, and his two prophetesses, Prisca and Maximilla. The province of Phrygia gave its name to these because they appeared there, and lived there, and even now they have adherents in the same parts. They assert that the advent of the Holy Spirit promised by the Lord has been granted to themselves rather than the apostles. They hold a second marriage as fornication, and, therefore, they say that the apostle Paul permitted it because he knew in part and prophesied in part, "for that which is perfect had not yet come" (cf. 1 Cor 13:9-10). This perfection, however, they rave has come in Montanus and his prophetesses. They are said to hold funereal sacraments. For they are said to prepare their eucharist, as it were, from the blood of a year old child, which they draw off from its whole body by means of minute puncture wounds, and to mix it with the flour, and thence make bread. If the child die, they consider him to be a martyr; if he live, he is considered to be a high priest.

(27) The Pepuzians have been named from a certain place which Epiphanius says is a deserted city. They, however, thinking it to be something divine, call it Jerusalem. They give so much pre-eminence to women that they are also honored with the priesthood among them. For they say that Christ was revealed in the form of a woman to Quintilla and Priscilla in the same city of Pepuza, whence they are also called Quintillians. These also do with the blood of an infant what we said above that the Cataphrygians

supra diximus, nam et ab eis perhibentur exorti. denique alii hanc Pepuzam non esse ciuitatem, sed uillam dicunt fuisse Montani et prophetissarum eius Priscillae et Maximillae, et quia ibi uixerunt, ideo locum meruisse appellari Ierusalem.

(28) Artotyritae sunt quibus oblatio eorum hoc nomen dedit. offerunt enim panem et caseum dicentes a primis hominibus oblationes de fructibus terrae et ouium fuisse celebratas. hos Pepuzianis iungit Epiphanius.

129. Ibid. 86 (CC 46, ed. Plaetse et Beukers, p. 339).

Non ergo ideo est Tertullianus factus haereticus; sed quia transiens ad Cataphrygas, quos ante destruxerat, coepit etiam secundas nuptias contra apostolicam doctrinam tamquam stupra damnare, et postmodum etiam ab ipsis diuisus sua conuenticula propagauit.

Pseudo-Chrysostom

130. *De spiritu sancto* 10 (PG 52.824-25).

Ἀνέκυψε Σίμων καὶ λέγει· Πνεῦμα ἔχω. ἀπὸ τῆς ὄψεως οὐδεὶς ᾔδει τίς ἔχει, τίς οὐκ ἔχει, ἢ τίς ἔχει πνεῦμα ἀκάθαρτον, ἢ τίς ἔχει πνεῦμα ἅγιον· εἰ μὲν γὰρ ὄψις ἦν, οὐκ ἂν ὑπέκλεπτεν· ἀπὸ γὰρ τῆς διαγνώσεως εἶχε τὸν ἔλεγχον. ἦλθε Μοντανὸς λέγων· Πνεῦμα ἅγιον ἔχω. ἦλθε Μανιχαῖος λέγων· Πνεῦμα ἅγιον ἔχω· οὐκ ἦν δὲ δῆλον.

Inscription

131. *Corpus Inscriptionum Latinarum* 8,1 ([1881] p. 252, no. 2272).

FLABIUS ABUS DOMESTICUS I(N) NOMINE PATRIS
ET FILII DONI MUNTANI QUOD PROMISIT COMPLEUIT.

Codex Theodosianus

132. *Theodosiani libri xvi* (ed. Mommsen et Meyer I,2 [1905] p. 866).

IDEM A. A. EUTYCHIANO P(RAEFECTO) P(RAETORI)O.

Eunomianae superstitionis clerici seu Montanistae consortio uel conuersatione ciuitatum uniuersarum atque urbium expellantur. qui si forte in rure degentes aut populum congregare aut aliquos probabuntur inire conuentus, perpetuo deportentur, procuratore possessionis ultima animaduersione punito, domino possessione priuando, in qua his consciis ac tacentibus

do, for they are said to originate from the former. Others, in fact, say that
this Pepuza is not a city, but was the village of Montanus and his prophetesses Priscilla and Maximilla, and because they lived there the place de-
served to be called Jerusalem.

(28) There are the Artotyrites whose offering gave them this name, for
they offer bread and cheese, saying that the offerings from the first men
were celebrated with the fruits of the earth and sheep. Epiphanius joins these
to the Pepuzians.

129. Ibid. 86.

It is not for this that Tertullian became a heretic, but because, when he
passed over to the Cataphrygians whom he had previously demolished, he
began also to condemn a second marriage as a disgrace in opposition to
apostolic teaching. Later he was also separated from them and propagated
his own assemblies.

Pseudo-Chrysostom

130. Sermon on the Holy Spirit 10.

Simon lifted up his head and said: "I have the Spirit." No one knows,
on the basis of sight, who does or who does not have the Spirit, or who has
an unclean spirit, or who has the Holy Spirit. For if it were a matter of sight,
he could not keep it secret, for he would have the refutation on the basis
of discernment. Montanus came saying: "I have the Holy Spirit." Manichaeus came saying: "I have the Holy Spirit." But this was not apparent.

Inscription

131. *Corpus of Latin Inscriptions,* vol. 8,1 n. 2272.

Flavius Avus, the domestic, has completed what he promised in the name
of the Father, and of the Son, and of the lord Montanus.

Codex Theodosianus

132. *Codex Theodosianus* 16.5.34.

The same Augustuses to Eutychianus, Praetorian Prefect.

Let the clerics of the superstition of Eunomius or of Montanus be expelled from the fellowship or frequentation of all municipalities and cities.
If perhaps those who live in the country are proven either to assemble the
population or to participate in any assemblies, let them be banished forever. Let the administrator of the property suffer the supreme penalty, and
let the owner be deprived of the property in which, with his knowledge and

infausti damnatique conuentus probabuntur agitati. si uero in qualibet post publicatam solemniter iussionem urbe deprehensi aut aliquam celebrandae superstitionis gratia ingressi domum probabuntur, et ipsi ademptis bonis ultima animaduersione plectantur et domus, in qua ea sorte qua dictum est, ingressi nec statim a domino dominaue domus expulsi ac prodite fuerint, fisco sine dilatione societur.

(I) Codices sane eorum scelerum onmium doctrinam ac materiam continentes summa sagacitate mox quaeri ac prodi exerta auctoritate mandamus sub aspectibus iudicantum incendio mox cremandos. ex quibus si qui forte aliquid qualibet occasione uel fraude occultasse nec prodidisse conuincitur, sciata se uelut noxiorum codicum et maleficii crimine conscribtorum retentatorem capite esse plectendum.
DAT. IIII NON. MART. CONST(ANTINO)P(OLI)
HONOR(IO) A. IIII ET EUTYCHIANO CONSS.

Socrates

133. *Historia ecclesiastica* 7.32.20 (PG 67.812).

Οὐ μὴν ὡς Φωτεινὸς καὶ ὁ Σαμοσατεὺς, ἀναιρεῖ αὐτοῦ τὴν ὕπαρξιν. τοῦτα γὰρ καὶ Μανιχαῖοι καὶ οἱ ἀπὸ Μοντανοῦ δογματίζειν ἐτόλμησαν

Sozomen

134. *Historia ecclesiastica* 2.32.1,2,6 (SC 306, ed. Bidez, pp. 370-74).

(1) Τὸ δὲ ᾿Αρείου δόγμα, εἰ καὶ πολλοῖς ἐν ταῖς διαλέξεσιν ἐσπουδάζετο, οὔπω εἰς ἴδιον διεκέκριτο λαόν, ἢ ὄνομα τοῦ εὑρόντος· ἀλλὰ πάντες ἅμα ἐκκλησίαζον καὶ ἐκοινώνουν, πλὴν Ναυατιανῶν, καὶ τῶν ἐπικαλουμένων Φρυγῶν, Οὐαλεντινιανῶν τε καὶ Μαρκιωνιστῶν καὶ Παυλιανῶν, καὶ εἴ τινες ἕτεροι ἑτέρας ἤδη ηὑρημένας αἱρέσεις ἐπλήρουν. (2) Κατὰ τούτων δὲ πάντων νόμον θέμενος ὁ βασιλεύς, προσέταξεν ἀφαιρεθῆναι αὐτῶν τοὺς εὐκτηρίους οἴκους, καὶ ταῖς ἐκκλησίαις συνάπτεσθαι, καὶ μήτε ἐν οἰκίαις ἰδιωτῶν, μήτε δημοσίᾳ ἐκκλησιάζειν. κάλλιον δὲ τῇ καθόλου ἐκκλησίᾳ κοινωνεῖν εἰσηγεῖτο, καὶ εἰς ταύτην συνιέναι συνεβούλευσε. διὰ τοῦτον δὲ τὸν νόμον τούτων τῶν αἱρέσεων οἶμαι τὴν πολλὴν ἀφανισθῆναι μνήμην. . . . (6) Φρύγες δὲ κατὰ τὴν ἄλλην ἀρχο-

compliance, these unpropitious and condemned meetings are proven to have been held. If, indeed, after this order has been formally published, they are discovered in any city, or are proven to have entered any house for the purpose of celebrating their superstition, their goods shall be confiscated, they themselves shall suffer the supreme penalty, and the house they have entered in the manner mentioned shall be attached to the imperial treasury without delay, unless the lord or lady of the house immediately expelled and reported them.

I. We command that the books indeed which contain the teaching and materials of all their crimes be sought out immediately and produced with extreme keenness and obvious authority. They are to be burned immediately under the supervision of the judges. If, by chance, someone is convicted of having hidden any of these books under whatever pretext or deceit, and of having failed to bring them forward, let him know that he will suffer capital punishment as a retainer of harmful books and as guilty of the crime of sorcery.

Given on the sixteenth day before the kalends of June at Milan in the year of the consulship of the Most Noble Theodorus. —May 17, 399.

Socrates

133. *Ecclesiastical History* 7.32.20.

He does not do away with his substance as Photinus and the Samosatan. For both the Manicheans and the followers of Montanus have dared to declare this.

Sozomen

134. *Ecclesiastical History* 2.32.1,2,6.

(1) And although the doctrine of Arius was zealously supported by many in the disputations, they were not yet set apart as a distinct group bearing the name of the founder, but all assembled together and were in fellowship, except the Novatians, those called Phrygians, the Valentinians, the Marcionites, the Paulianians, and some others who were adherents of heresies already invented. (2) The emperor, however, enacted a law against all these and ordered that their houses of prayer be destroyed and that they join themselves to the Churches and assemble neither in the houses of private individuals nor in a public place. He judged it better that they share in the Catholic Church, and he advised them to come together there. And because of this law, I think, most of the memory of these heresies has vanished. . . . (6) The Phrygians suffered the same things as the others in the

μένην, παραπλήσια τοῖς ἄλλοις ὑπέμειναν, πλὴν Φρυγίας, καὶ τῶν ἄλλων ἐθνῶν τῶν ἐκ γειτόνων· ἔνθα δὴ ἐκ τῶν κατὰ Μοντανὸν χρόνων πλῆθος ἀρξάμενοι καὶ νῦν εἰσι.

135. Ibid. 7.18.12-14 (PG 67.1472-73).

(12) Μοντανισταὶ δὲ, οὓς Πεπουζίτας καὶ Φρύγας ὀνομάζουσε, ξένην τινὰ μέθοδον εἰσαγαγόντες, κατὰ ταύτην τὸ Πάσχα ἄγουσι. τοῖς μὲν γὰρ ἐπὶ τούτῳ τὸν τῆς σελήνης δρόμον πολυπραγμονοῦσι καταμέμφονται. φασὶ δὲ χρῆναι μόνοις τοῖς ἡλιακοῖς ἕπεσθαι κύκλοις τοὺς ὀρθῶς ταῦτα κανονίζοντας· καὶ μῆνα μὲν ἕκαστον εἶναι ἡμερῶν τριάκοντα ὁρίζουσιν. ἄρχεσθαι δὲ τὴν πρώτην ἀπὸ τῆς ἐαρινῆς ἰσημερίας, ἢ ῥηθείη ἂν κατὰ Ῥωμαίους, πρὸ ἐννέα καλανδῶν Ἀπριλλίων· ἐπειδὴ, φασίν, οἱ δύο φωστῆρες τότε ἐγένοντο, οἷς οἱ ἐνιαυτοὶ δηλοῦνται. (13) Καὶ τοῦτο δείκνυται τὸ τὴν σελήνην διὰ ὀκταετηρίδος τῷ ἡλίῳ συνιέναι, καὶ ἀμφοῖν κατὰ ταὐτὸν νουμηνίαν συμβαίνειν. καθότι ἡ ὀκταετηρὶς τοῦ σεληνιακοῦ δρόμου πληροῦται ἐννέα καὶ ἐνενήκοντα μησὶν, ἡμέραις δὲ δισχιλίαις ἐννακοσίαις εἴκοσι δύο ἐν αἷς ὁ ἥλιος τοὺς ὀκτὼ δρόμους ἀνύει, λογιζομένων ἑκάστῳ ἔτει τριακοσίων ἑξήκοντα ἡμερῶν, καὶ προσέτι τετάρτου ἡμέρας μιᾶς. (14) Ἀπὸ γὰρ τῆς πρὸ ἐννέα καλανδῶν Ἀπριλλίων, ὡς ἀρχῆς οὔσης κινήσεως, ἡλίου καὶ πρώτου μηνός, ἀναλογίζονται τὴν εἰρημένην ταῖς ἱεραῖς γραφαῖς τεσσαρεσκαιδεκαταίαν. καὶ ταύτην εἶναι λέγουσι τὴν πρὸ ὀκτὼ ἰδῶν Ἀπριλλίων· καθ' ἣν ἀεὶ τὸ Πάσχα ἄγουσιν εἰ συμβαίη καὶ τὴν ἀναστάσιμον αὐτῇ συνδραμεῖν ἡμέραν, [εἰ δὲ μὴ] ἐπὶ τῇ ἐχομένῃ Κυριακῇ ἑορτάζουσι. γέγραπται γὰρ, φησὶν, ἀπὸ τεσσαρεσκαιδεκάτης μέχρι εἰκοστῆς πρώτης.

Theodoret

136. *Haereticarum fabularum compendium* 3.2 (PG 83.401-404).

Τῆς δὲ κατὰ Φρύγας καλουμένης αἱρέσεως ἤρξατο Μοντανὸς, ἀπὸ κώμης τινὸς ἐκεῖ διακειμένης ὁρμώμενος, Ἀρδαβᾶν καλουμένης. οὗτος οἰστρηθεὶς ἔρωτι φιλαρχίας παράκλητον ἑαυτὸν προσηγόρευσε, καὶ προφήτιδας ἐποιήσατο δύο, Πρίσκιλλαν καὶ Μαξιμίλλαν, καὶ τὰ τούτων συγγράμματα προφητικὰς προσηγόρευσε βίβλους, Πέπουζαν δὲ τὴν κώμην ὠνόμασεν Ἱερουσαλήμ. οὗτος καὶ γάμον διαλύειν ἐνομοθέτησε, καὶ νηστείας καινὰς παρὰ τὸ τῆς ἐκκλησίας ἐπεισήγαγεν ἔθος. τὸν δὲ περὶ τῆς θείας Τριάδος οὐκ ἐλυμήνατο λόγον, καὶ τὰ περὶ τῆς τοῦ κόσμου δημιουργίας ὁμοίως ἡμῖν ἐδογμάτισεν. οἱ δὲ τῆς τούτου διδασκαλίας ἐξηρτημένοι, καλοῦνται μὲν ἀπὸ τούτου Μοντανισταὶ, καλοῦνται δὲ κατὰ Φρύγας ἀπὸ τοῦ ἔθνους, Πεπουζηνοὶ δὲ ἀπὸ τῆς κώμης, ἣν Ἱερουσαλὴμ ἐκεῖνος ὠνόμασεν. αἱ δὲ τῆς Πρισκίλλης καὶ Μαξιμίλλης προφη-

other province, except in Phrygia and in the neighboring countries, where from the times of Montanus they had begun to be a multitude, and are still today.

135. Ibid. 7.18.12-14.

(12) The Montanists, who are called Pepuzites and Phrygians, celebrate the Passover according to a strange system which they introduced. They censure those who inquire into the course of the moon for this purpose. And they say that those who regulate these matters correctly must follow only the sun's cycles. They also ordain that each month consist of thirty days. And they say the first day after the vernal equinox is the beginning of the year, or, as the Romans would say, the ninth day before the Calends of April, since, they say, the two luminaries by which the years are indicated were created then. (13) This is proven by the fact that the moon and the sun come together every eight years, and the new moon occurs when both are at the same point. The eight year cycle of the moon's course is fulfilled in ninety-nine months, and in two thousand nine hundred and twenty-two days, in which the sun completes eight revolutions, three hundred sixty-five and one-fourth days being reckoned in each year. (14) For they calculate the fourteenth day mentioned in the Holy Scriptures from the ninth day before the Calends of April, since it is the beginning of the creation of the sun and the first month. And they say this is the eighth day before the Ides of April. They always celebrate the Passover on this day if it happens also to fall on the day of the resurrection. Otherwise they celebrate the feast on the following Lord's day. For it is written, he says, "from the fourteenth day to the twenty-first" (cf. Exod 12:18).

Theodoret

136. *Compendium of Heretical Falsehood* 3.1.

Montanus was the leader of the heresy called Cataphrygian, starting from a certain village located there called Ardaba. This man, driven mad by a lust for power, called himself the Paraclete, and procured two prophetesses for himself, Priscilla and Maximilla, and called what they wrote prophetic books, and named the village of Pepuza Jerusalem. He also ordained the dissolution of marriage, and introduced new fasts contrary to the custom of the Church. But he brought no dishonor on the doctrine of the Holy Trinity, and he taught the same things we do concerning the creation of the world. The adherents of his teaching are called Montanists from the man himself, and they are called Cataphrygians from the nation, and Pepuzians from the village which he named Jerusalem. But they honor the prophecies of Priscilla and Maximilla more than the holy Gospel. Some

τεῖαι ὑπὲρ τὸ θεῖον εὐαγγέλιον τετίμηνται παρ' αὐτοῖς. περὶ δὲ τῶν μυστηρίων τινὲς μὲν θρυλλοῦσί τινα, ἐκεῖνοι δὲ οὐ συνομολογοῦσιν, ἀλλὰ συκοφαντίαν τὴν κατηγορίαν καλοῦσι. τινὲς δὲ αὐτῶν τὰς τρεῖς ὑποστάσεις τῆς θεότητος Σαβελλίῳ παραπλησίως ἠρνήσαντο, τὸν αὐτὸν εἶναι λέγοντες, καὶ πατέρα, καὶ υἱὸν, καὶ ἅγιον πνεῦμα, παραπλησίως τῷ ᾿Ασιανῷ Νοητῷ. κατὰ τούτων συνέγραψεν ᾿Απολινάριος, ὁ τῆς κατὰ Φρυγίαν ἱερᾶς πόλεως ἐπίσκοπος γεγονὼς, ἀνὴρ ἀξιέπαινος, καὶ πρὸς τῇ γνώσει τῶν θείων καὶ τὴν ἔξωθεν παιδείαν προσειληφώς. ὡσαύτως δὲ καὶ Μιλτιάδης, καὶ ᾿Απολλώνιος, καὶ ἕτεροι συγγραφεῖς. κατὰ δὲ Πρόκλου τῆς αὐτῆς αἱρέσεως προστατεύσαντος συνέγραψε Γάϊος, οὗ καὶ πρόσθεν ἐμνήσθημεν.

Præstinatus

137. *Praedestinatorum haeresis* 1.26-28 (PL 53.596-97).

(26) Vicesima et sexta haeresis Cataphryges orti sunt, qui hoc nomen a prouincia, non a dogmate assumpserunt; quorum auctores fuerunt Montanus, Prisca et Maximilla. Hi itaque aduentum Spiritus sancti a domino promissum in se potius quam in apostolis fuisse asserunt redditum. Secundas nuptias pro fornicationibus habent, et ideo dicunt eas permisisse apostolum Paulum, quia ex parte sciebat, et ex parte prophetabat. Nondum enim uenerat quod perfectum est. hoc autem perfectum in Montanum et in eius prophetissas quas supra diximus uenisse delirant. Hactenus dixerim de Cataphrygis. Caetera quae dicuntur quasi incerta praetereo, de infantis sanguine eos accipere, quod ideo dicimus, ne uideamur ignorare omnia quae de eis dicuntur: hi enim qui contra eos scripserunt nihil hinc penitus memorarunt. scripsit contra eos librum sanctus Soter papa urbis, et Apollonius Ephesiorum antistes. contra quos scripsit Tertullianus presbyter Carthaginiensis. Qui cum omnia bene et prime et incomparabiliter scripserit, in hoc solum se reprehensibilem fecit, quod Montanum defendit, agens contra Soterem supra dictum urbis papam, asserens falsa esse de sanguine infantis, trinitatem in unitate deitatis, poenitentiam lapsis, mysteriis eisdem unum pascha nobiscum. "Hoc solum discrepamus, inquit, quod secundas nuptias non recipimus, et prophetiam Montani de futuro iudicio non recusamus." obiciunt quidam Tertulliano quod animam ex traduce, id est animam dixerit ita gigni ex anima, sicut ex corporibus corpus; quod catholica fides uehementer exsecratur.

(27) Vicesima septima haeresis Pepuzianorum, qui a loco quodam nominati sunt. quam desertam ciuitatem dicit Epiphanius: hanc autem

raise certain objections concerning their mysteries, but others do not agree, but say the accusation is a misrepresentation. Some of them deny the three hypostases of the divinity like Sabellius, saying like the Asian Noetus, that the Father, Son, and Holy Spirit are the same. Apolinarius, who was bishop of Hierapolis in Phrygia, a man worthy of praise, who in addition to his knowledge of divine matters had also received a profane education, wrote against them. Miltiades also, and Apollonius, and others likewise wrote against them. Gaius, whom we mentioned earlier, wrote against Proclus, who was a leader of the same heresy.

Praedestinatus

137. Praedestinatus 1.26-28.

(26) The Cataphrygians were the twenty-sixth heresy to spring up. They received this name from the province, not from their teaching. Their initiators were Montanus, Prisca, and Maximilla. These assert accordingly that the coming of the Holy Spirit promised by the Lord had been granted to themselves rather than to the apostles. They hold a second marriage to be fornication, and for this reason they say the apostle Paul permitted it because he knew in part and prophesied in part, for that which is perfect had not yet come (cf. 1 Cor 13:9-10). But they rave that this perfection has come in Montanus and in his prophetesses whom we mentioned above. This is as much as I have to say about the Cataphrygians. I pass over other things which are said, as they are uncertain. We mention that they accept the blood of an infant that we may not appear to be ignorant of all the things which are said about them, for those who have written against them mention nothing at all on this point. The holy Soter, pope of Rome, wrote a book against them, and Apollonius, overseer of the Ephesians. Tertullian, presbyter of Carthage, wrote against these men. While Tertullian wrote all things well, first-rate, and incomparably, he made himself reprehensible only in this, that he defended Montanus, acting contrary to Soter, pope of Rome mentioned above, asserting that the story was false about the blood of an infant. He accepts the Trinity in the unity of the divinity, the penitence of the lapsed, one Passover in the same mysteries with us. "We will disagree in this alone," he says, "that we do not admit a second marriage, and we do not refuse the prophecy of Montanus about a future judgment." Some reproach Tertullian because he said the soul is from a slip, that is a soul comes to be from a soul, like a body from bodies. The Catholic faith strongly execrates this view.

(27) The twenty-seventh heresy is that of the Pepuzians, who have been named from a certain place which Epiphanius says is a deserted city, but

isti diuinum aliquid esse arbitrantes, Hierusalem vocant. Tantum dantes mulieribus principatum, ut sacerdotio quoque apud eos honorentur. dicunt enim duas ecclesias, Quintillae et Priscillae, in eadem civitate Pepuza. Unum sunt cum Cataphrygis. Contemptui autem eos habent, quod se isti Pepuziani caeteris aestiment meliores. Dicunt enim hanc Pepuzam uillam fuisse Montani, Priscae et Maximillae, et quia ibi coeperunt praedicare et ibi uixerunt, ideo locum appellari Hierusalem. Et quia habitatores loci sunt, ideo caeteris se esse meliores ascribunt. Hos Apollonius superauit Ephesiorum episcopus.

(28) Vicesima octaua haeresis Artotyritas suos uocat, quibus hoc nomen oblatio dedit. Offerunt enim panem et caseum, dicentes a primis hominibus oblationes deo de fructibus terrae et ouium fuisse celebratas. Hos Pepuzianis iungit Epiphanius, contra quos nullus dignatus est nec loqui.

138. Ibid. 1.86 (PL 53.616-17).

Tertullianistas olim a Sotere papa Romano damnatos legimus. cur autem octogesimam et sextam eos haeresim dicamus arripuisse haec causa est, quod quaedam Octauina ueniens ex Africa, cuius uir, Hesperius nomine, uidebatur duci Arbogasti ualde coniunctus, qui etiam apud Maximum tyrannum multum potuit, haec Octauiana adduxit secum quemdam tergiuersatorem uersutumque daemonem, cui uix centum occurrerent uerbosanti atque in hominem confidenti. hic cum se presbyterum diceret Tertullianistam, meruit per sacrum scriptum, ut sibi collegium extra muros urbis fabricaret. quod dum impetrasset a tyranno Maximo, sanctorum nostrorum exclusit locum, id est duorum fratrum Processi et Martiniani, dicens eos Phryges fuisse, et ideo hanc legem tenuisse quam Tertullianus: atque hoc ordine per occasionem martyrum dei populum seducebat. deo autem Theodosio religioso Augusto dante uictoriam, punitoque satellite Maximi, de cuius se Tertullianista potestate iactabat, statim fugit cum matrona quae uenerat, nec uiuentis nec mortui rumore renouato. martyrum suorum deus excubias catholicae festiuitati restituit.

Tertullianus autem fuit ciuis et presbyter Carthaginensi. opuscula eloquentissima et feruentia in defensione edidit ueritatis. hic apud Carthaginem basilicam habuit, ubi populi ad eum conueniebant. quae basilica usque ad Aurelium episcopum fuit. agente enim Augustino Hipponiensi episcopo et rationabiliter cum eis disputante, conuersi sunt, ecclesiamque suam sanctae ecclesiae contulerunt.

they, thinking it to be something divine, call it Jerusalem. They give so much pre-eminence to women that they are also honored with the priesthood among them. For they say that there are two Churches in the same city of Pepuza, that of Quintilla and that of Priscilla. They are one with the Cataphrygians, but they hold them in contempt because those Pepuzians think they are better than the others. For they say that this Pepuza was the village of Montanus, Prisca, and Maximilla, and that they began to preach there and lived there, and for this reason the place is called Jerusalem. And because they are the inhabitants of the place, they regard themselves to be better than the others. Apollonius, bishop of the Ephesians, subdued them.

(28) The twenty-eighth heresy is that of the Artotyrites. They get this name from their offering, for they offer bread and cheese, saying that the first offerings to God were celebrated by the first men from the fruits of the earth and sheep. Epiphanius joins these with the Pepuzians. No one has considered it worthwhile to speak against them.

138. Ibid. 86.

We read that the Tertullianists were once condemned by the Roman pope Soter. Here is why we say they have been accused of being the eighty-sixth heresy. There was a certain Octaviana whose husband, named Hesperius, was closely tied to the general Arbogast who also had much influence with the tyrant Maximus. This Octaviana, coming from Africa, brought with her a certain evasive and clever demon, whom scarcely a hundred could resist in verbosity and confidence among men. When he said he was a Tertullianist presbyter, by a sacred writing he was entitled to form an association for himself outside the walls of the city. Once he had obtained this from the tyrant Maximus, he removed the place of our saints, that is of the two brothers Processus and Martinianus, saying that they were Phrygians and, therefore, observed this same law which Tertullian did, and he misled the people of God in this rank by the occasion of the martyrs. But when God gave victory to the pious emperor Theodosius, and when the attendant of Maximus of whose power the Tertullianist used to boast himself was punished, he fled immediately with the matron who had come from Africa, nor has a rumor been spread of his being alive or dead. God restored the religious services of their martyrs with catholic festivity.

But Tertullian was a citizen and presbyter of Carthage. He published the most eloquent and fiery little works in defense of the truth. He had a basilica at Carthage where the people used to gather to him. This basilica existed until the episcopate of Aurelius. For while Augustine was serving as a bishop of Hippo and was arguing with them rationally, they were converted and gathered their Church to the holy Church.

Tertullianum autem catholica hinc reprehendit auctoritas, quod animam ex anima nasci dicit, et defendit Montanum et Priscam et Maximillam contra fidem catholicam et contra Apollonium episcopum orientis et contra Soterem papam urbis Romae, ut supra diximus, dum Cataphryges haereticos detegeremus: a quibus postea diuisus, ne plebs Montani nomen Tertulliani uideretur excludere, fudit a se omnem Phrygiae uanitatem et Tertullianistarum conuenticula propagauit: nihil tamen in fide mutauit. Nam et secundas nuptias condemnat, ut diximus, animam ex traduce uenire asserit, et nos catholicos psychicos titulat. ubicumque autem legeris Tertulliani aduersum psychicos, scias eum contra catholicos agere.

Isidore of Pelusium

139. *Epistolarum libri quinque* 1.242 (PG 78.329-32).

Εἰ καί σοι ἀνήκοος ἦν μέχρι δεῦρο, ὡς ἔγραψας, ἡ Μοντανοῦ βλασφημία. ἀλλ᾽ ἀρχαία ἐστὶ καὶ μακρά, σηπεδόνα πολλήν ἐργασαμένη [καὶ] λώβην καὶ λύμην. χρὴ δὲ προτροπάδην αὐτὴν καὶ φεύγειν καὶ ἀποπέμπεσθαι, τοσαύτην τίκτειν βλάβην τῇ ψυχῇ δυναμένην, ὅσην αὐτὸς εὗρεν τῆς πλάνης τεχνίτης. μαγγανείαις γὰρ καὶ παιδοκτονίαις, μοιχείαις τε καὶ εἰδωλολατρείαις συντίθεται. καὶ δαίμοσι χαλεποῖς συγκροτεῖται· ἧς μετέχων, ἐκείνων εὐθὺς ἀναπίμπλαται.

140. Ibid. 1.243 (PG 78.332).

Πολλῆς μὲν δεῖται μακρηγορίας ἡ παράστασις τῆς δυσσεβείας. ὡς ἐν συντόμῳ δὲ φράσαι, ἀνελεῖν σπουδάζουσι τὸ πανάγιον πνεῦμα, οὐκ ἐν τῇ ἡμέρᾳ τῆς Πεντηκοστῆς ἐπιφοιτῆσαι τοῦτο τοῖς ἱεροῖς λέγοντες ἀποστόλοις, ἀλλ᾽ ἐς ὕστερον μακρῷ Μοντανοῦ διακονοῦντος δεδόσθαι, ἀνθρώπου οὐδὲν μὲν βαρύ, ὡς οὗτοί φασι, πεπραχότος, μοιχοῦ δὲ φανερῶς ἑαλωκότος, καὶ τῷ κατορθώματι τούτῳ θεοφάνειαν λέγοντος πεπιστεῦσθαι.

Pseudo-Gelasius

141. *Notitia librorum apocryphorum qui non recipiuntur* (PL 59.163.64).

Opuscula Montani, Priscillae et Maximillae, apocrypha. . . .

Haec et omnia his similia, quae . . . Montanus quoque cum suis obscenissimis sequacibus . . . docuerunt uel conscripserunt . . . sub anathematis indissolubili uinculo in aeternum confitemur esse damnata.

But the Catholic authority censures Tertullian because he says the soul is born from a soul, and he defends Montanus, Prisca, and Maximilla contrary to the Catholic faith, and contrary to Apollonius, bishop of the Orient, and Soter pope of the city of Rome, as we said above when we were exposing the Cataphrygian heretics. He later separated from the Cataphrygians (lest it appear that the followers of Montanus removed Tertullian's name) and cast off every Phrygian vanity, and propagated associations of Tertullianists. He did not, however, change anything in his faith, for he condemned second marriages, as we said, and asserted that the soul comes from a shoot, and he gave the title "psychics" to us Catholics. Whenever you read of Tertullian against the psychics, you should know that he is speaking against the Catholics.

Isidore of Pelusium

139. Epistle 1.242.

Although, as you wrote, you had not heard of the blasphemy of Montanus till now, nevertheless it is ancient and long, having caused much corruption and disgrace and outrage. We must both flee it with utmost speed and banish it, since it can give birth to such great damage in the soul as the architect himself of this error discovered. For it consents to trickeries, to the murders of children, to adultery and idolatry. It is assisted by grievous demons. He who participates in it is immediately filled with them.

140. Ibid. 1.243.

The exposé of the impiety would take a long time. But to declare it in brief: they are eager to destroy the all-holy Spirit by saying he did not visit the holy apostles on the day of Pentecost, but was given much later through Montanus as his minister, a man who has done nothing important, as these say, but who was manifestly caught as an adulterer, and for this upright action he says he was entrusted with a theophany.

Pseudo-Gelasius

141. *List of Apocryphal Books which are not Received.*

The little works of Montanus, Priscilla, and Maximilla are apocryphal.

. . .

We make known that these, and all the works like them which Montanus, along with his most repulsive followers, . . . taught or wrote are to be condemned under anathemas with an indissoluble bond forever.

Timothy of Constantinople

142. *De iis qui ad ecclesiam accedunt* (PG 86.20).

Μοντανὸς παράκλητον ἑαυτὸν προσηγόρευσεν· δύο πορνικὰς ἐπαγό-
μενος γυναῖκας, Πρίσκιλλαν καὶ Μαξίμιλλαν, ἃς καὶ προφήτιδας ὠνό-
μασεν· καὶ Πέπουζαν, κωμήδιον Φρυγίας, Ἱερουσαλήμ ὠνόμασεν, καὶ
γάμους ἐπέτρεπεν λύεσθαι, καὶ βρωμάτων ἀποχάς· καὶ τὸ Πάσχα διέ-
στρεψε· καὶ τὰς τρεῖς ὑποστάσεις τῆς ὁμοουσίου θεότητος εἰς ἓν συν-
αιρεῖ πρόσωπον χεόμενον. οἵτινες αἷμα συμφύρουσιν ἀλφίτοις εἰς
μετάληψιν· οὗ τὴν μέθεξιν ἀρνοῦνται αἰδούμενοι.

Isidore of Spain

143. *Etymologiarum libri XX* 8.5.27 (PL 82.300).

Cataphrygiis nomen prouincia Phrygia dedit, quia ibi exstiterunt auctores eorum Montanus, Prisca et Maximilla: hi aduentum Spiritus sancti
non in apostolis, sed in se traditum asserunt.

Chronicon Paschale

144. *Chronicon Paschale* 240 (PG 92.641-44).

Ἡ κατὰ Φρύγας ἄθεος ψευδοπροφητεία Μοντανοῦ καὶ τῶν σὺν αὐτῷ
παραπλήγων γυναικῶν αὐτοῦ Πρισκίλλας καὶ Μαξιμίλλας συνέστη, ἔτι
δὲ καὶ Ἀλκιβιάδου καὶ Θεοδότου· καθ' ὧν συνεγράψατο ὁ ἐν ὁσίᾳ τῇ μνήμῃ
Ἀπολλινάριος Ἱεραπόλεως ἐπίσκοπος καὶ Μιλτιάδης συγγραφεὺς, καὶ
ἄλλοι πολλοί, ἐν οἷς καὶ Σαραπίων Ἀντιοχείας ἐπίσκοπος.

Germanus of Constantinople

145. *Ad Antimum diaconum narratio de sanctis synodis et de subortis iam inde ab ori-
gine apostolicae praedicationis haeresibus*, 4-5 (PG 98.41-44).

(4) Ἔτι δὲ Μανιχαῖοι καὶ Μοντανοί, καὶ οἱ τούτοις προσόμοιοι
ἀνέστησαν κατ' αὐτῆς, οὐ τοὺς τυχόντας αὐτῇ παρέχοντες ἀγῶνας. . . .

(5) Τῶν δὲ Μοντανῶν διάφορος εἶναι λέγεται δόξα, καὶ οὐ μονομερής,
ἀλλὰ πολύτροπος. τὸ δὲ τέλειον αὐτῶν δόγμα ἐν τούτοις ἐστὶν, ὅτι τε
αὐτὸν τὸν Μοντανὸν λέγουσιν εἶναι τὸ πνεῦμα τὸ ἅγιον, καὶ πάλιν τὸν
αὐτὸν λόγον καὶ πνεῦμα. ἔτι δὲ καὶ ὀκτὼ οὐρανοὺς εἶναι νομοθετοῦσι,
κολαστήριά τε φοβερὰ ἐν τῷ μέλλοντι αἰῶνι ἐξηγοῦνται, δράκοντάς
τινας καὶ λέοντας ἐκ τῶν μυκτήρων πῦρ ἀποπέμπειν μέλλοντας καὶ κατα-
καίειν τοὺς ἀδίκους καὶ ἑτέρους ἀποκρέμασθαι ἀπὸ τῶν σαρκῶν, καὶ
ἄλλα τινὰ πλήρη ματαιοσύνης μυθολογοῦσιν. εἰς κρίσιν δὲ τοὺς ἐκ πορ-

Timothy of Constantinople

142. *Concerning those who approach the Holy Church.*

Montanus called himself Paraclete; he procured two courtesans whom he also named priestesses; he named Pepuza, a little village of Phrygia, Jerusalem; he commanded the dissolution of marriages and abstinence from foods (cf. 1 Tim 4:3). He also perverted the Passover, and contracted the three hypostases of the homoousios divinity into one confused person. They mix blood with meal for partaking, the participation in which they deny from a sense of shame.

Isidore of Spain

143. *Etymologies* 8.5.27.

The province of Phrygia provided the name for the Cataphrygians because their founders, Montanus, Prisca, and Maximilla, appeared there. These assert that the Holy Spirit came not in the apostles, but in themselves.

Chronicon Paschale

144. *Chronicon Paschale* 240.

The atheistic pseudo-prophecy in Phrygia came into existence from Montanus, along with his mad women, Priscilla and Maximilla, and in addition also Alcibiades and Theodotus. Apollinarius of sacred memory, bishop of Hierapolis, wrote against them, and the writer Miltiades, and many others, among whom also was Serapion, bishop of Antioch.

Germanus of Constantinople

145. To Antimus the deacon, a narration of the holy synods and of the heresies which have arisen since the origin of the apostolic preaching, 4-5.

(4) Further, the Manicheans and Montanists, and those like them, arose against the Church and presented it no common struggles. . . .

(5) Now the opinion of the Montanists is said to differ. It is not single, but manifold. Their complete doctrine consists of the following. They say that Montanus himself is the Holy Spirit, and again, that the same man is the Word and the Spirit. And they further ordain that there are eight heavens, and they explain that there will be fearful punishments in the age to come, dragons and lions which will breathe fire from their nostrils to burn up the unjust, and to suspend others by their flesh. They also invent certain other tales full of vanity. And they say that those born of fornication or

178 THE MONTANIST ORACLES AND TESTIMONIA

νείας ἢ μοιχείας γεννηθέντας ἄγεσθαι καὶ κολάζεσθαι, ὑπὸ κολαστήρια
τὰ δεινότατα, ὅτι τε μόνον ἐκ τούτων γεγέννηνται, κἂν αὐτῶν ὁ βίος μὴ
παράνομος πέφυκεν. Ἀλλ' οὐδὲ τοὺς ἁμαρτάνοντας ἔτι εἰς μετάνοιαν
δέχονται, ἢ τοὺς διγαμοῦντας συναχθῆναι μετ' αὐτῶν ἐν ταῖς συναγωγαῖς αὐτῶν ἀνέχονται, καὶ ἕτερα δὲ πάμπολλα παρόμοια τούτων ἐπι-
τελεῖται αὐτοῖς.

Photius

146. *Bibliotheca* 48 (ed. Henry, Tome I [1959] pp. 34-35).

Εὗρον δὲ ἐν παραγραφαῖς ὅτι οὐκ ἔστιν ὁ λόγος Ἰωσήπου, ἀλλὰ Γαίου
τινὸς πρεσβυτέρου ἐν Ῥώμῃ διατρίβοντος, ὅν φασι συντάξαι καὶ τὸν
λαβύρινθον. οὗ καὶ διάλογος φέρεται πρὸς Πρόκλον τινὰ ὑπέρμαχον τῆς
τῶν Μοντανιστῶν αἱρέσεως.

Libellus Synodicus

147. *Ex libello synodico (Mansi Sacrorum Conciliorum Nova et Amplissima Collectio* I
[1960/1901] pp. 723-25).

Σύνοδος θεία καὶ ἱερὰ τοπική, ἐν Ἱεραπόλει τῆς Ἀσίας, συναθροισθεῖσα ὑπὸ Ἀπολλιναρίου, ιοῦ ταύτης ὁσιωτάτου ἐπισκόπου καὶ ἑτέρων
εἰκοσιέξ ἐπισκόπων, ἀποκηρύξασά τε καὶ ἐκκόψασα Μοντανὸν καὶ Μαξιμίλλαν, τοὺς ψευδοπροφήτας· οἱ καὶ βλασφήμως, ἤτοι δαιμονιῶντες, καθὼς
φησιν ὁ αὐτὸς πατήρ, τὸν βίον κατέστρεψαν. σὺν αὐτοῖς δὲ, κατέκρινε
καὶ θεόδοτον τὸν σκυτέα.

Σύνοδος θεία καὶ ἱερὰ μερική, συναθροισθεῖσα ὑπὸ τοῦ ὁσιωτάτου
ἐπισκόπου Ἀχιλῶν, Σωτᾶ, καὶ ἑτέρων δυοκαίδεκα ἐπισκόπων· ἥτις ἐλέγξασα
ἀπεκήρυξε τὸν σκυτέα θεόδοτον, καὶ Μοντανὸν, σὺν Μαξιμίλλῃ, ὀκτα-
κοσίους καὶ ἑβδομήκοντα ὀκτὼ αἰῶνας δογματίζοντα, καὶ πνεῦμα ἅγιον
ἑαυτὸν εἶναι ἐπιφημίζοντα.

Σύνοδος θεία καὶ ἱερὰ τοπικὴ ἐν Γαλλίᾳ, συναθροισθεῖσα ὑπὸ τῶν
ὁμολογητῶν, ἀποκηρύξασα Μοντανὸν καὶ Μαξιμίλλαν, ἧς ὁ ὅρος πρὸς τοὺς
ἐν Ἀσίᾳ πιστοὺς διέβη.

Inscription

148. *Corpus Inscriptionum Graecarum* 4, 8953 (1877) p. 400.

ΛΑΟΔΙΚΕΑ
[Ἡ] ἁγία σύνοδος ἡ ἐν Λαοδικείᾳ τῆς Φρυγίας τῶν κε ἐπισκόπων
γέγ[ον]εν διὰ Μοντανὸν κὲ [τ]ὰ[ς] λοιπὰς ἐρέσεις· τού[τους] ὡς αἱρε-
τικοὺς καὶ ἐχθροὺς τῆς ἀλεθείας ἡ ἁγία σύνοδος ἀνεθεμάτισεν.

adultery are brought to judgment and punished with the most terrible punishments for the fact alone that they have been born of these, even if their life has not been lawless. But neither do they admit to penitence those who sin further, nor do they permit those who have married twice to assemble with them in their gatherings, and numerous other things closely resembling these are performed by them. . . .

Photius

146. *Library* 48.

But I discovered in marginal notes that the treatise is not by Josephus, but Gaius, a certain presbyter who lived in Rome, whom, they say, also composed the *Labyrinthe*. A dialogue of his with Proclus, a certain champion of the Montanist heresy, is also cited.

Libellus Synodicus

147. *Libellus Synodicus.*

An august and holy local synod was assembled in Hierapolis of Asia by Apollinarius, the most holy bishop of this city, and twenty-six other bishops, to renounce publicly and excommunicate the false prophets Montanus and Maximilla, who in a blasphemous manner, or demon possessed as the same Father says, ended their life. With them they also condemned Theodotus the leather-worker.

An august and holy special synod was assembled by the most holy bishop of Achilles, Sota, and twelve other bishops. It reproved and publicly renounced the leather-worker Theodotus, along with Montanus and Maximilla, who taught that there are eight hundred and seventy-eight ages, and claimed that he himself was the Holy Spirit.

An august and holy local synod was assembled in Gaul by the confessors to publicly renounce Montanus and Maximilla. Its ruling passed over to the faithful in Asia.

Inscription

148. *Corpus of Greek Inscriptions.* vol. 4, 8953.

LAODICEA

The holy synod of the bishops in Laodicea of Phrygia was held because of Montanus and the other heresies. The holy synod anathematized them as heretics and enemies of the truth.

Index
of Scriptures

Index
of Persons, Places, and Groups

Index
of Selected Greek Words

Index
of Selected Latin Words

amentia, 68

castratus, 78

charisma, 52, 70, 72, 76, 84, 88

Christus, 58, 62, 64, 66, 68, 70, 78, 80, 84, 86, 90, 94, 96, 100, 138, 150

continentia, 76, 78, 80

conubium, 66

conversatio, 62

crux, 6, 70

daemon, 64, 102, 172

delictus, 6, 92, 150

deus, 6, 52, 60, 64, 66, 68, 70, 74, 76, 78, 80, 82, 84, 88, 90, 92, 100, 104, 128, 150, 156, 172

diabolus, 62, 84, 88

disciplina, 62, 64, 74, 76, 78, 80, 84, 86, 90, 92, 104

dominus, 6, 52, 60, 64, 70, 72, 76, 78, 82, 84, 88, 90, 92, 96, 100, 104, 148, 150, 160, 162, 164, 170

donativum, 60

donum, 52, 94

ecclesia, 6, 52, 60, 66, 70, 86, 88, 92, 96, 98, 100, 104, 128, 138, 148, 150, 154, 158, 160, 162, 172

ecstasis, 68, 104, 152, 156, 158

effundo, 52, 60, 74, 90, 148

episcopus, 86, 88, 92, 150, 152, 154, 156, 172, 174

epistola, 52, 100, 128, 150, 152, 154, 156

femina, 64, 150, 156, 158, 162

filius (dei), 58, 60, 88, 90, 92, 100, 104, 138, 150, 156, 164

gratia, 52, 60, 68, 74, 84, 90, 100, 104, 110

haeresis, 8, 62, 74, 76, 82, 88, 136, 148, 154, 158, 170, 172

ieiumium, 82, 84, 156

ieiunatio, 86

ieiuno, 82, 150, 156, 158

manifestus, 4, 66

martyr, 62, 70, 150, 162, 172

martyrium, 6, 60, 70, 72, 88

matrimonium, 66, 76, 80, 82

minister, 4, 64

monogamia, 76, 80, 156

mulier, 52, 102, 126, 128, 162, 172

novus, 60, 68, 70, 74, 76, 80, 86, 90, 92, 100, 104, 148, 150, 154

nuptiae, 76, 78, 80, 82, 90, 150, 162, 164, 170, 174

occultus, 4, 66

paracletus, 4, 6, 52, 58, 62, 64, 66, 70, 72, 74, 76, 78, 80, 82, 84, 86, 88, 90, 92, 94, 96, 110, 138, 148, 160, 162

pater, 52, 58, 88, 90, 92, 100, 104, 138, 148, 150, 164

presbyter, 102, 154, 170, 172

propheta, 4, 6, 8, 64, 74, 84, 88, 92, 96, 104, 128, 138, 148, 150, 152, 154, 158, 162, 164

prophetia, 52, 60, 68, 72, 74, 80, 82, 88, 90, 98, 100, 148, 154, 156, 170

propheticus, 52, 64, 92

prophetissa, 162, 170

The Patristic Monograph Series

"We can only be grateful to the . . . Patristic Monograph Series
for making available such quality research. . . . " —*Church History*

The Montanist Oracles and Testimonia is number 14 in the Patristic
Monograph Series (PMS) sponsored by the North American Patristic Society (NAPS). The series originated under the auspices of the Philadelphia Patristic Foundation, organized to meet the need of producing and
publishing high-quality, scholarly studies about early Christianity. Mercer University Press is now (beginning with PMS 13) publisher of the
series for the NAPS and distributor of previously published titles still
available. Future volumes will be announced as published, as will re-
printings of previous numbers now out of stock.

PMS 14
**The Montanist Oracles
and Testimonia**
by Ronald E. Heine
0-86554-333-X   xiv + 190 pp. $25.00

PMS 8

A History of Neo-Arianism
by Thomas A. Kopicek
0-915646-07-2   2vv./v + 553 pp. $12.00

PMS 13
**Dogma and Mysticism
in Early Christianity
Epiphanius of Cyprus
and the Legacy of Origen**
by Jon Dechow
0-86554-311-9   xii + 584 pp. $25.00

PMS 7

**The Dynamics of Salvation
A Study in Gregory of Nazianzus**
by Donald F. Winslow
0-915646-06-4   vii + 214 pp. $12.00

PMS 12

**The Biographical Works
of Gregory of Nyssa**
ed. Andreas Spira
0-915646-11-0   viii + 374 pp. $12.00

PMS 6
**Disciplina Nostra
Essays in Memory
of Robert F. Evans**
ed. Donald F. Winslow
0-915646-05-6   iv + 212 pp. $12.00

PMS 9
**The Easter Sermons
of Gregory of Nyssa
Translation and Commentary**
ed. Andreas Spira and Christoph Klock
0-915646-08-0   x + 384 pp. $12.00

PMS 5

**Sacrificial Ideas
in Greek-Christian Writers**
by Frances M. Young
0-915646-04-8   iv + 317 pp. $12.00

Ronald E. Heine most recently was Recognized Lecturer in the theology department of the University of Birmingham (1985–1989) and half-time director of the Institute for the Study of Religion and Culture (Birmingham, England, 1986–1989). In August 1989 Professor Heine became director of the Institut zur Erforschung des Urchristentums in Tübingen. His previous publications include *Perfection in the Virtuous Life,* number 2 in the Patristic Monograph Series (Philadelphia Patristic Foundation, 1975).

The Montanist Oracles and Testimonia is a new edition and translation of the oracles attributed to the earliest Montanist prophets and prophetesses, and of the testimonia related to the debate between the Montanists and the church from the late second century through the ninth century. This is the first translation into English of the testimonia relating to Montanism (as opposed to translations of the few oracles). The fragments are arranged in reference to the geographical areas from which they have come or to which they relate, and in the chronological order of the sources themselves rather than that of the Fathers who preserve the sources in quotations.

The Montanist Oracles and Testimonia

Interior typography designed by Edd Rowell.
Binding designed by Margaret Jordan Brown.
Composition by MUP Composition Department.

Production specifications:
     text paper—50-lb. Glatfelter's Natural
     endpapers—80-lb. Glatfelter's Natural
     cover (on .088 boards)—Kivar 5 black,
          stamped with black and red foil.

Printing (offset lithography) and binding by
     Braun-Brumfield, Inc., Ann Arbor, Michigan.